RANTERS RUN AMOK

BOOKS BY LEONARD W. LEVY

The Law of the Commonwealth and Chief Justice Shaw
Legacy of Suppression: Freedom of Speech and Press in Early American History
The American Political Process, editor
Jefferson and Civil Liberties: The Darker Side
Major Crises in American History: Documentary Problems, editor
Congress, editor
The Judiciary, editor
Political Parties and Pressure Groups, editor
The Presidency, editor
American Constitutional Law: Historical Essays
Freedom of the Press from Zenger to Jefferson
Freedom and Reform, editor
Origins of the Fifth Amendment: The Right Against Self-Incrimination
Essays on the Making of the Constitution, editor
The Fourteenth Amendment and the Bill of Rights, editor
Judgments: Essays on American Constitutional History
The Supreme Court Under Warren, editor
Blasphemy in Massachusetts, editor
Treason Against God: A History of the Offense of Blasphemy
Emergence of a Free Press
Constitutional Opinions: Aspects of the Bill of Rights
The Establishment Clause: Religion and the First Amendment
Encyclopedia of the American Constitution, editor
The Framing and Ratification of the Constitution, editor
The American Founding, editor
Original Intent and the Framers' Constitution
Encyclopedia of the American Constitution, Supplements One and Two, editor
Blasphemy: Verbal Offense Against the Sacred from Moses to Salman Rushdie
Encyclopedia of the American Presidency, editor
Seasoned Judgments: Constitutional Rights and American History
A License to Steal: The Forfeiture of Property
Origins of the Bill of Rights
The Palladium of Justice
Against the Law
Judicial Review and the Supreme Court
Jim Crow Education, editor

RANTERS RUN AMOK

And Other Adventures in the
History of the Law

LEONARD W. LEVY

Chicago
IVAN R. DEE
2000

Library of Congress Cataloging-in-Publication Data:
Levy, Leonard Williams, 1923–
    Ranters run amok : and other adventures in the history of the law / Leonard W. Levy.
      p. cm.
    Includes bibliographical references.
    ISBN 1-56663-277-3 (alk. paper)
     1. Constitutional history—United States.   I. Title.
KF4541 .L385 2000
342.73'029—dc21   99-052807

For Aaron Harris and Natalie Glucklich,
who like to see my books in their school's library

Lovingly, Grandpa

Preface

*I*N 1972 Ivan R. Dee, then at Quadrangle Books, published *Judgments*, the first anthology of my writings. This book is the third such compilation, and I'm very pleased that he is my editor and publisher, this time under his own name. I am also glad to have a public occasion to thank him for his interest, knowledge, and constructive assistance. He is a good friend, a splendid editor, and a publisher of fine books. If I were not dedicating this book to my grandchildren, I would have dedicated it to him.

L. W. L.

Ashland, Oregon
October 1999

Contents

RANTERS RUN AMOK

The Ranters:
Antinomianism Run Amok

REMINISCING about the years 1649–1651, when he was called "Captain of the Rant," Laurence Clarkson wrote:

> I brake the Law in all points (murther excepted:) and the ground of this my judgement was, God had made all things good, so nothing [was] evil but as man judged it; for I apprehended there was no such thing as theft, cheat, or a lie, but as man made it so; for if the creature had brought this world into no propriety [property], as *Mine* and *Thine*, there had been no such title as theft, cheat, or a lie; for the prevention hereof Everard and Gerrard Winstanley did dig up the Commons, that so all might have to live of themselves, then there had been no need of defrauding, but unity one with another.

The reference by the Ranter Clarkson to Everard and Winstanley, the Digger leaders, showed a kinship. They did not believe in private property or in sin as organized religion taught it, although they differed radically about the meaning of sin. In England in the spring of 1649, the Diggers, those religious mystics who sought to establish a Christian communist community, had occupied St. George's Hill in Surrey. They dug the ground and planted vegetables because, as Winstanley explained in *The True Levellers Standard*, "the great Creator Reason made the Earth to be a Common Treasury" for all mankind. The government fined them for trespass and prosecuted them for both unlawful assem-

3

bly and disorderly conduct; soldiers destroyed their little utopian community.[1]

"Digger," like "Ranter" and "Leveller," was a term of contempt. In a political tract of 1647 advocating the sovereignty of the common people, Clarkson spoke of the "True Levellers," a name which the Diggers adopted. Cromwell despised them all—Levellers, True Levellers, and Ranters. "Did not the levelling principle," he asked, "tend to reducing all to an equality . . . to make the tenant as liberal a fortune as the landlord?" Winstanley, knowing that poor people worked for only four pence a day and that the price of flour was high, remembered the prediction "The poor shall inherit the earth," and he added, "I tell you, the scripture is to be really and materially fulfilled. . . . You jeer at the name Leveller. I tell you Jesus Christ, who is that powerfull Spirit of Love, is the Head Leveller."[2]

Men of the "true" leveling principle, Diggers and Ranters, were a tiny minority in England who posed no military or political threat, but their theory resonated subversion of Christian society. Even the Socinians, as well as the Baptists and other autonomous congregational sects, could agree on that. If Paul Best,

[1]Laurence Clarkson, *The Lost Sheep Found* (1660), p. 27. (All seventeenth-century tracts cited here were published in London.) A. L. Morton, *The World of Ranters: Religious Radicalism in the English Revolution* (London, 1970), ch. 5, is a study of Clarkson; ch. 4 is on the Ranters generally. Christopher Hill, *The World Turned Upside Down: Radical Ideas During the English Revolution* (New York, 1973), ch. 9, treats the Ranters. Jerome Friedman, *Blasphemy, Immorality, and Anarchy: The Ranters and the English Revolution* (Athens, Ohio, 1987), is comprehensive and disappointing. Norman Cohn, *The Pursuit of the Millennium: Revolutionary Millenarians and Mystical Anarchists of the Middle Ages* (New York, 1970, rev. ed.), has a valuable appendix containing extracts from Ranter and anti-Ranter documents, pp. 287–330. Robert Barclay, *The Inner Life of the Religious Societies of the Commonwealth* (London, 1876), appendix to ch. 5, includes abbreviated Ranter documents by Joseph Salmon and Jacob Bauthumley. Nigel Smith, ed., *A Collection of Ranter Writings from the 17th Century* (London, 1983), contains works by Abiezer Coppe, Laurence Clarkson, Joseph Salmon, and Jacob Bauthumley.

[2]On the Diggers, see introduction, George H. Sabine, ed., *The Works of Gerrard Winstanley* (Ithaca, N.Y., 1941); David W. Petegorsky. *Left-Wing Democracy in the English Civil War* (London, 1940), ch. 4. On Clarkson's tract of 1647, see Morton, *World of the Ranters*, p. 132; Perez Zagorin, *A History of Political Thought in the English Revolution* (London, 1954), pp. 31–32. For Cromwell, see Wilbur Cortez Abbott, *Writings and Speeches of Oliver Cromwell* (Cambridge, Mass., 1937–1947, 4 vols.), vol. 3, p. 435. The Winstanley quotation is from *A New-Yeers Gift for the Parliament and the Armie* (1650), in Sabine, ed., *Works of Winstanley*, pp. 389–390.

John Fry, and John Biddle had converted much of the nation to their anti-Trinitarianism, England's momentum toward intellectual freedom and an open society would have accelerated, but the future would not have significantly differed. If the Levellers, the constitutional radicals led by John Lilburne, Richard Overton, and John Wildman, had triumphed, political democracy would have come swiftly, followed by some amelioration of the injustices of the class system and the economic order. If Winstanley, Clarkson, and Abiezer Coppe had prevailed, law and order, the Protestant ethic, private property, the class system, and even Christianity itself might have disintegrated in a revolutionary and blasphemous upheaval. Although the threat of such an upheaval remained rhetorical, the government summarily squashed it. The Ranters could not be ignored; they were too blatantly offensive, deliberately going to extremes to shock, to show contempt for society, and to scorn its right to judge them. As political radicals, the Ranters had the clout of pipsqueaks, but as antinomian libertines, they stirred envy, disgust, and hostility, as did their late-medieval precursors, the Brethren of the Free Spirit.

Antinomianism defies definition even more than Puritanism or Independency. The word in its narrowest sense means being against the law—generally, the moral law; specifically, the Ten Commandments. But antinomianism need not be taken in its narrowest sense except, perhaps, in the case of those who, like the Ranters, wholly repudiated the concept of sin. Too narrow a definition of antinomianism misses its religious argument—namely, that, God's grace being unbounded, eternal salvation is open to all, that salvation begins here on earth and not beyond the grave, and that the righteous or moral man does not, or cannot, sin. A world of difference exists, of course, between "does not" and "cannot." The antinomians lived in that contradictory world and could not consistently resolve its contradiction.

Antinomianism begins with the proposition that human nature is perfectible and is perfected even in this world through the gift of divine grace. God makes the moral law subordinate to His grace or love, just as He makes the spirit of the Bible transcend its letter. Antinomians such as Behmenists, Familists, Grindletonians, Seekers, and Quakers believed that divine inspiration and spiritual regeneration perfected the soul, making the acts of a righteous or perfected man correspond with and even supersede the moral law. In Christ none can sin; sin is a temporary aberration pardonable through spiritual regeneration. Antinomians magnified the compelling nature of grace. They emphasized man as redeemed, not man as the fallen and depraved Adam. They focused on Paul's doctrine that salvation is attained not by observance of the Law but by faith inspired by the divine spark within the soul. Christ, Paul proclaimed, lived within him (Galatians 2:20). "The Father is in me" is also a doctrine of the Gospel of John 10:38. An Epistle of John reinforced antinomianism's mystical principles: "No one born of God commits sin; for God's nature abides in him" (1 John 3:9), and "God abides in us and his love is perfected in us" (1 John 4:12).[3]

Antinomian readings of such texts were intensely exalting, personal, and liberating. Antinomianism was not easily communicable or understandable to someone not on the same spiritual wavelength. Antinomians scarcely agreed among themselves. Perhaps there were as many brands of antinomianism as there were inner selves. The Ranters reflected an extreme: antinomianism run amok into religious anarchism. Not that there was a different sort of rant for every Ranter, but Ranters differed sharply. Joseph Salmon, George Foster, Laurence Clarkson, William Franklin, and John Robins were dissimilar Ranters but

---

[3]Gertrude Huehns, *Antinomianism in English History* (London, 1951), unfortunately dismisses the Ranters with a paragraph (p. 109) but is otherwise instructive. The Grindletonians, an obscure sect named after the place of their origin in Yorkshire, believed in universal grace, the indwelling Christ, and the possibility that sin does not exist for Christians; see Hill, *World Upside Down*, pp. 65–68. The Behmenists, a similarly mystical sect, were named for the founder of their movement, Jacob Boehme; see Rufus M. Jones, *Spiritual Reformers of the 16th and 17th Centuries* (1914; Boston, 1959 reprint), which is mainly about Boehme and his English followers, including the Seekers, so named because they looked for the true church, found none, and joined none. Unlike the Familists and Behmenists, the Seekers did not form a sect. Hill, *World Upside Down*, pp. 148–158, treats the Seekers, as does Rufus M. Jones, *Studies in Mystical Religion* (London, 1909), pp. 449–500, which includes, with little understanding, some references to Ranters.

definably Ranters. A former Ranter fancifully classified seven types of schools of Ranters and to each gave an exotic name— Familists, Shelomethes, Clements, Athians, Nicholartanes, Marcions, and Seleutian Donatists. The Ranters themselves made no such distinctions, did not worship in churches of any sort, and never organized into sects.[4]

The conduct and opinions of Abiezer Coppe suggest why he became the most notorious of the Ranters, although he was no more "typical" than any other Ranter. The repressions of Coppe's early life suggest reasons for his later libertinism. So puritanical was his upbringing that thoughts of hell consumed him; he kept a daily register of his sins and "did constantly confess." His tears, he wrote, were his drink; ashes, his meat; and his life, "zeal, devotion, and exceeding strictness." At seventeen he entered Oxford as a "poor scholar" to study for the ministry, but the civil war ended his formal education. An enthusiast for the parliamentary cause, he became a preacher to an army garrison. Drifting from Presbyterianism to Baptism, he continued his search for religious satisfaction. The histrionic powers that Coppe later displayed as a Ranter must have been at his command as an itinerant Baptist preacher, for he claimed to have "dipped" about seven thousand people.

In 1649, a year that began with the execution of Charles I and ended in the sudden emergence of Ranterism, Coppe underwent a spiritual conversion that was not at all uncommon at the time. He heard terrifying thunderclaps and saw a light as dazzling as the sun and as red as fire; "with joy unspeakable in the spirit, I clapt my hands and cryed out, *Amen, Halelujah, Halelujah, Amen.*" Trembling and sweating, he felt divine grace sweeping over him. "Lord," he shouted, "what wilt thou do with me," and the "eternal glory" in him answered that he would be taken into the everlasting kingdom after first being thrown into "the belly of hell." He was among all the devils, he reported, but "under all this ter-

---

[4] Gilbert Roulston, *The Ranters Bible. Or, Seven Several Religions by Them Held and Maintained* (1650), pp. 1–6.

rour, and amazement, there was a little spark of transcendent, transplendent, unspeakable glory . . . triumphing, exulting, and exalting itself," till at last he was the "Eternal Majesty" and heard a voice saying, "The spirits of just men made perfect." It was the antinomian message: a pure or sanctified man can do no evil. After four days and nights of revelations, Coppe received his divine commission: he must go to the great city of London to spread his new gospel. Thus he explained his conversion to Ranterism as a spiritual experience, although by conventional standards of morality and religion Ranterism was obscene, blasphemous, and seditious.[5]

In London, Coppe preached his antinomian version of the doctrine of the Free Spirit: Christ's death liberated mankind from sin, God dwells within everyone, and all shall be saved, all except perhaps the prosperous and powerful. Coppe's theology was saturated with a hatred of the rich. He assaulted "men and women of the greater rank" in the city streets, ranting and gnashing his teeth at them, while proclaiming that the day of the Lord, the "great Leveller," had come. He embraced the poor and the diseased, and he became a libertine. "Twas usual with him," recorded an Oxonian biographer who knew him, "to preach stark naked many blasphemies and unheard-of Villanies in the Daytime, and in the Night to drink and lye with a wenche, that had been also his hearer, stark naked." He was imprisoned for fourteen weeks, possibly for similar conduct. In London he fell in with Laurence Clarkson and an orgiastic group of Ranters who called themselves "My One Flesh," probably to symbolize their unity with all God's creatures. A 1650 vignette of "Ranters ranting" depicts Coppe, "their Ring-leader," as having drunkenly "bestowed an hours time in belching forth imprecations, curses, and other such like stuffe, as is not fit to be once named among Christians." He was supposed to have retired that night with two

---

[5]*Copps Return to the Wayes of Truth* (1651) describes his upbringing; his account of his conversion is in his first *A Fiery Flying Roll* (1649), preface. For a similar account of a conversion, see George Foster, *The Sounding of the Last Trumpet* (1651), pp. 1–10.

of his "she-Disciples." The rumor was that "he commonly lay in bed with two women at a time." The cursing, nudity, adultery, drunkenness, and generally immoral behavior (none of it sinful to Coppe) reflected the Ranter repudiation of Puritan middle-class conventions.[6]

Coppe's eloquent and cadenced biblical rhetoric was a mix of mystical ravings and social radicalism. Antinomianism (a repudiation of the moral law), pantheism (the doctrine that God dwells within all creatures), and a repudiation of private property suffused Coppe's utterances. In late 1649 he wrote his sensational tract *A Fiery Flying Roll* [of Thunder] and its successor of the same title. The two tracts purported to be Coppe's witness to a divine warning issued against "all the Great Ones of the Earth." Their dreadful day of judgment was at hand. God would save England with a vengeance. The gospel, according to Coppe, was "I overturn, overturn, overturn." The bishops, lords, and king had had their turn, and the surviving great ones would be next. Although Coppe identified God as "Universal Love," served by "perfect freedom, and pure Libertinisme," the love did not extend to those who could not endure "levelling." "Behold, behold, behold, I the eternall God, the Lord of Hosts, who am that mighty Leveller, am comming (yea even at the doores) to Levell in good earnest . . . putting down the mighty from their seats; and exalting them of low degree." God would level riches and bring "parity, equality, community" to avenge the deaths of the army Levellers who had been shot for mutiny. Coppe himself was a pacifist who repudiated "sword levelling, or digging levelling"; rather than fight, he preferred to be drunk "every day of the weeke, and lye with whores." The real sins, he declared to the great ones, were wealth, pomp, and property—and taking the "enslaved ploughmans money from him." Coppe would rather starve than do that, although stealing from the rich was not sin.

[6]Anthony à Wood, *Athenae Oxoniensus* (London, 1721, 2nd ed., 3 vols.), vol. 2, p. 501. *Routing of the Ranters* (1650), p. 3. *The Ranters Ranting* (1650), p. 2.

Mine eares are filled brim full with cryes of poor prisoners, New-gate, Ludgate cryes (of late) are seldome out of mine ears. Those dolefull cryes, Bread, bread, bread, for the Lords sake, pierce mine eares, and heart, I can no longer forbeare.

Werefore high you apace to all prisons in the Kingdome,

Bow before those poore, nasty louisie, ragged wretches, say to them . . . we let you go free, and serve you,

Do this or (as I live saith the Lord), thine eyes (at least) shall be boared out, and thou carried captive in a strange Land.

. . . undo the heavy burdens, let the oppressed go free, and breake every yoake. Deale thy bread to the hungry, and bring the poore that are cast out (both of houses and Synagogues) to thy house. Cover the naked: Hide not thy self from thine own flesh, from a creeple, a rogue, a begger, he's thine own flesh. From a Whoremonger, a thief, &c. he's flesh of thy flesh, and his theft, and whoredome is flesh of thy flesh also, thine own flesh.[7]

In an anticlerical passage, Coppe represented God as demanding that branding with the letter "B" for "blasphemy" be ended. The clergy could not judge "what is sinne, what not, what evill, and what not, what blasphemy, and what not." They served God and Jesus for money, and for all their learning could not understand the real meaning of sin: oppressing the people. Coppe reversed orthodox values when he declared his belief that what was called good was evil, "and Evill Good; Light Darknesse, and Darknesse Light; Truth Blasphemy, and Blasphemy Truth." To the pure, all things are pure. Cursing by some was more glorious than praying by others. What God cleansed should not be called unclean.[8]

The second *Fiery Flying Roll* warned those who had "many baggs of money" that the Great Leveller would come "as a thief in the night" with sword drawn, and say "deliver your purse, deliver sirrah! deliver or I'll cut thy throat." The rich should turn over their wealth to the cripples, lepers, rogues, thieves, whores,

---

[7]*Fiery Flying Roll*, vol. 1, pp. 1–5 passim, and, for the long quotation, pp. 6–7.
[8]Ibid., pp. 6–8.

and to all the poor, "who are flesh of thy flesh, and every whit as good as thy self in mine eye." The "fat swine of the earth" would soon "go to the knife," if they did not obey the command to "give, give, give, give up, give up your houses, horses, goods, gold, Lands, give up, account nothing your own, have ALL THINGS common, or els the plague of God will rot and consume all that you have." In other chapters Coppe explained how he had found "unspeakable glory" in the basest things, how he had found God in gypsies and jailbirds ("mine own brethren and sisters, flesh of my flesh, and as good as the greatest Lord in England"), and how the path to salvation lay in abandoning "stinking family duties," biblical laws, and personal possessions. The presence of God within him filled his life with joy and beauty, not to mention "concubines without number." In his final chapters, Coppe returned to the theme that kings, princes, and lords, "the great ones," who pleaded "priviledge and Prerogative from Scripture," must yield to "the poorest Peasants" to fulfill the grand design: "equality, community, and universall love." His closing jeremiad (from James 5:1)—"Howl, howl, ye nobles, howl honourable, howl ye rich men for the miseries that are coming upon you"—revealed Coppe's utopian vision: "For our parts, we that hear the APOSTLE preach, will also have all things in common; neither will we call any thing that we have our own. . . . Wee'l eat our bread together in singleness of heart, wee'l break bread from house to house." The same thought is in Winstanley.[9]

Abiezer Coppe was a religious eccentric and a spiritual anarchist, but he was not demented and, judged by his time, was not a capricious sport. Millenarian and mystical traditions reached back into the Middle Ages. The foremost doctrine of Ranterism, that God lives within every creature, was an old heresy bolstered by scriptural evidence. That heresy thrived in the thirteenth and fourteenth centuries in most of Europe as the Free Spirit movement, and it cropped out in an entirely different form in Elizabethan England when Dutch and German immigrants imported

[9]Ibid., vol. 2, pp. 2–4, 13–15, 19. Sabine, ed., *Works of Winstanley*, p. 262.

Hendrik Nicholas's Familist beliefs. Christopher Vitell, a disciple of Nicholas, translated his works into English. The Familists survived royal persecution and the libels of even radical sectarians. Henry Ainsworth, a Separatist, in 1698 said that no one wrote "more blasphemously" than Nicholas; and Edmond Jessop, who despised English Anabaptists, described the Familists as "the most blasphemous and erroneous sect this day in the world." Yet Nicholas explicitly repudiated libertinism and preached that personal righteousness bears witness to a new life, which showed that one has experienced the inward revelation that God or Christ is within one's spirit. Such mystical knowledge led to the Familist belief that regenerated people, in whom Christ dwells, have reached perfection and cannot sin; that belief opened Familists to the antinomian charge. They also invited denunciation by exalting the spirit above Scripture. Anabaptists advocated similar principles, and so did the Behmenists. Others, called Seekers, believing that there was no true church yet, wandered in search of a revelation of God's glory. Even John Murton, the tolerant Baptist leader, condemned Familists and Seekers (although he would not silence them) for advocating the "libertine doctrine" that people need not hear preaching or read the Bible. Gilbert Roulston, who was once a Ranter, designated a particular school of them as Familists or members of the Family of Love, which he traced to a German of Elizabeth's time. Another anti-Ranter writer entitled his tract *The Bottomless Pit Smoaking in Familisme*.[10]

Familism influenced Coppe and the Ranters. In 1649, the turning point in the history of Ranterism, four of Nicholas's English books were reprinted. But Ranterism was more directly a product of the civil war of the 1640s and of the revolutionary up-

---

[10]Cohn, *Pursuit of the Millennium*, and Jones, *Studies in Mystical Religion*, cover the Middle Ages. Jones, pp. 428–448, is good on Familism, and on p. 445 quotes Ainsworth; on p. 455, Murton. See also Barclay, *Inner Life*, for background on religious mysticism and belief in the indwelling Christ, ch. 5, pp. 9–10. Champlin Burrage, *Early English Dissenters* (Cambridge, England, 1912, 2 vols.), vol. 1, pp. 212–214, reprints Jessop. Roulston, *Ranters Bible*, p. 2, describes Ranters as Familists. John Tickell wrote *The Bottomless Pit Smoaking in Familisme* (1651).

heavals that accompanied it. The period was both disruptive and creative. The overthrow of the episcopacy and of their ecclesiastical courts, which had maintained law, order, and status, and helped keep people in subjugation to state and church, snapped religious restraints. People formed "gathered churches" or voluntary congregations and separated from society. They advocated universal grace and took up all sorts of old heresies as if they were new revelations. The inner light in the soul of the individual believer, whatever he believed, became the highest standard of authority in spiritual matters. Judging what was sinful was left to personal conscience, and men were saying that the clergy, with the support of the rulers, had invented sin as a means of suppression. People felt emancipated. They were free from sin and from prosecutions for sin; they were free to form their own congregations, to preach as they pleased, or to choose lay preachers. They felt free to argue against and reject the orthodoxies of the past. In the absence of effective censorship, those who dreamed of new worlds freely expressed themselves. Infinite liberty and utopia seemed within the realm of possibility, especially in religious matters. Next to instinctual needs, religion was still the most important aspect of life—and of death. John Biddle, the Socinian, rationally rejected original sin and eternal damnation, while uneducated people—herdsmen, tinkers, soap makers, and weavers—instinctively came to the same conclusions.

In 1644 a conservative identified "Antinomians and Familists" as "enemies of civil government, who seek to overthrow the eternall Law of God, on which the civil law is built. . . ." He was saying, in effect, that religious questions contain or mask political and social issues. That inference can also be drawn from a sermon preached before the House of Commons in 1647 by Thomas Case. Case warned that, if liberty were granted to sectaries, people would claim their birthright to be free from parliaments and kings and even rebel against them. "Liberty of conscience, falsely so called," Case added, "may in good time improve itself into liberty of estates and liberty of houses and liberty of wives." Within a year, Levellers mutinied in the army, and in the next year a king was beheaded, while Diggers, Ranters, and others proclaimed that property should be shared in common and that there should be free love. The free exercise of religion, coming almost all at once in the 1640s, after the sudden breakdown of the usual controls, burst forth in a torrent of exotic and eccentric religious opinions, many of which were precursors of Ranterism. And many openly or implicitly expressed political positions.[11]

In that, nothing was new. When there was a dispute, provoked by Laud, within the Church of England on the placement of the altar, the issue was as much over who should control the church as it was theological. If the altar was at the far end of the church, above the congregation and railed off from them, the people received the sacrament from the priest on their knees before the railing; if the altar was a table within the nave, on a level with the congregation, they could take the sacrament closer to God, seated, and on equal terms with the priest. Presbyterians wanted the elders to select the minister, whereas the Independents said that the whole congregation should choose him: the theological issue pitted ecclesiastical oligarchy against congregational democracy. So did the sectarian demand for lay preachers, especially because the pulpit was a public rostrum for the expression of political and social ideas. Thomas Edwards, the Presbyterian cataloguer of the heresies and blasphemies that infected England in 1646, believed, rightly, that many disorders attributable to wrong opinions and practices derived from "mechanics taking upon them[selves] to preach and baptize, as [did] Smiths, Taylors, Shoo-makers, Peddlars, Weavers," and even women.[12]

The Calvinist doctrine of predestination was obviously theo-

---

[11]The 1644 quote is from Thomas Clarkson, *A Confutation of the Anabaptists* (1644), p. 4. Hill, *World Upside Down*, p. 81, quotes Case; Hill is best on the emergence of radical ideas, but he tends to exaggerate and selects evidence, sometimes out of context, to suit his political interpretation.

[12]Thomas Edwards, *Gangraena: or a Catalogue and Discovery of many of the Errours, Heresies, Blasphemies and pernicious Practices of the Sectaries of this time* (1646), p. 116.

logical but was as surely political in its implications. Sin having corrupted human nature, eternal damnation was the just reward for all mankind. God in His mercy, however, had for His own reasons predestined some people for salvation; they were the elect. Although they could not know they were the saints, their spiritual rigor and material prosperity were a sign, which made them best qualified to govern church and state. But if Christ had died for all mankind and all were saved, then all were equally qualified to govern. Amid the "gangrene" in Protestantism, Edwards reported, was the common doctrine "That by Christs death, all the sins of all the men in the world, Turks, Pagans, as well as Christians committed against the morall Law and first Covenant, are actually pardoned and forgiven, and this is the everlasting Gospel," meaning universal salvation. Edwards listed corollary doctrines that the Ranters would popularize. The Creator was responsible for people's sins and for the "Pravity, Ataxy, Anomy" which is in them. God loves them whether they pray or sin, do good or evil. It could not stand with the goodness of God to damn his own creatures eternally, "nor would he pick and choose" among people in showing mercy, for if He manifested His love to only a few, "it is far from being infinite."[13]

Two other "errours" in Edwards's catalogue concern Ranterism. One was the argument for religious liberty made by Roger Williams in a book of 1644 which Parliament ordered burned. Some "eminent sectaries" endorsed the argument, Edwards said, and they added that, where conscience was concerned, "the Magistrate may not punish for blasphemies, nor for denying the Scriptures, nor for denying there is a God." The second "errour," in Aesopian language, was "That God the Father did reign under the Law, God the Son under the Gospel, and now God the Father and God the Son are making over the Kingdom to God the holy Ghost, and he shall reign and be poured out upon all flesh." That was remarkably like the message of *A Rout, A Rout,* the first Ranter tract, which appeared in early 1649. Its author, Joseph

---

[13]Ibid., no. 32, p. 22; no. 11, p. 20; no. 77, p. 26; no. 165, p. 35; no. 176, p. 36.

Salmon, believed that God had progressively manifested himself: first when he gave the Law to Moses, then when he revealed himself through Jesus, and finally in the present age, when he destroyed the monarchy and was spreading his spirit upon all the people of England. But Parliament and the army, Salmon wrote, had made themselves "as absolute and tyrannicall as ever the King"; the "Grandees," he warned, should watch out, "for the Lord is now comming forth to Rip up your bowels." If the grandees laid down their swords and sought deliverance, they would replace oppression with "a blessed Freedom."[14]

Salmon wrote shortly after Charles had been beheaded, when the Rump Parliament—the approximately fifty Independents who survived Pride's Purge of the Presbyterians—and the Council of State governed England. For people like Salmon, Clarkson, and Coppe, "the fall of the monarch," as A. L. Morton observed, "was only the first stage in vast changes by which the whole social order would be turned upside down." Radicals versed in the Bible expected that "the world would be turned upside down" (Acts 17:6). England had become a republic; even the House of Lords had been abolished. Yet the country was governed as autocratically as ever. The government represented substantial property owners and the generals of the New Model Army. "We were before ruled by King, Lords, and Commons," said a Leveller leader, "now by a General, A Court Martial, and House of Commons: and we pray you what is the difference?"[15]

Ranterism probably developed because the difference was so very little, blasting the expectations of many people and leading them back to religious expression as their only consolation—and their only way of venting defiance against everything their rulers stood for. The "tyranny" of the generals and of Commons was a Ranter theme. For a time there had been a reasonable

---

[14]Ibid., no. 13, p. 20 (quoting *The Bloudy Tenet of Persecution*); no. 166, p. 35; Joseph Salmon, *A Rout, A Rout* (1649), pp. 1–11 passim; pp. 3, 4, 11 for the quotations.

[15]On the Ranter theme, see Coppe, *Fiery Flying Roll*, vol. 1, p. 10; Foster, *Last Trumpet*, pp. 7–10, 14, 17–19; Salmon, *A Rout*, pp. 2–4. Morton, *World of the Ranters*, p. 84. The Leveller was Richard Overton, *The Hunting of the Foxes* (1649), reprinted in Don M. Wolfe, ed., *Leveller Manifestoes of the Puritan Revolution* (New York, 1944), p. 371.

expectation that a New Jerusalem would arise in England. The constitutional radicals, the Levellers under John Lilburne, demanded popular sovereignty, a genuinely democratic government, and civil and religious liberty. The common soldiers of the New Model Army constituted the rank and file of the Leveller movement and of the gathered churches of the sectaries. The civil war seemed to them a revolution signaling the reconstruction of society. William Dell, one of the leading preachers of the army, told his congregation of soldiers, "the power is in you, the people; keep it, part not with it." He said of them, after a victory over royalist forces, "Poor illiterate, mechanic men turned the world upside down." Leveller leaders encouraged the vision that the ordinary people were on the threshold of inheriting the earth. Richard Overton, in his *Appeale . . . to the . . . free people in general,* wrote, "I am confident that it must be the poor, the simple and mean things of this earth that must confound the mighty and strong." But the Levellers miscalculated their strength when negotiating with the generals, "the Grandees," for a united front in securing their program from Parliament. The people, a Leveller despairingly wrote, grieved; "they are deceived, their expectations . . . frustrated, and their liberty betrayed." A royalist commentator pointed to the reason: "The Grandees and the Levellers can as soon combine as fire and water; the one aim at pure democracy, the others at an oligarchy."[16]

When the generals rejected the Leveller program, the radicals had no choice but to submit or rebel. Their leaders repudiated the government and the generals in a manifesto calling for the abolition of the Council of State because it was a front for military despotism. The House of Commons condemned that seditious tract as tending to cause mutiny in the army and branded its authors as traitors. The next day, Cromwell arrested

---

[16]Hill, *World Upside Down,* pp. 47, 75, quotes Dell, and, p. 31, Overton. The other Leveller quote is in Abbott, *Writings of Cromwell,* vol. 2, p. 69, and the royalist in G. P. Gooch, *English Democratic Ideas in the Seventeenth Century* (1898; New York, 1959 reprint), p. 167.

Lilburne, Overton, and two others, sending them to the Tower of London on a charge of treason. From the Tower they published further incitements, including the third *Agreement of the Free People*, the climax of Leveller thought. A week later mutiny broke out in the army, but Cromwell responded with overwhelming force. His defeat of the Levellers at Burford destroyed their military power. By no coincidence, Ranterism soon became prominent. "You have killed the Levellers," Coppe accused the "Great Ones," and "Ye have killed the just." That refrain, like his assault on the rich, was an echo from James 5:6.[17]

Ranterism was a religious phenomenon among the defeated and disillusioned political left. Politics had failed, pamphleteering had failed, mutiny had failed. Only religion remained. When the Stuart tyrant was beheaded in January 1649, there had been talk about King Jesus succeeding King Charles. Regicide, the defeat at Burford, and the dispersion of the Diggers later the same year were shattering events that provoked a crisis of faith. If the time of deliverance was at hand, millenarian expectations and social radicalism required further revelations. George Fox began his travels throughout England in 1649, proclaiming his "Quaker" message of love and the divinity within all persons. Those who became Fifth Monarchists first insisted in 1649 that the kingdom be turned over to them, to be governed by officers appointed by the power of Christ. Others survived their despair by becoming Ranters.[18]

---

[17]The seditious tract was *The Second Part of England's New Chaines* (1649), reprinted in William B. Haller and Godfrey Davies, eds., *The Leveller Tracts, 1647–1653* (New York, 1944), p. 177ff. "The Third Agreement" is in Wolfe, ed., *Leveller Manifestoes*, p. 397ff. See also Pauline Gregg, *Free-born John: A Biography of John Lilburne* (London, 1961), pp. 207–284; H. N. Brailsford, *The Levellers and the English Revolution* (London, 1961), pp. 481–522, Coppe, *Fiery Flying Roll*, vol. 1, p. 11.

[18]Louise Fargo Brown, *The Political Activities of the Baptists and the Fifth Monarchy Men in England during the Interregnum* (Washington, D.C., 1912), pp. 11–18; B. S. Capp, *The Fifth Monarchy Men* (London, 1972), pp. 14, 20–22, 50–58. The "Fifth Monarchy" was to be the successor of the four "beasts" or empires mentioned in Daniel's vision (Daniel 7:1–14), which millenarians of the seventeenth century construed as Babylon, Assyria, Greece, and Rome. The Fifth Monarchists of England expected the imminent kingdom of Christ on earth and claimed the religious duty of taking up arms against Cromwell and Parliament in order to usher in the millennium.

The Ranter message was a peculiar one to be cast in religious terms; but religion was then the universal language, and Ranterism was an expression of religious conviction, not a loss of religion. The Ranters shared the universal craving for a communion with God, although they understood Him differently. Ranters saw the inhumanity of man to man, and they could not stand their pain. They lost their revolution and could not stand their grief. And they reacted extravagantly in a form of religiously inspired surrealism, which was anchored in the familiar Familist heresy of the immanence or indwelling of God as the activating force of the universe.

What set the Ranters apart, though, was the surrealistic way they translated their visions. They acknowledged no authority but their own intuition and emotional satisfactions. They allowed their subconscious to reveal itself in their theology and in the uncensored conduct of their daily lives. Their imagery was nonrational, their style frenzied, their subjectivity intense. They exaggerated everything for emotive purposes. Their fantasy that they were truly liberated people led them from spiritual ecstasies to crude and energetic sensationalism. They made a principle out of unsocial conduct, sexual promiscuity, and even madness. And, of course, they raved vehemently and interminably, giving rise to the name by which they were called. They smoked tobacco even as they preached, drank and cursed heavily, fornicated lustily, ate gluttonously, tended to shiftlessness, and in every way imaginable tried to be shocking. If a Ranter had known French, his motto would have been "Épater les bourgeois!"

Their extravagant flouting of normative conduct also reflected the Ranters' belief that the normative principles were no longer right and authoritative. Depression, war, revolution, and betrayal led to an erosion of confidence in the guides that conventionally defined conscience. The Fifth Monarchist, the Familist, the Behmenist, the Leveller, the Digger, the Seeker, the Quaker, and other radicals were not libertines, although each in his own way, like the Ranter, was a symptom of and a response to widespread social breakdown. Only the Ranter greedily practiced a rejection of the moral law. The values and institutions of England no longer commanded the respect of tens of thousands of people, but all radicals except the Ranters belonged to the overwhelming majority who still professed the conventional standards of morality. The majority determined what was eccentric, crazy, and dangerous; the same majority defined blasphemy. By every standard but their own, the Ranters were blasphemous. A basically Puritan society had to prosecute them. Yet Ranter blasphemy, although calculated, perverse, and threatening, was usually harmless defiance. Its harmlessness did not mitigate its offensiveness. But its offensiveness was chiefly a matter of sensibility. Cursing, whoring, and theft appalled moralists, but war, profit making, and poverty were at least as shocking to Ranter sensibilities as Ranter blasphemy was to Puritan sensibilities. Ranter blasphemy—which is to say, Ranter theology—was a symptom of anomie, unlike Socinian blasphemy, which was a reflection of rationalism. Ranters believed that people were not responsible for the "Pravity, Ataxy, Anomy" within them. In that belief they were not wholly wrong. But they did not blame society for their abnormal convictions and behavior. They blamed no one. They gave credit where credit was due: all that is in man, all that he feels, all that he does, is God-given, for God is the Creator, omnipotent and all-wise.

God was that and much more to the Ranters, because they carried every principle to its logical extreme—and beyond. John Holland, "an eye and ear witness" who wrote a reliable description of their theology, not surprisingly condemned their "Atheistical blasphemies." They maintained, he wrote, that God is as much in a leaf as in an angel. He heard one Ranter say that God did not exist except in creatures and that men should pray to no god "but what was in them." They called God "the Being, the Fulnesse, the Great motion, Reason, the Immensity," and one Ranter said that, if there was any god, he was it. When Holland called that blasphemy, because man could not create as God could, the Ranter replied, "he was not The God, but he was God,

because God was in him and in every creature in the world."
Jacob Bauthumley, who spoke reverentially for a Ranter, had
their usual pantheistic view; he saw God in every flower—indeed, in "Man and Beast, Fish and Fowle, and every green thing
from the highest Cedar to the Ivey on the wall." God was the life
and being of all, "doth really dwell in all," framed men's
thoughts, and was in all their acts—all of them. Like other
Ranters, Bauthumley abandoned an anthropomorphic concept of
God as well as a God who favored an elect of any sort. His god
was little more than a divine spirit suffusing everything alive. To
some Ranters, God was even in inanimate things, incarnate in
the furniture in the room. Edward Hide reasoned logically that,
if God was in all things, "then he is sin and wickedness; and if he
be all things, then he is this Dog, this Tobacco-pipe, he is me,
and I am him." Bauthumley said that man could not know, believe in, or pray to God. Richard Coppin concluded that if God
was perfect and was in every man, each person was perfect—so
none could sin. To Abiezer Coppe, God was not only the great
Leveller; He was base things, unspotted beauty, and the Divine
Being. "My spirit dwells with God," said Coppe, "sups with him,
in him, feeds on him, with him, in him."[19]

Whatever God was to the Ranters, he was never evil to them,
or connected with evil. They attributed to God everything useful or enjoyable—a table, sex, children, a daisy, comradeship.
They did not find godliness in the things they opposed—war,

---

[19]John Holland, *Smoke of the Bottomlesse Pit* (1651), pp. 1–2. Jacob Bauthumley, *The Light and Dark Sides of God* (1650), p. 17. Edward Hide, *A Wonder Yet No Wonder* (1651), pp. 36–37. Lodowick Muggleton, *The Acts of the Witnesses of the Spirit* (1699), reprinted in Joseph Frost and Isaac Frost, eds., *The Works of John Reeve and Lodowicke Muggleton* (London, 1831, 3 vols.), vol. 3, p. 56, where Muggleton said: "So that the life of a Dog, Cat, Toad, or any venomous Beast, was the Life of God: Nay That God was in a Table, Chair, or Stool. This was the Ranters God, and they thought there was no better God at all." Muggleton, who had known Ranters personally and was briefly attracted to their move-ment at its outset, wrote *Acts of the Witnesses* in 1677. All books and tracts in *Works of Reeve and Muggleton* contain the pagination of the original editions or, in some instances, of their eighteenth-century reprints. The table of contents is detailed, making it easy to locate any item, even though the three volumes do not have continuous pagination or an index. See also Richard Coppin, *Divine Teachings* (1649), pp. 8–9; Coppe, *Fiery Flying Roll*, vol. 2, p. 18.

disease, wealth, inequality, churches. Yet they insisted, illogically, that God created everything and dwelt in everything. Christ had no significance for them, except as a rarely used synonym for God; the Christ of the Bible meant as little to them as the Bible. Laurence Clarkson "really believed [in] no Moses, Prophets, Christ or Apostles, no resurrection at all."[20]

The Bible laid down the moral law, the Ten Commandments. To Ranters it was merely the work of men, a human invention, a figment of the imagination. Some Ranters construed the Bible as a collection of allegories. The Resurrection, for example, was spiritual, not of the body. Christ's coming meant the saving of all men, or free grace. For others, who rejected the Bible altogether, scriptural truths had no meaning. The sense of God within man should be his guide, not the Bible. It was, they said, a "dead letter," a "piece of Witchcraft," and "but a meer Romance." One said that it consisted of tales "to keep People in subjection," and had as much truth in it as the history of Tom Thumb. The commandments of both Old and New Testaments were "fruits of the curse" from which the grace of God freed mankind. Heaven, hell, the afterlife, and sin were fictions, said the Ranters, to enslave people and make them content with their lot. Clarkson thought there was nothing after death. He would "know nothing after this my being was dissolved." Even as a stream was distinct from the ocean till it entered the ocean, he said, so he was distinct from God until death returned his spirit to God and he "became one with God, yea God it self." He spoke too of death as no more than rot and corruption. Heaven was pleasure in this world; hell was poverty, sickness, or, in Bauthumley's phrase, "an accusing conscience." The Ranters had fun with the concept of the devil. He was, they said, just an old woman stuffed with parsley, or the rear end of God, and not really a bad fellow, because he too was a creation of God.[21]

---

[20]Clarkson, *Lost Sheep*, p. 33.
[21]Holland, *Smoke*, pp. 2–5. J. M., *The Ranters Last Sermon* (1654), pp. 4, 7. Clarkson, *Lost Sheep*, p. 28. Bauthumley, *Light and Dark Sides*, pp. 28–31. *The Arraignment and Tryall with a Declaration of the Ranters* (1650), p. 4. *Routing of the Ranters*, p. 2.

Sin, another fiction, was the invention of churches to make a living for priests. Ranters were fond of the royal motto "Evil to him who evil thinks," and insisted, like Coppe and Clarkson, "To the pure all things are pure." "Whatever I do," said Clarkson, "is acted by that Majesty in me." From this he concluded that "Scripture, Churches, Saints, and Devils are no more to me than the cutting off of a Dog's head." God was good; He was in every act; therefore every act was good. Clarkson applied his simple logic to swearing, drunkenness, adultery, and theft. He drew the line at murder and, perhaps, at praying in church. All else was the product of God and perfected by His wisdom. The very name "sin," Clarkson said, was but "a name without substance, hath no being in God, nor in the Creature, but only of the imagination." Men reached perfection and grew closer to divinity if they could commit "sins" with no remorse or shame. None could be free from sin "till in purity it be acted as no sin." Clarkson clinched his point by claiming that a man would continue to feel sin until he "can lie with all women as one woman, and judge it not a sin." In an anti-Ranter tract by "a late fellow-Ranter," an eyewitness described a Ranter meeting in a tavern as affirming

> that that man who tipples deepest, swears the frequentest, commits adultery, incest, or buggers the oftenest, blasphemes the imprudentest, and perpetrates the most notorious crimes with the highest hand, and rigedest resolution, is the dearest darling to be gloriously placed in the tribunal Throne of Heaven, holding this detestable Opinion, (equalizing themselves with our blessed Redeemer) that it is lawful for them to drink healths to their Brother *Christ*, and that in [drinking] their liquor, each Brother ought to take his Fellow-Female upon his knee, saying Let us lie down and multiply. . . . *O most horrible blasphemy!*

People believed that Ranters regarded sexual intercourse as the highest sacrament and therefore that they supposed it was no sin for "hundreds of Men and Women (savage like) to lie with each other, publickly all together, either in Houses, Fields, or Streets, which is their constant course." Pornographic woodcuts depicting lascivious conduct by Ranters illustrated *Strange Vewes from Newgate and the Old Baily*, a tract that retailed the sensational evidence given at the trial of two Ranters charged with blasphemy. Ranters were amusing as well as repellent. One of them took a candle and in broad daylight began hunting about the rooms of a tavern, saying "that he sought for his sins, but there were none, and that which they [the police] thought so great unto him, was so small, that he could not see it."[22]

Ranters liked to meet in taverns—houses of God, Clarkson called them. Ephraim Pagitt, in a clever phrase, called Ranters "the merriest of devils." They sang bawdy songs, often to the tune of church hymns; they whistled, danced, clapped hands, and reputedly enjoyed orgies. One critic spoke of their "prodigious pranks, and unparalleled deportments," and another entitled his comic, anti-Ranter play *The Jovial Crew, or the Devill turn'd Ranter* (1651). Dining was a ritual that some Ranters turned into a travesty on the Christian Mass. One police informant testified that he saw a group in a tavern eating a piece of beef and "one of them took it in his hand, tearing it asunder said to the other, *This is the flesh of Christ, take and eat.* The other took a cup of Ale and threw it into the chimney corner, saying, *There* is *the bloud of Christ.*" They discussed God over their meal, and one said he could go to the outhouse "*and make a God every morning, by easing his body.*"[23]

Some Ranters were undoubtedly scatological and coarse, and much in Ranterism was outrageous and deliberately disrespectful. But by pushing the doctrines of free grace and human perfection to the outermost limits of antinomian practice, the

---

[22]"To the pure all things are pure" is from Titus 1:15, quoted by Coppe, *Fiery Flying Roll*, vol. 1, p. 8, and Clarkson, *Lost Sheep*, p. 25. See also Laurence Clarkson, *Single Eye*, pp. 7–9, 11, 15–16, and *Lost Sheep*, pp. 26–27. The long quotation is from M. Stubs, *The Ranters Declaration* (1650), p. 2. *Arraignment and Tryall*, p. 3. *The Ranters Religion* (1650), p. 5. Roulston, *Ranters Bible*, p. 5. *Strange Newes from Newgate and the Old Baily* (1651), pp. 3–4. *Routing of the Ranters*, pp. 4–5.

[23]Clarkson, *Lost Sheep*, p. 28. Ephraim Pagitt, *Heresiography* (1654, 5th ed.), p. 144. *Strange Newes from Newgate*, pp. 2–3. *Ranters Religion*, p. 8, also reported the travesty.

Ranters seized upon what was for them an enormous truth—organized religion stifled human expression. They blamed religion for muzzling people's emotional lives. Using theological terms disabled the Ranters from saying that religion had failed man; they intended what Freud meant when he said religion was the universal neurosis. Their intense subjectivity, which was based on hopelessness, was no program, but it was no more unrealistic than the Diggers' economics or the Levellers' politics, both of which had failed. By vomiting away moral repressions, Ranters sought to emancipate the inner lives of people. Their way of living was an invitation for all to live out relatively harmless but socially disruptive fantasies; Ranterism was a purge for sickening anxieties and for an oppressive sense of guilt, especially about sex. Coppe and Clarkson, wild as they were, spoke to the alienated person, alienated from his own inner life as well as from his "fellow Creatures."

The Ranter fantasy was that man could return to Eden, the godly inheritance which religion denied. Before the Fall, God was a benefactor, the world was good, and man did not know evil. After the Fall, the Ranters were saying, the God of theology appeared, vengeful and arbitrary; it was He whom they rejected. Orthodox theology represented Adam as the sinner and Eve as temptation, not as love or fulfillment. The Ranters offered an alternative theology as well as an alternative way of life. Unfortunately we have no Ranter statements by women, but the sexual content of the writings of the Ranter men and even of the anti-Ranter writings implies that Ranter women were willing believers and partners. The first Ranter sermon that Clarkson heard was preached by a Mary Lake. In a titallating pamphlet, *The Ranters Last Sermon*, "Mistress E.B.," in mixed company, went to one of the men and offered "to unbutton his Cod-piece." When her partner asked why, she is supposed to have replied, "For sin: whereupon . . . in the sight of all the rest, they commit Fornication." If she did reply "For sin," she was jesting, because, as the author of the pamphlet acknowledged, Ranters believed that "whatsoever they did was Good and not Evill, there being no such thing as sin in the world."[24]

The England of the Ranters was a Puritan society in which the foremost connotation of sin was sexual. John Holland, an accurate though hostile reporter, depicted women as equal beneficiaries of free love. "They say," he wrote, "that for one man to be tied to one woman, or one woman to one man, is a fruit of the curse; but, they say, we are freed from the curse, therefore it is our liberty to make use of whom we please." The lack of contraceptives doubtless robbed women of that equality. Gerrard Winstanley, the Digger, warned women to "beware this ranting practice." It burdened them with excessive childbearing. The mother and the children were likely, he said, "to have the worst of it, for the man will be gone and leave them . . . after he hath his pleasure." Winstanley was probably right, but he missed the point that the Ranters hungered for an emotional expression, of which sex was a part, that religion inhibited. Nor did he understand that the Ranter advocacy of extreme individual freedom represented a desperate search for psychological health. It was present even in Jacob Bauthumley's attempt to understand God: "If I say I love thee, it is nothing so, for there is in me nothing can love thee but thy self; and therefore thou dost but love thy self: My seeking of thee is no other but thy seeking of thy self: My delighting enjoying thee, is no other but thy delighting in thy self, and enjoying thy selfe after a most unconceivable manner." Bauthumley's narcissistic illusion that he loved the God within him expressed a drive to fulfill himself through someone else.[25]

The Ranters fed a hunger in people. John Taylor wrote in 1651 that heretics used to emerge one by one, "but now they sprout by huddles and clusters (like locusts out of the bottomless pit). They now come thronging upon us in swarms, as the Caterpillers of Aegypt." He was speaking of the Ranters. Samuel

[24]Clarkson, *Lost Sheep*, p. 25. *Ranters Last Sermon*, p. 3.
[25]Holland, *Smoke*, p. 4. *Routing of the Ranters*, p. 6. Winstanley, *A Vindication*, in Sabine, ed., *Works of Winstanley*, pp. 400–401. Bauthumley, *Light and Dark Sides*, p. 26.

Sheppard, who thought the devil had turned Ranter, claimed that same year, "All the world now is in the Ranting humour." In 1652 Durant Hotham, a justice of the peace, told George Fox, the founding Quaker, that "all the justices of the nation" could not have prevented England from being "overspread with Ranterism." These were no doubt exaggerated statements; although Ranters existed throughout England, in both town and country, their strength lay in London among the teeming poor. They attracted unskilled workers, petty artisans, the unemployed, vagabonds, former soldiers, and underworld elements. Ranterism had a lower-class character. Coppe romantically identified with thieves, whores, and beggars. Salmon addressed *A Rout, A Rout* to fellow soldiers "of inferior rank and quality." The caterpillars of Egypt notwithstanding, Ranters usually congregated in small groups. Even before the government launched its campaign to suppress them, they tended to be a secretive, underground movement. When Clarkson first tried to meet the Ranters who called themselves "My One Flesh," he had to be given introductions to one intermediary after another. In London the Ranters probably numbered thousands, but their constituency never competed with the organized denominations or with the gathered churches. Ranterism was more boisterous and articulate than truly dangerous. Focusing on what their leaders said can make them sound dangerous. A. L. Morton observed that leveling, as the Ranters understood it, "involved a far greater social upheaval than the political changes advanced by Lilburne and his associates, or Winstanley's quite limited proposals for a joint cultivation of the commons and waste land." But for all their militancy, Ranters were pacifists and appealed "only to the defeated and declassed, the lower strata of the urban poor, and upon these no substantial movement could possibly be built." They were also badly organized, if organized at all, and schismatic. They did not even have a program. Men who left the movement revealed that a "Ranter's Parliament" in London lost half its attendance of three hundred when the speakers could not satisfactorily answer questions about the problems of poverty.

People should borrow money without paying it back, the leaders said, and steal, and "not only make use of a Man's wife, but of his Estate, Goods, and Chattels also, for all things were common." Even the poor understood that the "strategem" was "no wayes feasible."[26]

Most people perceived the Ranters as spiritual fanatics and libertines. Their critics usually lambasted them as "Atheistical blasphemers," but a few who condemned them for having abandoned all religion spoke contradictorily. One referred to their "irreligious Religions." The titles of some anti-Ranter tracts show the same ambivalence: *The Ranters Religion, The Ranters Creed,* and *The Ranters Bible.* One writer, noting the dualism in Ranter thought, perceptively defined a particular gang of Ranters as "Marcions," an allusion to second-century Christian Gnostics; the "Marcions," like the old Gnostics, believed in two deities, one of which was the creator of all evil. Another writer, appalled by the "horrid" blasphemy that sin was imaginary, said, "These Ranters are but the Gnosticks of former Ages brought backwards among us." Yet the Presbyterian divine Richard Baxter, although esteemed for his learning and his attempts to be tolerant, discerned in Ranterism no more than its run-of-the-mill opponents did. The Ranters, Baxter claimed, made it their business, "under the Name of Christ in Men," to dishonor all churches, the Bible, the clergy, and worship. They demanded that men and women should "hearken to Christ within them," Baxter wrote, but

> they conjoyned a Cursed Doctrine of *Libertinism,* which brought them to all abominable filthiness of Life: They taught, as the familists, that God regarded not the Actions of the Outward Man, but of the Heart; and that to the Pure all things are Pure, (even the most forbidden): And so as [if] allowed by God, they

[26]John Taylor, *Ranters of Both Sexes* (1651), p. 4. Sheppard's prologue to his *The Joviall Crew* (1651), opposite the title page, is: "Bedlam broke loose? Hell is open'd too. / Madmen & Fiends, & Harpies to your view / We do present: but who shall cure the Tumor? / All the world now is in the Ranting Humor." Hotham is quoted in *The Journal of George Fox,* ed. John T. Nickalls (Cambridge, England, 1952), p. 90. Salmon, *A Rout,* p. 1. Clarkson, *Lost Sheep,* pp. 24–25. Morton, *World of the Ranters,* pp. 87, 112. Stubs, *Ranters Declaration,* pp. 5–6.

spoke most hideous Words of Blasphemy, and many of them committed Whoredoms commonly . . . and this all uttered as the Effect of Knowledge, and a part of their Religion, in a Fanatick Strain, and fathered on the Spirit of God.

Quakers and Presbyterians agreed on Ranters, although the early Quakers often suffered the indignity of being confused with Ranters. George Fox first encountered Ranters in a Coventry prison in late 1649. When he met them, "a great power of darkness struck me," and they said they were God. Fox asked them whether it would rain tomorrow; they did not know. God knew, he rejoined, and after reproving them for their blasphemies, he left, because "I perceived they were Ranters, and I had met with none before."[27]

Although Gerrard Winstanley and the Ranters shared some fundamental tenets, he publicly repudiated them to still the slanders that Diggers and Ranters were indistinguishable. Winstanley believed that man should earn his bread by the sweat of his brow; labor, hard and productive, was a virtue with him. He scorned the Ranters as slothful and condemned them for cheating others of their earnings. Winstanley, who was very Quaker-like, condemned libertinism. Righteous and quietistic, he spurned the Ranters' materialism. Theirs, he wrote, was the "Kingdome that lies in objects; As in the outward enjoyment of meat, drinke, pleasures, and women; so that the man within can have no quiet rest, unlesse he enjoy those outward objects in excesse." They believed, he complained, only in the life of the senses, "which is the life of the Beast." Overindulgence, he warned, impaired the "Temple" of the body and brought eventual "sorrow of mind." He thought too that "excessive copulation with Women" broke up families, caused quarrels, and burdened women with childbearing. Winstanley was the only critic of the

---

[27]Holland, *Smoke*, p. 1, used "Atheistical," and Taylor *Ranters of Both Sexes*, p. 1, "irreligious." Roulston, *Ranters Bible*, p. 4, used "Marcions." "Gnostics" appears in *Ranters Religion*, p. 4. *Reliquiae Baxterianae, or . . . Baxter's Narrative*, ed. M. Sylvester (London, 1696), pp. 76–77. *The Journal of George Fox*, ed. Norman Penney (Cambridge, England, 1911, 2 vols.), vol. 1, p. 47.

Ranters who did not castigate their theology, nor would he suppress them. Let him who was without sin, he wrote, "cast the first Stone at the Ranter." He counseled patience and righteous living, "and thou shalt see a returne of the Ranters."[28]

The government pursued a different policy. Coventry was probably the first town to jail its Ranters. Among the group that George Fox visited in prison there in late 1649 was Joseph Salmon, the former soldier and itinerant preacher who had written *A Rout, A Rout.* Abiezer Coppe, who had just written the two installments of his lurid *Fiery Flying Roll,* was probably in the same Coventry prison with Salmon and his group. The charge against them may have been based on a provision in the Blasphemy Act of 1648 for publishing the heretical belief that the moral law of the Ten Commandments is not a rule of Christian life. Too little is known about the Coventry case to be certain. In January 1650 the two *Fiery Flying Rolls* were republished as one, adding to their notoriety. The authorities in Coventry did not know they had the book's author in custody, nor did the House of Commons know that Coventry had him when, on February 1, the House directed that a search be made for him. The House censured the book for its "horrid Blasphemies" and ordered that all copies be seized throughout the realm and burned by the public hangmen. According to George Fox, the Coventry Ranters won their release by recanting their beliefs "not long after" he encountered them. Salmon had to promise to put his recantation into public print. Coppe, who was probably using an assumed name to escape detection, recanted orally; he and Salmon were at liberty in mid-1650.[29]

Ranters had not the stuff of which martyrs were made. They renounced their beliefs with comparative ease. Believing in neither heaven nor hell, that even the soul died with the body, and that there was no afterlife, they had nothing to win if they stood fast by their beliefs and nothing to lose by repudiating them.

---

[28]Winstanley, *Vindication,* in Sabine, ed., *Works of Winstanley,* pp. 399–403.
[29]*Journals H.C.,* vol. 6, p. 354 (Feb. 1, 1650). *Journal of Fox,* ed. Penney, vol. 1, p. 47.

Life was to be enjoyed here and now rather than be wasted in prison. Anyway, the Ranters were amoral enough to say what had to be said to gain their freedom. As Justice Hotham told Fox in 1652, they would have said and done as the magistrates commanded "and yet kept their principle still." Salmon, in his book of recantation, professed a "sincere abdication of certain Tenets, either formerly vented by him, or now charged upon him." The very title of his *Heights in Depths and Depths in Heights* was a clue that he had not fundamentally changed. Ranters were fond of oxymorons, rhetorical figures that joined contradictory and incongruous meanings, as when Coppe spoke of his "filthy, nasty holiness," or said that one could not know unspotted beauty without knowing base things. The oxymorons reflected Gnostic dualism.[30]

Salmon recanted after he suffered "above halfe a years imprisonment under the notion of a blaspheamer; which through want of air and many other conveniences, became very irksome and tedious to my outward man." Those are Ranter sentiments. Similarly, Salmon, supposedly repentant, defined God as "one simple, single, uncompounded glory: nothing lives in him or flows from him, but what is his pure individual self." A minister, commenting on the Ranter practice of using Aesopian language, declared that Ranters say "one thinge and mean another. . . . They will say and unsay in one breath." Their expressions had "wayes and windings, to keep themselves from being known, but to their owne."[31]

In 1650 Clarkson published his libertine manifesto, *A Single Eye All Light, no Darkness; or Light and Darkness One.* The "Devil is God, Hell is Heaven, Sin Holiness, Damnation Salvation, this and only this is the first Resurrection," Clarkson announced.

---

[30]*Journal of Fox*, ed. Penney, vol. 1, p. 90. Joseph Salmon, *Heights in Depths and Depths in Heights* (1651), title page for quotation. Coppe, *Fiery Flying Roll*, vol. 2, pp. 13, 14. Salmon clearly recanted, but *Heights in Depths*, pp. 37–54, is unorthodox on God, heaven, hell, sin, and the Trinity.

[31]Salmon, *Heights in Depths*, p. A4 in preface ("To the Reader"), p. 52. Tickell, *Bottomless Pit*, pp. 37–38.

The House of Commons, in June 1650, after listening to a reading of *A Single Eye*, empowered a committee that was investigating "a Sect called Ranters" to find and imprison them. The House also ordered the committee to prepare a bill to suppress such blasphemies "and to make the same Offences capital."[32]

New legislation was needed because the Blasphemy Act of 1648, having been passed before the emergence of the Ranters, did not speak to their principles or conduct. The heresy clause on the denial of the Ten Commandments, the only one applicable to the Ranters, allowed recantation as an alternative to a prison term. The act of 1648, a Presbyterian product, required death for a conviction of any of the blasphemies it proscribed, and in the main they were Socinian in character. The heresy clauses of the same act were so broad that, if enforced, they would have ensnared Cromwell, members of the Rump Parliament, and a large part of the army. The Independents, who controlled the government, were reluctant to enforce a Presbyterian measure, especially at a time when Presbyterian Scotland was engaged in a war against England for the purpose of placing Charles II on the throne. As the House of Commons debated a new measure on offenses against religion, Scottish divines charged that the English Independents were guilty of blasphemies and heresies. Repudiating that charge, Cromwell declared that he abhorred the detestable blasphemies "lately broken out amongst us," and he called attention to the fact that "We have already punished some among us for blasphemy, and are further ready to do it." On the same day in July when the House of Commons received a copy of Cromwell's declaration, it voted against death as the punishment for Ranter blasphemy by accepting a six-month prison term for the first offense. The House also voted against a proposal that punishment for the second offense should be boring through the blasphemer's tongue with a hot iron. Banishment was to be the recidivist's sentence; death was reserved only for those who, having

---

[32]Clarkson, *A Single Eye*, p. 14. *Journals H.C.*, vol. 6, p. 427 (June 21, 1650).

been banished, returned to England without permission from the House.[33]

On August 9, 1650, the House passed its "Act against several Atheistical, Blasphemous and Execrable Opinions, derogatory to the honor of God." By comparison with any previous standard in English history, this was not an enactment into law of bigotry; it was carefully framed to cover only Ranter professions and practices. No persons whose religious beliefs were recognizably Christian, not even the Familists, who upheld the teachings of Hendrik Nicholas, or any of the novel and recent sects such as the Quakers and Fifth Monarchists, came within its terms. From the standpoint of its framers, the target of the statute was not the unorthodox but the irreligious, or those who made a religion of immorality. John Milton supported the act of 1650 because, he said, blasphemy "or evil speaking against God" was not a reflection of religious conscience. He offered the act of 1650 as a definition of blasphemy that was plainer and more judicious than the clergy had produced "in many a prolix volume." Actually, all the act did was to catalogue Ranter precepts and call them blasphemous.[34]

The act applied to anyone who maintained any of the following opinions: that he or another living person was God, was equal to God, or possessed His attributes; that God dwells within man "and no where else"; that unrighteousness or sinfulness was not immoral; or that heaven and hell, or salvation and damnation, did not exist or could not be distinguished. The act also applied to anyone who denied or blasphemed God, cursed Him, or swore falsely or profanely in His name; and to anyone who claimed that it was not sinful to speak obscenely, or steal, cheat, and defraud, or commit adultery, fornication, incest, or sodomy, or that any of

---

[33]*Journals H.C.*, vol. 6, pp. 430 (June 21), 437 (July 5), 440 (July 12), 443–44 (July 19). "A Declaration of the Army," July 19, 1650, in Abbott, *Cromwell*, vol. 2, p. 286.

[34]C. H. Firth and R. S. Rait, eds., *Acts and Ordinances of the Interregnum, 1642–1660* (London, 1911, 3 vols.), vol. 2, pp. 109–112. *Journals H.C.*, vol. 6, p. 453. John Milton, "Of Civil Power," in *The Works of John Milton*, ed. Frank Allen Patterson (New York, 1931–1938, 18 vols.), vol. 6, p. 11.

the enumerated sins was as holy as praying or preaching. In addition, the act covered anyone who professed that whatever he did, "whether Whoredom, Adultery, Drunkenness or the like open Wickedness," could be done without sin or expressed the God within him; and anyone who professed that heaven consisted in acting out the things that were sinful, or that one committing them was closer to God or reached perfection by feeling no remorse, or that sin had God's approval, or that there was no such thing as sin.

A month later the same House of Commons passed an act that repealed all enactments requiring uniformity in religious belief and practice, or establishing any form of religion in England. That statute of September 1650 also advanced the cause of religious liberty by implying that no establishment of religion should exist and by allowing every variety of Christian worship. As an alternative to Sunday worship, one might privately preach, pray, read the Bible, or discuss it. In effect, toleration existed for anyone not subject to the provisions of the Blasphemy Acts of 1648 (Socinianism) and 1650 (Ranterism). The Toleration Act was fittingly denoted an act for the relief of "religious and peaceable people."[35]

On the very day of the passage of the Toleration Act, the House tried two Ranters who had been arrested, Laurence Clarkson and Major William Rainborough, a former Leveller. Clarkson was a great prize, for his *Single Eye* was the immediate provocation of the Blasphemy Act of 1650, although Coppe claimed credit for it. He too had been captured and awaited his turn to be examined. The House's committee on Ranters had already examined Clarkson. He was a difficult witness, for he admitted nothing, demanded that his accusers prove that he wrote the book whose title page bore only the initials "L.C.," and refused to answer incriminatory questions. The committee, however, reported that he had confessed, and the House summarily

---

[35] "An Act for Relief of Religious and Peaceable People," in Firth and Rait, eds., *Acts and Ordinances*, vol. 2, pp. 423–425.

condemned him as guilty and ordered the burning of his book. They sentenced him to a month in jail, after which he was to be banished "and not to return, upon Pain of Death." The sentence of banishment was not carried out, probably because it was illegal. Indeed, the entire trial of Clarkson by the House of Commons was illegal. By the terms of the Blasphemy Act of 1650 the accused was to be held for trial before a judge, a justice of the peace, or a mayor, and the sentence of banishment could be imposed only after a second lawful conviction. Clarkson was released from prison after about fourteen weeks. Rainborough, for his Ranter conduct, was simply stripped of his rank and discharged from the army.[36]

When the same committee of the House examined the author of the *Fiery Flying Rolls*, "the wild deportment of Mr. Copp the great Ranter" made news. He disrupted the proceedings by acting like a lunatic—talking to himself and flinging fruit and nuts about the room. His having "disguised himself into a madnesse" was rational, because the act of 1650 exempted persons "distracted in brain," and Coppe apparently believed that appearing mad was the appropriate response of a sane man in an insane world. The tactic failed; they returned him to Newgate Prison and left him there. Although the statue of limitations had run out on Coppe's offense, the House of Commons did not stick at a legal nicety. Like John Biddle, Coppe received no trial, not even a formal condemnation by the House, and they had already done him the honor of burning his book.[37]

In Newgate, Coppe was as feisty as ever, at first. He received visitors with éclat and converted some fellow prisoners. But he had little of Biddle's courage and consistency. Ranters were not cut out to suffer for a cause. A few months later Coppe published

[36]*Journals H.C.*, vol. 6, p. 475 (Sept. 27, 1650). Clarkson, *Lost Sheep*, pp. 30–31.

[37]*Weekly Intelligencer*, Oct. 1–8, 1651, quoted in William M. Clyde, *Freedom of the Press from Caxton to Cromwell* (London, 1934), p. 206, and Morton, *World of the Ranters*, p. 103. *Routing of Ranters*, p. 2. *Journals H.C.*, vol. 6, p. 475 (Oct. 1, 1650). Coppe's book was reprinted in January 1650; the House ordered it burned in February; the committee examined him in September, more than six months after the offense.

a hemidemisemiquaver of a recantation; it was a protest, denying that he held blasphemous opinions and complaining that he had been defamed. The government paid no attention to him. After fourteen months of incarceration, Coppe published his *Return to the wayes of Truth*, begging Parliament's pardon. He renounced his blasphemous opinions, although he retained his social radicalism. While damning the conventional sins, he emphasized hypocrisy, a lecherous heart, and tyranny over the poor as the worst sins. If a "fellow creature" hungered, Coppe would feed him: "If I have bread it shall, or should be his, else all my religion is in vain. I am for dealing bread to the hungry, for cloathing the naked, for breaking of every yoak, for the letting of the oppressed go free." Doing otherwise was sinful—not in a religious sense but sinful nonetheless. But he was on the side of the angels on the issue of righteous living, so the government set him free. As part of the bargain, he had to preach a recantation sermon at Burford, where Cromwell had suppressed the Leveller mutiny. A minister who heard Coppe's sermon remained unconvinced. Coppe, he wrote, used "melting words, Honey-sweet, smooth as oyle, but full of poison."[38]

The act of 1650 punished the Ranter conviction that, if God was in man, man was God. Some Ranters took that literally, among them William Franklin, a ropemaker of London. His spiritual adventure and apprehension occurred before the passage of the statute. Its "Franklin clause" was intended to remedy a gap in the law. Franklin had been a pious Congregationalist, but, on recovering from an illness that affected his mind, he announced that he was God and Christ. In 1649 he fell in with Ranters, abandoned his wife, and began practicing free love. One of his women, Mary Gadbury, was a religious eccentric given to visions. That Christ had been reborn in Franklin came to her in a revelation, and she spread the glad tidings. When a minister questioned the morality of her living with Franklin, she replied that

---

[38] *A Remonstrance of the sincere and zealous Protestation of Abiezer Coppe* (1651). *Copps Return to the Wayes of Truth*, pp. 14, 19–21. Tickell, *Bottomless Pit*, p. 38.

Adam and Eve had lived naked in their innocence and had been unashamed till sin brought shame into the world; but Christ had taken sin away. She called herself the spouse of Christ and claimed to be equal to God. In late 1649 Franklin and Gadbury left London to bring their gospel to the Southampton countryside. They made converts and even found disciples. "Now," wrote an eyewitness, "doth this poysonous infection begin to amaine [at full speed] to spread itself, having gotten many, and these also very active persons, to be the Preachers, Spreaders, and publishers of it abroad to the people. . . . They perswade others to imbrace and entertain also, that this Franklin is the Son of God, the Christ, the Messiah." Millenarians expected King Jesus but not that he would spout Ranter doctrines. Franklin, Gadbury, and their disciples were arrested in 1650. At first, they all claimed, and Franklin agreed, that he was literally Christ. The disciples, having been reborn when they met him, dated their ages from that event. They were steadfast in their new beliefs until their leader betrayed them. Confronted with prison, he recanted, angering his disciples and causing them to abandon him. Mary Gadbury, unrepentant, was sent to Bridewell Prison, where she was whipped intermittently for several weeks. The men received prison sentences but were released on giving sureties for good behavior. Franklin, who was penniless, joined Gadbury in Bridewell. When the next impostors came along, the law was readier to deal with them.[39]

The act of 1650 and the imprisonment of Salmon, Clarkson, Coppe, and Franklin did not intimidate some Ranters. George Foster published his *Sounding of the Last Trumpet*, apocalyptically restating the social doctrines of the early Coppe. Foster presented God as the Great Leveller who would usher in King Jesus' communist utopia after overthrowing the rich, the clergy, and Parliament—all oppressors of the poor. Jacob Bauthumley's *Light and Dark Sides of God* was quietistic but anti-Trinitarian and

[39]Humphrey Ellis, *Pseudochristus: Or, A true and fanciful Relation of the Grand Impostures, Horrid Blasphemies, Abominable Practices* (1650), pp. 33–38, 42–51.

pantheistic. Bauthumley, once a cobbler from Leicester, wrote his little book when he was a soldier. The army, following its own law, made an example of him: he was punished by being bored through the tongue with a hot iron. The army suppressed its Ranters remorselessly. Cromwell himself cashiered one Ranter officer for denying that man could sin. Ranter officers lost their commissions and, like rank-and-file Ranters, were publicly whipped. Some soldiers were suspended by their thumbs, and one, a "W. Smith," was hanged by the neck at York, at the close of 1650, "for denying the Deity, Arianlike," and for other unnamed Ranter practices. Following the act of 1650, the police cracked down on civilian Ranters. Systematic raids resulted in scores of arrests. In one case, eight Ranters, taken in a London tavern, were sent to Bridewell to beat hemp, and the two who were the most offensive were put on trial at Old Bailey, the seat of the central criminal court in London, and sentenced to six months in prison. Other Ranters, a gang of them, were sentenced to be whipped at Bridewell. The police raids continued into 1651. We may disbelieve one report that a Ranter, supposedly in league with the devil, escaped after he "called for . . . a pissepot, and in an instant, upon a great flash of fire, vanished, and was never seen more."[40]

Undoubtedly some Ranters were mentally deranged. One writer classified "these Atheistical Creatures" as either Free Will Ranters or your mad Ranters, for they are lunatics very often." They were punished anyway because of the enormity of their blasphemous conceits. Two women, both named Elizabeth Sorrell and related to each other, were arrested for blaspheming the "Holy Trinitie" and claiming the power to raise the dead. Four

[40]George Foster's *Sounding of the Last Trumpet* (1651) sounds like the work of an antinomian Seeker, not a Ranter. Cohn, *Pursuit of the Millennium*, p. 303, reported that Bauthumley's tongue was bored—I could not verify the fact from a primary source; Morton, *World of the Ranters*, p. 96, and Hill, *World Upside Down*, p. 176, retail the same incident. Samuel Rawson Gardiner, *History of the Commonwealth and Protectorate* (London, 1894–1901, 3 vols.), vol. 1, p. 396; Jones, *Studies in Mystical Religion*, p. 479 n. 2; and Morton, *World of the Ranters*, pp. 104–105, describe the treatment of Ranters in the army. See also *Arraignment and Tryall*, p. 4; *The Ranters Recantation* (1650), p. 5; *Routing the Ranters*, pp. 2–3; *Ranters Last Sermon*, pp. 6–7; *Strange Newes from Newgate*, p. 6.

of their followers were also arrested, and at least one of the Sorrells was sent to jail. Messianic delusions were not uncommon among Ranters. In the same year, 1651, Richard King was imprisoned for the blasphemous claim that his pregnant wife was about to give birth to the Holy Ghost. Mary Adams also went to jail for claiming that her unborn child was Jesus Christ, although Joan Robins contested that claim by saying the same about her own child; she too earned a sentence for blasphemy, also in 1651. It was a vintage year for messiahs. The two most notorious were Joan's husband, John Robins, and Thomas Tany.[41]

John Robins was a blasphemer who inspired blasphemy in others. Thomas Tilford, first arrested as a follower of the Sorrells, transferred his allegiance to Robins and, like Robins, whom he called "God the Father, and the Father of our Lord Jesus Christ," landed in jail for blasphemy. Robins, as well as the Sorrells, claimed the power to raise the dead, but he went further. By his own statement he had already raised Cain, Benjamin the son of Jacob, the prophet Jeremiah, and Judas; he had not only raised but redeemed them. Lodowick Muggleton, then as associate of Robins and later a great heresiarch, recorded that he had had "nine or ten of them at my house at a time, of those that were said to be raised from the dead. For I do not speak this from a Hear-say from Others, but from a perfect Knowledge, which I have seen and heard from themselves." Robins, whom an enemy called "the Shakers god" and "the Ranters' god," allowed his followers to worship him. He was fluent in the Scriptures, claimed to have been Adam and then Melchizedek in previous incarnations, and came by his Hebrew, Greek, and Latin, he said, "by inspiration." He had a plan to lead 144,000 people out of England to the Mount of Olives in the Promised Land. Joshua Garment, his Moses, would part the waters of the Red Sea for the pilgrims, and Robins would feed them with manna from heaven. In May

[41]Stubs, *Ranters Declaration*, p. 4. John Cordy Jeafferson, ed., *Middlesex County Records* (London, 1886–1892, 7 vols.), vol. 3, p. 204. *A List of some of the Grand Blasphemers and Blasphemies* (1654), broadsheet. *The Ranters Creed, Being a true copie of the Examination of a blasphemous lot of people called Ranters* (1651), pp. 1–6. Taylor, *Ranters of Both Sexes*, pp. 2–3.

1651 Robins, his wife, and eleven disciples, including the Kings and the Sorrells, were imprisoned. After a year in jail, Robins addressed a letter of recantation to Cromwell, which won him a discharge.[42]

Thomas Tany, an associate of Robins, spent six months in Newgate for his blasphemies. He had abandoned his business as a goldsmith to proclaim that God had personally spoken to him, giving him to understand that he was a Jew of the tribe of Reuben whose mission was to lead the Jews back to the Promised Land and rebuild the Temple. By divine command, Tany changed his name to Theaurau John and, according to Muggleton, circumcised himself. Tany had many silly ideas, some of them sublime. He claimed to be the earl of Essex, heir to the throne of England, and in a pamphlet of 1651 debated Magna Carta "with the Thing called Parliament." He ranted madly in the streets about his mission as high priest of the Jews and the indwelling of God. Following his prison term he was quiet for several years, but in 1654 he was claiming that, as a descendant of Charlemagne, he was entitled to the crown of France. As that year closed, he publicly burned the Bible and then assaulted the House of Commons while it debated the fate of John Biddle, the Socinian. With a long, rusty sword, Tany hacked away at the doors of Parliament, slashing at people nearby. After he was subdued and brought before the bar of the House, he explained, irrationally, that the people were ready to stone him (the Old Testament punishment for blasphemy) because he had burned the Bible. Asked why he had burned it, he said it had deceived him: it was only letters and idolatry, not "Life" and "the word of God." But he "did it not of himself: And

---

[42]*List of Grand Blasphemers. A Declaration of John Robins, the false prophet*, by G.H., an Ear-witness (1651), pp. 1–6, includes statements by Robins in which he exalted himself as the "third Adam," who was divinely inspired, but denied being God or immortal. *Ranters Creed*, pp. 1–6. Taylor, *Ranters of Both Sexes*, pp. 1–6, alleged, in the subtitle and elsewhere, that Robins "doth Accuse himselfe to be the great God of Heaven." See also Lodowick Muggleton, *Acts of the Witnesses*, in Frost and Frost, eds., *Works of Reeve and Muggleton*, vol. 3, pp. 20–23, 45–48; the quotation is on p. 21.

being asked, Who bid him do it; saith, God." The House, taking him for a Quaker, resolved that, for drawing his sword, burning the Bible, and declaring that it was not the word of God, he be committed to the Gatehouse Prison. After his liberation some months later, he revived his project for restoring the Jews in Jerusalem. There being no Jews in England, Tany sailed to Amsterdam but perished at sea.[43]

Robert Norwood, a friend of Tany, was a more conventional Ranter, if Ranters of any stripe can be said to have been conventional. A former army captain, he came to the Ranter way of thinking by abandoning belief in the immortality of the soul, the physical existence of heaven and hell, and the literalness of the resurrection. Convicted in Old Bailey in 1652 for the crime of blasphemy, he was sentenced to six months' imprisonment under the act of 1650. Richard Faulkner of Petersfield was lucky that Parliament did not get him before the criminal courts did. He not only drank a toast to the devil; he said "our saviour Christ was a bastard," and, with the class consciousness of a Ranter, added that Joseph was only a poor carpenter. He too got six months.[44]

When Parliament got hold of William Erbury in 1652, it was scraping the barrel. Although Erbury's record made him a likely suspect, he was no Ranter. After attending Oxford he had been an Anglican priest frequently in trouble with the Court of High Commission. In 1640 he became a Puritan, later an Independent. During the civil war he was a chaplain in the army. Thomas Ed-

[43]Muggleton, *Acts of the Witnesses*, in Frost and Frost, eds., *Works of Reeve and Muggleton*, vol. 3, pp. 20, 42–45. Tany, *The Nations Right in Magna Charta discussed with the Thing called Parliament* (1651) and *Theaurau John his Aurora* (1651). *D.N.B.* on Tany, vol. 19, pp. 363–364.

[44]Norwood wrote the preface to Tany's *Theaurau John his Aurora*. See also *The Case and Trial of Capt. Robert Norwood* (1651) and *A Brief discourse made by Capt. Robert Norwood . . . upon an indictment . . . in Old Bayly* (1652); *List of Grand Blasphemers*. Norwood denied the charges of blasphemy and professed Christianity, yet he was anticlerical and said, "Verily I cannot but abhor the Doctrines and Principles of most Christians," which he condemned as "Doctrines of devils." He embraced antinomianism, and declared we sin "by oppression, by injustice, and by deceit" (*Case and Trial*, pp. 7, 13, 15, 17).

wards charged that he vented antinomian doctrines, which could mean merely that he advocated universal salvation. Cheynell, another Presbyterian, debated Erbury publicly and accused him of Socinian blasphemies. Like Biddle, Erbury denied the divinity of Christ while preaching the "inner Christ," a doctrine of universal incarnation in believers. He defied all labels, except that of Seeker. His politics were as radical as his religion. Although he flirted with Ranterism and shared some of its views, much in Ranterism offended him. When examined by the parliamentary investigating committee, he denounced the Ranters, but that occurred in 1652, after the law had turned against them and the craze had subsided. That the committee examined Erbury is proof that by that date the Ranter heresiarchs had been silenced or driven underground. There were still some Ranters around, but if they did not keep to themselves they risked being caught like Henry Walker, a tavern keeper who pronounced "a poxe on Jesus Christ" and said he would rather be in bed with his girlfriend than in paradise with Jesus.[45]

The prosecution of John Reeve and Lodowick Muggleton under the act of 1650 was as misdirected as the investigation of Erbury. Worse, their prosecution, like that of Biddle, reflected religious prejudice against mere doctrinal novelty. Reeve and Muggleton were upright men with exceedingly strange ideas, too strange to countenance. These two cousins were not Ranters, although Reeve had briefly consorted with John Robins and Thomas Tany, and Muggleton had been fascinated by them. Muggleton had also avidly read the works of Jacob Boehme, one of the mystics who believed in the indwelling of God and in universal salvation. By 1653, however, when Reeve and Muggleton were arrested, they had completely repudiated Ranterism; in-

---

[45]Herbert John McLachlan, *Socinianism in Seventeenth Century England* (London, 1951), pp. 226–237, is good on Erbury; see also Hill, *World Upside Down*, pp. 154–159. The primary source is *The Testimony of William Erbury* (1658), which includes his encounter with Cheynell and his denunciation of the Ranters, pp. 3–18, 315–337. On Walker, see *Middlesex County Records*, vol. 3, p. 215, May 25, 1653.

deed, they felt so repelled by it that they cursed its advocates—
and when they cursed anyone, he was damned everlastingly.[46]

Thomas Babington Macaulay amusingly referred to a "mad
tailor, named Lodowick Muggleton, [who] wandered from pothouse to pothouse, tippling ale, and denouncing eternal torments
against all those who refused to believe, on his testimony, that
the Supreme Being was only six feet high, and that the sun was
just four miles from the earth." Muggleton, who knew nothing of
astronomy, was more sober than Macaulay and no madder. His
logic told him that if God made man in His own image, God was
human in form and size, exactly like Jesus Christ. Muggleton,
like Reeve, was only a tailor. If the Old Testament prophets
could have been herdsmen, and Christ's apostles fishermen, he
asked, then why couldn't tailors be the two witnesses mentioned
in Revelation 11:3? Reeve and Muggleton, like the new faith
they had the boldness to imagine, were Interregnum period
pieces fashioned by the religious turbulence of their time, but
"Muggletonianism" survived it. Of all the sects spawned in that
period, only two have endured, Quakerism and Muggletonianism, the two which in the seventeenth century hated each other.
The Muggletonians are doubtless the most obscure and tiny sect
in all Christendom.[47]

Reeve and Muggleton no more advocated sin than a believing Presbyterian did. No Ranter shared their fantastic opinion
that Eve, the Ranter's sex symbol, was the devil come to flesh.
The two witnesses, Reeve and Muggleton, thought that prose-

---

[46]Frost and Frost, eds., *Works of Reeve and Muggleton*, contains books, pamphlets, and
letters. Alexander Gordon, who did the *D.N.B.* essay on Muggleton (and those on Reeve,
Coppe, Tany, and Robins), published two lectures which constitute all the scholarship on
Muggletonianism: "The Origin of the Muggletonians," paper read before the Liverpool
Literary and Historical Society, April 5, 1869, and "Ancient and Modern Muggletonians,"
paper read before the same society a year later. The only other writings on the subject are
James Hyde, "The Muggletonians and the Document of 1729," *New-Church Review*, vol.
7 (1900) pp. 215–227; George Charles Williamson, *Lodowick Muggleton: A Paper Read Before Ye Sette of Odd Volumes* (London, 1919), which derives wholly from Gordon.

[47]T. B. Macaulay, *The History of England, from the Accession of James II* (London,
1849–1865, 5 vols.), vol. 1, p. 164.

cuting them for their beliefs was blasphemous. The act of 1650 aimed at those who made a religion out of immorality or who justified sin by blasphemous opinions. Reeve and Muggleton, by contrast, were puritanical; as men of rectitude, they were industrious, believers in Christ, faithful to their wives, and opposed to drunkenness and gambling. Muggleton, who died at the patriarchal age of eighty-nine, proudly recorded that he had never lived off the Gospel as the apostles had; he had always earned his livelihood from his craft as a tailor, accumulated property, paid his taxes, and had no debts. Although he was not given to religious enthusiasm, spiritual fires smoldered within him. He had lost his zeal as a Calvinist after the civil war fractured Puritanism into squabbling factions, and he stopped the habit of praying. If anything followed death, he wrote in his autobiography, he would leave it to God to do "what He would with me." God did not wait for Muggleton's death. In 1651 he began getting revelations that opened to him "the Paradise of heaven, within man upon earth," and he began reading the Bible again. Reeve, long envious of Muggleton's serenity, finally experienced similar revelations. Reaching a state of peace, the two thought they would never again dispute with anyone about religion. Then, in 1652 Muggleton recalled, "we were made the greatest meddlers in Religion of all Men in the World. Because our faces were against all Mens Religion in the World, of what Sect or Opinion soever."[48]

Reeve got the message first. As he recorded in a tract of 1652, the one that got them into trouble for blasphemy,

> the Lord Jesus, the only wise God, whose glorious person is resident above or beyond the stars, . . . spake to me Reeve, saying, I have given thee understanding of my mind in the Scriptures, above all men in the world. . . . I have chosen thee my last messenger for a great work unto this bloody unbelieving world; and I have given thee Lodowicke Muggleton to be thy mouth. . . . I

---

[48]Muggleton, *Acts of the Witnesses*, in Frost and Frost, eds., *Works of Reeve and Muggleton*, vol. 3, pp. 38–39.

have put the two-edged sword of my Spirit into thy mouth, that whoever I pronounce blessed through thy mouth is blessed to eternity, and whoever I pronounce cursed through thy mouth is cursed to eternity.

Reeve and Muggleton had a divine commission to teach the Word as they understood it, and they were armed with a unique power. In compliance with other messages from the Lord Jesus, they pronounced curses of damnation upon Theaurau John Tany and John Robins. The curse on Robins, a marvel of hellfire and brimstone, damned him eternally as the Antichrist. Robins, who was in Bridewell Prison at the time, put his hands on the grates of his cell and uttered, "It is finished; the Lord's will be done," and soon after he recanted. The new prophets began attracting the crowds that had thronged around Tany and Robins.[49]

In their revised version of Christianity, Reeve and Muggleton renounced the Trinitarian principle. No point was clearer at the time of their arrest in 1653. Reeve, until his death in 1658, and Muggleton thereafter, continued to develop their theology without ever resolving some contradictions. From the beginning, though, they believed that the Father, the Son, and the Holy Ghost were synonymous expressions for one real person, the God Jesus Christ. In the beginning, when He was the Creator, He was Spirit, but He came to earth as Jesus the man, to die so that He would understand the human predicament. On the cross He cried out to Elijah, whom He had left on the throne of glory as His representative while He was mortal. When Jesus died, God died, but rose again body and soul, and thereafter paid no further attention to man. Having set everything in motion, God would not concern Himself with the human race again until Judgment Day. So wars, plagues, famine, and human cruelty were the work of the devil, a fallen angel who had planted his seed in Eve and lived in all her descendants through Cain.

---

[49]Ibid., pp. 47–48. The Reeve quotation is from his *A Transcendent Spiritual Treatise* (1652), in ibid., vol. 1, pp. 1–2, reprinted the 2nd ed. of 1756. My description of the Reeve-Muggleton theology is from this work.

God, having fixed a conscience in man's heart, allowed him to work out his own destiny. Thus, every person had within him both the spirit of God and that of the devil; as the voice heard by Reeve had said, the kingdoms of heaven and hell were in man's body. On Judgment Day, God would resurrect the righteous, body and soul. Till then, He would do nothing. After that time, this earth would become hell, inhabited by the damned. One need only believe and live righteously. All else was pointless: worship, churches, sacraments, ceremonies, clergymen, and their ordinances. Anyone who heard the message of God's last prophets, Reeve and Muggleton, and willfully disbelieved was damned.

Some angry readers delivered copies of Reeve's book to the lord mayor of London and demanded an arrest. Reeve and his "mouth," Muggleton, said that God had died, repudiated the doctrine of the Trinity, and claimed that the soul was mortal. It was too much. The mayor ordered their arrest. When the two witnesses appeared before him, he had a copy of their book and copies of their letters to the Presbyterian ministers of London ordering them to quit preaching or be damned eternally for the unpardonable sin of blasphemy against the Holy Spirit. Reeve admitted writing the book, Muggleton the curses. "You are accused," the mayor said, "for denying the three Persons in the Trinity: You say there is but one Person Christ Jesus, you deny the Father." Reeve replied that they accepted the Trinity as "all but one person." When the mayor answered that the devil had spoken to Reeve, the prisoner damned his lordship and demanded an explanation of God. He was an "infinite, incomprehensible Spirit," the mayor said, with "no Body or Person at all." Reeve insisted that Jesus had a body "in form like Man, Sin excepted." Then the mayor read from the act of Parliament "newly made against Blasphemy," which condemned any man who said that he was God and that God was nowhere else. Reeve and Muggleton had not, of course, made that claim. Muggleton informed the mayor that, as a mere temporal magistrate, he was "not to judge of Blasphemy against God; not those that made this

Act neither." And, with stupefying arrogance, Muggleton added that God had chosen only his two witnesses to be judges of blasphemy. The mayor sent them to Newgate.

After a month in jail they were tried before a jury, with the mayor presiding, at Old Bailey. The charge of blasphemy was based on the denial of the Trinity in Reeve's book. After a few questions and direct answers, the trial was done, "and the Jury laid their Heads a little together" and found them guilty. They were sentenced to six months in Bridewell. When they got out they wrote *A Remonstrance from the Eternal God,* which they addressed to the government. They restated their mission as the Lord's messengers and lamented their unjust sentence, but in the main they pleaded for liberty of conscience. They did not understand that the power they claimed, to damn willful disbelievers, conflicted with conscience, "which belongs not to man to judge, but to God only that knows the heart." But they made a ringing plea in behalf of "the free people of England, that they should not only enjoy their civil liberties, but the liberty of consciences towards God."[50]

The government, which paid no attention to their demand, did not understand that in Reeve and Muggleton it had had behind bars a pair of heresiarchs whose opinions violated the act of 1648, not the one of 1650. When Reeve died four years after coming out of prison, Muggleton took command of the new sect, and he survived until 1698. He would be troubled three times more with the charge of blasphemy, but he was a witness with a divine commission. He could not be stopped by a government that did not impose crippling sentences and could not distinguish a Muggletonian from a Ranter.

The government never did stamp out all the Ranters. In time they faded away; they were never more than a passing craze. Coppe changed his name, became a physician, and was buried in the town church. As late as 1655 he reciprocated a visit that

---

[50]The imprisonment and trial of 1653 are reported in ibid., vol. 3, pp. 67–78. *A Remonstrance,* in ibid., vol. 1, pp. 15–22.

George Fox had once paid him in a Coventry jail; when Fox was in jail, Coppe and Bauthumley and a company of Ranters visited him. Fox called Bauthumley a "great Ranter" in 1655, but Bauthumley too lapsed into respectability; he became keeper of the library in Leicester. Salmon emigrated to Barbados. Coppin became a Seeker, and Clarkson a Muggletonian. That Ranterism survived throughout the 1650s is evident from occasional glimpses of it. In 1655 R. Forneworth, a Quaker, published a denunciation of blasphemous Ranterism in this sketch of Robert Wilkinson of Leicester:

> ... he said he was both God and Devill, and he said there was no God but him, and no Devill but him, and he said whom he blest was blest, and whom he curst was curst, and he said he was a serpent, and so he is, and he said the Apostles were lyars and deceivers, and I gave him a Bible to prove that, and he said the Bible was a pack of lyes, and there was neither heaven nor hell but here, and yet he was both in heaven and hell, and had as lieve be in hell, as in heaven, and he said he was a serpent, and a whoremaster, and before he said he was born of God, and could not commit sin.

That is Ranterism, straight and pure. As late as 1659, Richard Hickcock, another Quaker, also published a tract "against the People call'd Ranters," in which he complained about those who cursed, lied, fornicated, believed that one sinned only if he thought so, and contended that God is the author of sin.[51]

When Ranters surfaced publicly, the government prosecuted. Richard Coppin, a founding Ranter, would never have served time for blasphemy if he had shunned publicity. His first tract, *Divine Teachings* (1649), for which Abiezer Coppe wrote the preface, became a source that other Ranters looted for ideas and im-

---

[51]*Journal of Fox*, pp. 182, 195. Morton, *World of the Ranters*, pp. 97, 138. Hill, *World Upside Down*, p. 176. R. Forneworth, *Ranter Principles and Deceits Discovered*, p. 19. Richard Hickcock, *Testimony against the People call'd Ranters*, pp. 2–4. Fox referred to "Ranters" as late as 1668 (*Journal*, ed. Nickalls, p. 622), but he meant rude, disruptive people, a standard by which Fox and all Quakers of the 1650s were Ranters.

agery. After the act of 1650, Coppin was quiet for a while. He claimed later that he had never abandoned his beliefs of 1649, although he explicitly repudiated Ranterism as well as Quakerism and every other religion but his own. Coppin the Seeker was an antinomian but no libertine. For him Scripture had become "dead letter" unless understood through the revelation that God had given to the Christ in Coppin. Yet his God was as much in everyone as in Christ, and made every person perfect. Coppin also denied the physical existence of heaven and hell. A Worcester jury convicted him of blasphemy in 1652, but the judge, noting that the beliefs proscribed by the act of 1650 did not precisely correspond with those charged against Coppin, bound him over for retrial. A jury in Oxford found him guilty too, but again a judge, disagreeing, persuaded the jury to reconsider its verdict; it divided indecisively. That was in 1653. In the next year Coppin was again arrested for blasphemy because he preached in violation of the act of 1650, but once more a judge strictly construed the statute in his favor. Coppin had clearly repudiated Ranterism, but few conventional Christians could tell the difference.[52]

In 1655 Coppin foolishly agreed to a public debate in Rochester on theological matters—against a Presbyterian, no less. Major General Thomas Kelsey heard Coppin. Assisted by justices of the peace, Kelsey accused him of blasphemy for having declared that Christ as a human being had been defiled by sin, that all men would be saved, and that heaven and hell existed only in man. Kelsey recommended to Cromwell that Coppin should be banished like Biddle, but Cromwell let the law take its course. Belatedly, Coppin received the statutory six-month sentence.[53]

---

[52]On Coppin, see *D.N.B.*, vol. 9, pp. 1117–1118. For his earlier beliefs on the indwelling God, see his *Divine Teachings*, pp. 8–9. His *Truth's Testimony* (1654), p. 25, reports his rejection of Ranters; that tract describes his later beliefs and five blasphemy prosecutions in which he ably defended himself.

[53]Kelsey to Cromwell, 1653, in T. Birch, ed., *A Collection of Sate Papers of John Thurloe* (London, 1742, 7 vols.), vol. 4, p. 486.

The same fate awaited two weavers in the village of Lacock in Wiltshire. William Bond and Thomas Hibbord rantingly maintained in public that there was no God, no Christ, only the sun overhead. Bond said that his friend Tom Lampire of Melksham could write better Scriptures than the Bible. Heaven was good fortune in this world, and hell was poverty. Hibbord, who believed that God was in anything thought sinful, said he "would sell all religions for a jug of beer." That was in 1656. The grand jury that indicted them deplored the fact that there were "many" people wandering about spreading such blasphemies.[54]

Ranterism could persevere in a free and disordered society like that of the England of the Interregnum, but not in Presbyterian Scotland. The Scots did not have the problem that Kelsey described to Cromwell after Coppin's arrest: "people are ready to cry out for liberty of conscience, and not backward to say it's persecution worse than in the bishops time, and the like." Uniformity in religion and severe persecution flourished in Scotland like heath and thistle. To a Scot of the established church, a sentence of merely six months for treason against God was coddling blasphemers. Alexander Agnew of Dumfries, a vagrant known as Jock of Broad Scotland, found that out. He was an atheist with the Ranter habit of talking too much and too offensively, but without sense enough to know when to shut up. His blasphemies, as his indictment stated, were frequent, uttered wherever he went. When asked whether he desired to attend church, he replied, "Hang God." God had given him nothing, and he was just as indebted to the devil, whom he thought the more powerful. When asked how many persons were in the Godhead, he replied only one person, God made all; Christ, a mere man, was not God. Jock denied that he was a sinner, scorned God's mercy, and mocked all worship. Declaring that he never had any religion and never would, he flatly said, "there was no God, nor Christ."

[54]Historical Manuscripts Commission, *Report on Manuscripts in Various Collections* (London, 1901), vol. 1, pp. 132–133.

Only nature reigned. Heaven and hell did not exist, the Bible was false, and man had no soul. On that evidence, the jury found him guilty. On May 21, 1651, Jock of Broad Scotland was hanged from a gibbet.[55]

[55]Kelsey in Birch, ed., *Thurloe Papers*, vol. 4, p. 486. *Mercurius Politicus*, June 26–July 3, 1656, reported the case of Jock of Broad Scotland, reprinted in David Masson, *The Life of John Milton* (London, 1859–1894, 7 vols.), vol. 5, pp. 92–94.

A Humanist Confronts the Law

*O*NCE a humanist named W. H. Auden confronted the law and found it inexplicable in a poem that included this verse:

Law, says the judge as he looks down his nose
Speaking clearly and most severely
Law is, as I've told you before
Law is, as you know I suppose
Law is, but let me explain it once more
Law is the law.

I have less difficulty than Auden with the law. As an historian, I don't confront the law, I embrace it. I embrace it as a marvelously revealing humanistic field of study. For some the law may be a profession and for others a bewildering cluster of technical rules. For me law is a window on history, or, as Justice Oliver Wendell Holmes said, a magic mirror in which we see reflected not only our own lives but the lives of all men now and in the past—and that's what history is about. History is the collective memory of mankind, the broadest discipline of scholarship, and the most humane. It is an effort to understand what mankind was, is, and can be, and to make that effort we must try to discover what mankind has been and done and thought. Through the humanities we reflect on the fundamental question: What does it mean to be human? The law provides one of the clues that help reveal how people have tried to make moral and intellectual sense in a world in which irrationality, despair, loneliness, and death are as conspicuous as birth, friendship, hope, and reason.

Reason is the very basis and language of the law. Aristotle said law is reason free from passion. Cicero said law is right reason in agreement with nature. That reminds me of a story that shows an analogy to the judicial process. It shows that special blend of reason and nature, of logical insight and experience, that often characterizes the judicial process and legal reasoning.

It is a story about Jews who lived outside the ghetto communities of nineteenth-century Russia. Such Jews could not travel without official permission. After months of negotiation, an old Jewish scholar who lived in Odessa got permission to travel from Odessa to Moscow. He boarded the train, and after one stop a young man got on and sat down opposite him. The old scholar looked at the young man and said to himself:

He looks Jewish. He doesn't look like a peasant, and if he isn't a peasant, he probably comes from this district. If he comes from this district, he must be Jewish because this is a Jewish district. But if he's Jewish, where could he be going? I'm the only one in the district who has permission to travel to Moscow. To what place would he not need permission to travel? Oh, just outside Moscow there's the little village of Mozhaisk, and to Mozhaisk you don't need permission. But who could he be visiting in Mozhaisk? There are only two Jewish families in the whole of Mozhaisk, the Linskys and the Greenbaums. I know the Linskys are a terrible family, so he must be visiting the Greenbaums. But who would undertake a trip at this time of year unless he were a close personal relative? The Greenbaums have only daughters, so perhaps he's a son-in-law. But if he's a son-in-law, which daughter did he marry? Esther married that nice young lawyer from Budapest. What was his name? Alexander Cohen. Who did Sarah marry? Sarah married that no-goodnik, that salesman from Zhadomir. It must be Esther. So, if he married Esther, his name is Alexander Cohen and he comes from Budapest. Oh, the terrible anti-Semitism they have there now! He probably changed his name from Cohen. So what's the Hungarian equivalent of Cohen? Kovacs. However, to change his name because of anti-Semitism, a man would need status. So what kind of status could he have? A doctor's degree from the university.

At this point the old scholar got up, tapped the young man on the shoulder, and said, "Dr. Alexander Kovacs?" "Why, yes," said the young man, "but how did you know?" "Oh," replied the old scholar, "it stands to reason."

The story shows that legal reasoning springs from life. Law, Holmes said, is the witness and external deposit of our life. The history of law is the history of the development of people. Law is the point at which logic and life meet. As Holmes observed:

> The life of the law has not been logic: it has been experience. The felt necessities of the time, the prevalent moral and political theories, intuitions of public policy, even the prejudices which judges share with their fellow-men, have had a good deal more to do than the syllogism in determining the rules by which men should be governed.

Studying law as a branch of history is studying a dimension of human reality. Studying law, like studying religion, or philosophy, or literature, or politics, or art, can tell us about ourselves, can stretch our imaginations, can enrich our understanding of what it means to live in this time and this culture as well as in other times and in other cultures. To study history without studying law is to miss an essential part of the story: If we omit the law we cannot understand who we are and how we came to be as we are. We risk becoming partial amnesiacs groping to discover our identity as a people, our values and beliefs.

Studying legal history also introduces us to procedure. Law is preoccupied with procedure as well as with substance, and the history of liberty, as Justice Felix Frankfurter said, is largely the history of procedure. Constitutional rights are often procedural and are not technicalities. What is liberty if not the right to due process of law before the state can send us to prison or take our lives or our property: Without law there is no liberty, though there might be liberties. The difference between liberty and liberties is as great as the difference between God and gods. Because of his love of liberty, Justice Robert Jackson once said that he would rather live under Soviet substantive law enforced by our procedures than under our substantive law enforced by Soviet procedures.

A society reveals itself in its laws. Its points of growth and the interests that it most values may be disclosed even in the decision of seemingly technical and insignificant questions.

The ultimate question of legal history is, how does the law of a given time and place meaningfully connect with the society of which it is a part? In the United States the question is all the more pressing because, as was noted by Burke and Tocqueville, Americans are the most legal-minded of people. Accordingly, American legal history shows in striking fashion how law is shaped by and in turn shapes the thought and experience of the American people. Tocqueville, a jurist in his own country, was astonished to discover that "Scarcely any question arises in the United States which does not become, sooner or later, a subject of judicial debate. . . ." In the guise of legal disputes between private parties, matters of high policy involving great stakes are referred ultimately to the courts for decision, and this in a political democracy. Thus the opinions of judges are often political, economic, and social events as well as legal events.

Consider: The relation of the individual to the state and of the states to the nation; the role of the government in the economy; the private and public interests deemed important enough to secure in permanent and authoritative form; the comparative valuation placed on different activities and goals, and on liberty and order; the points of tension, of growth, and of power; and prevailing conceptions of rights, duties, and liabilities: all are exposed in the law.

We could, for example, take the great concept of individualism, which is based on the assumption that man is a creature of free will, and show how it manifests itself in our law and is central to our law. In constitutional law, individualism means equal protection of all individuals for the most personal rights. In criminal law, individualism is apparent in the fundamental premise that a crime may be committed only by a free moral agent who acts voluntarily, is accountable for his conduct, and is the object of retributive justice. Similarly in tort law and in contract law, the individual is free to work out his own destiny and is responsible for his decisions. Only a free responsible individual is capable of binding himself by contract or even committing a civil wrong upon another. The examples could be multiplied.

In sum, humanist learning, whether in the study of law or literature or art, is not merely contemplative and divorced from life. It is part of life and intensely practical, depending on how it is studied. Nothing is at one and the same time more philosophically contemplative and practically realistic than humanistic study.

Anecdotage

JUSTICE Felix Frankfurter was probably the foremost influence on my thinking about the Supreme Court. In 1953, as a young instructor at Brandeis University, I had published several articles lambasting judicial decisions that sustained Jim Crow laws. One of the articles appeared in *The New Republic*, for which Frankfurter had regularly written about the Court when he was a professor at Harvard Law School. Professor Frankfurter could be censurious and biting. My own articles were written in a similar spirit. One, which apparently outraged Frankfurter, dealt with "frauds and fallacies" in the law of segregation. I savaged not only *Plessy v. Ferguson* but decisions following *Plessy*, including the 1927 case of *Gong Lum v. Rice*,[1] in which the Court sustained a Mississippi ruling that classified a Chinese child as black and segregated her.

Frankfurter wrote a letter to my boss at Brandeis, his good friend Max Lerner, demanding to know who was the arrogant young instructor who dared to criticize even opinions of the Court that the "revered" Justices Oliver Wendell Holmes and Louis D. Brandeis had joined. Showing me Frankfurter's letter, Lerner suggested that I answer it and give him a copy. The response took a couple of weeks, as I researched the law on fraud; I defended my view of the Court's failures, covering not only the law of segregation but, on the issue of genteel criticism, prece-

[1] 275 U.S. 78 (1927).

dents of rancorous language by Professor Frankfurter. My letter led to a correspondence, and as a result Frankfurter invited me to Washington as his guest to hear the arguments in *Brown v. Board of Education.* He also asked me to meet him in his chambers.

The moment I entered his chambers, Frankfurter sharply exclaimed, "There's that damn Jeffersonian liberal!" He started baiting me and finally succeeded in provoking an argument in which I sought to defend liberal judicial activism rather than judicial self-restraint. At the time I was considering a book on the Court and the Bill of Rights, in which I expected to champion the position of Hugo Black. Frankfurter made several sharp remarks about Black's inconsistencies and against Black's activist impulses. He also was remarkably spirited in slamming my views. The argument grew intense and I lost my sense of deference. I must have been brazen in my counterassault, discrediting several of Frankfurter's opinions for inconsistencies.

While talking animatedly and pacing before his big desk, I suddenly noticed that Frankfurter's face was vividly reddening. Then the slight, distinguished-looking scholarly jurist rose from his high-backed chair and slowly approached me with a clenched fist. I froze and thought, "My God, I'm going to be struck by a Justice of the Supreme Court of the United States." He came around the side of the desk, walked right up to me, flushed and tightfisted, and suddenly, poking a finger under my nose, he declared, "Good point, young man!" Then he returned to his chair, sat back, and beamed at me. He seemed delighted that I had supported my argument even at his expense.

Frankfurter taught me to criticize my most cherished beliefs by demanding valid evidence for any proposition. I learned to see at least two sides to every question and to appreciate the values of judicial self-restraint even more than those of judicial activism. Frankfurter became, for me, a model of intellectual rectitude. And he became a friend. He invited me to his home whenever I was in Washington. Once, when lunching with him, I was thrilled to hear him tell his servant to hold all calls "except

from Dean" (Acheson). I had the pleasure of presenting Frankfurter with an honorary degree at Brandeis University.

He was instrumental in my receiving a Guggenheim Fellowship. I had a good project and several all-star scholars as references, including Paul Freund and Mark Howe of the Harvard
Law School, and Henry Steele Commager and Richard B. Morris of the Columbia University Department of History, but I have
always believed that Frankfurter's letter made the difference.
The secretary-general of the Guggenheim Foundation was a
man with a formidable reputation, the greatly respected Henry
Allen Moe. Frankfurter wrote him the following letter, with a
copy to me: "Dear Moe: Levy is a very bright young man. Some-
day he may write something important. Give him a fellowship.
Felix Frankfurter." The fellowship enabled me to begin research
on the origins of the right against self-incrimination, eventually
resulting in a book that won the Pulitzer Prize. Frankfurter was
important, too, in helping me decide whether I should accept the
offer to become the first dean of the Graduate School of Arts and
Sciences at Brandeis University. I wanted the position but felt
guilty about betraying scholarship. Frankfurter, in response to
my request for advice, urged me to accept, saying that Edward
Gibbon could never have written his *Decline and Fall* had he not
had the experience of being a sergeant-major in the British army.
I did not know at the time that Gibbon probably never was, but
I accepted the deanship.

Hugo Black was scarcely as open-minded as Frankfurter.
Black once rebuked me for not having submitted the manuscript
of my book *Legacy of Suppression* for criticism by people who
agreed with his absolutist interpretation of freedom of the press.
Black was always the partisan: Justice Black differed not much
from Senator Black. A former clerk to Black once told me that
Black had underlined much of my book and made aspersive marginal asides. The justice required him to spend an entire summer
checking the footnotes and sources for *Legacy of Suppression*, looking for mistakes. He found none. Black, he said, insisted that the
book was wrong even if its facts were right, because of its inter-

pretation. I thought the evidence dictated the interpretation that the framers of the Bill of Rights narrowly conceived freedom of the press.

A close friend of Black, Professor Edmond Cahn of New York University Law School, tried to persuade him that *Legacy of Suppression* had some merit. Cahn reviewed the book very favorably for the *New York Herald Tribune* and recommended it to Black. In the first draft of his reply to Cahn, Black wrote of *Legacy*, "In brief my judgment is that it is probably one of the most devastating blows that has been delivered against civil liberty in America for a long time." I do not know whether Black ranked me above or below Joe McCarthy. In any case, he regretted that, despite Cahn's description of me as a "great libertarian," I "had seen fit to take this reactionary view of the First Amendment's purposes." Cahn assured Black that the First Amendment would survive my book, but Black moodily replied, "I hope you are right but I am afraid you are not in believing that Dean Levy's book has done no damage to the First Amendment." Black absolutely refused to read my *Jefferson and Civil Liberties: The Darker Side*, because the subtitle indicated that he would disagree with my viewpoint. He was no different from the great Jeffersonian scholar, Julian Boyd, editor of Jefferson's papers, who admitted that he had not read the book but condemned it anyway, because, he wrote, if I was right, he had wasted the best years of his life.

Frankfurter's reaction to *Legacy of Suppression* had been wholly favorable. In a letter to me he said he found the book "fortifying and cheering" at a time when too many professing liberals succumbed to what Brandeis called the most odious of doctrines, that the end justifies the means. Frankfurter wrote me that he would "rather have said what you say . . . than have written *McCulloch v. Maryland*"—high praise because Frankfurter thought that the opinion by John Marshall was the greatest in our history.

In *Brown v. Board of Education*, Thurgood Marshall, then leader of the NAACP Legal Defense Fund, answered the arguments of counsel who defended segregation. Shortly after he concluded, the Court adjourned and I returned to Frankfurter's chambers. We were chatting when Justice Robert S. Jackson burst into the room and, without taking any notice of me, blurted out excitedly, "Wasn't that colored fellow magnificent! He simply creamed John W. Davis." Frankfurter, obviously upset by Jackson's breach of judicial reticence in the presence of an outsider, broke in on him, introduced me to him, and changed the subject. It had been an electrifying moment. Later, according to scholars, Jackson was indecisive for a while on the outcome of the case. I had glimpsed a different Jackson.

Chief Justice Earl Warren arrived in Boston on a cold November day in 1957 to spend the commencement weekend at Brandeis and to receive an honorary degree. I presented him and was his host on behalf of the university for the weekend. Warren carried informality to extremes. I went to the hotel dressed in a tuxedo to meet him and escort him to a formal dinner. Learning his room number at the hotel desk, I knocked at his door. He did not inquire who was knocking. In a hearty voice he just boomed out, "Come in, come in! It's open." I opened the door and walked in to see the Chief Justice of the United States, a big ruddy man, standing there before me in his old-fashioned BVDs. The next day, when we had some time together, he wore a torn baggy sweater as we composed a speech for him to deliver to an interfaith meeting a few days later.

When the weekend was over, I was glad to take Warren back to Logan Airport to catch his plane. The intense activities at school and being on my best behavior with the chief justice had wearied me. That Sunday afternoon was unnaturally cold and windy. The heating system at Eastern Airlines wasn't working properly. We stood in a long line of overcoated people as we awaited the call for Warren's plane to be boarded. An official of the airlines recognized Warren and approached us, saying, "Mr. Chief Justice, kindly step this way to our VIP room. It has a hot-air heater, and we will be glad to make you comfortable while you wait and give you a drink." I was relieved at the prospect of the rescue, but Warren astonished and dismayed me when he replied: "Thank you so very much. I should be pleased to accept your offer. And," with a sweeping gesture of his arm, "all these good folk in line are invited too?" The flustered airline official replied that he could not accommodate more than the two of us because the VIP facilities were too small. Warren quietly responded, "In that case, I'll just wait here, thank you." We waited our turn with everyone else. The press had not been present. The sentiments Warren expressed were genuine. He was a folksy democrat and would accept no special favors.

That episode with Warren reminds me of a later time when I had lunch with Eleanor Roosevelt in the faculty dining room at Brandeis. On the way out, she excused herself and walked through the doorway leading to the kitchen. I thought she had made a mistake and followed her into the kitchen to advise her on the location of the ladies' room. I found that she was where she wanted to be, shaking hands with the cooks and waitresses, thanking them for lunch.

Thurgood Marshall on another occasion was also a degree recipient whom I presented. At the time, in 1961, he was the solicitor general of the United States, having resigned a seat on the federal court of appeals. I addressed him as Judge Marshall, but he was as relaxed and informal as a big puppy. He affected slangy speech and a buddy-buddy attitude. At breakfast he asked me whether I had seen the *New York Times* story on the Freedom Riders. A racially mixed group of young people riding a bus through the South had been set upon in Anniston, Alabama. Their bus had been overturned and burned. We discussed the episode for a few minutes, and Marshall then confided in me, "You know, I could never have joined them. I just couldn't have been a Freedom Rider." Not quite believing him, I asked, "Why not?" "It's my back," he replied. "I have a broad yellow streak up my back"—and he roared with laughter.

A wholly different sort of person was Chief Justice Warren Burger, whom I first met in Birmingham in 1976 on the occasion of the centennial of Justice Black's birth. We were both speakers in the event. Burger was said to have arrived in a private plane, and he took the entire top floor of the hotel with his nine bodyguards, who worked eight-hour shifts in batches of three each. I have never met a more starchy person than Burger. Pomposity enshrouded him; he was blanketed with his own sense of self-importance.

I resented the treatment accorded to me as well as others when a party was given for the speakers. Before we could enter the room, Burger's guards frisked us for weapons and searched briefcases and purses. Later I tried to engage Burger in conversation but was as unsuccessful as others. In 1971 the Court had decided, in *Bivens v. Six Unknown Agents*,[2] that the Fourth Amendment permits damage suits for injuries sustained in an illegal federal search. Burger had dissented in an opinion recommending that Congress should enact a statute establishing a remedy against the government in order to provide compensation for persons whose Fourth Amendment rights had been violated. It was an interesting idea. Moreover, the Court had merely held that the wronged individual had a right to sue. I wondered what had happened subsequently. So I asked Burger about the outcome of the case when it was returned to the lower courts. Did Bivens win his suit? Did Congress ever give consideration to Burger's idea? He seemed not to know what I was speaking about, and when I tried to explain, to remind him of the case, he grunted, "I don't know" and turned away.

At another commencement, Brandeis University honored the two Massachusetts senators, Leverett Saltonstall and John F. Kennedy. My colleague, John P. Roche, had the luck of presenting the junior senator, Kennedy, while I was assigned to Saltonstall, a stuffy fellow. The four of us spent considerable time together. When the marshal of the academic procession called out that we would march out in five minutes, Kennedy excused

[2]403 U.S. 388 (1971).

himself. He leaned against a wall, pulled an envelope out of his pocket, and made notes on it for a few minutes. At the commencement, Saltonstall read a dull speech for an hour. When Kennedy got his turn, he put the envelope before him on the lectern and spoke brilliantly for about ten minutes in beautiful English and with some wit. He received a grand ovation.

Adventures in Scholarship

*E*XPOSING raw prejudice in the halls of ivy is like fornicating on a sacred altar. I was shaken, therefore, when Professor Dumas Malone, at the defense of my doctoral dissertation in 1951, objected to my critical assessment of the origins of the "separate but equal" doctrine by remarking in his pleasant drawl, "When Ah was a boy in Mississippi we jes' couldn' let a niggra go to a white man's school." Noel T. Dowling, the Harlan Fiske Stone Professor of Constitutional Law at Columbia Law School, added, "I associate myself with the remarks of the distinguished speaker." Henry Steele Commager, my dissertation supervisor, who sat next to me, kicked me under the table, a warning to shut up and let the point pass, while he deftly changed the subject.

Graduate students in history are trained to understand conflicting interpretations, to realize that one's presuppositions might color his understanding of a subject, and to strive for objectivity and intellectual rectitude. After more than four decades as a professional historian, I have come to realize what I should have sensed even before the defense of my dissertation: Truth is not necessarily the first criterion for writing or judging historical writing. When evaluating a book, an historian's deepest-felt values count most. That is probably true in any field of criticism. When one's book is being reviewed, the luck of the draw makes the greatest difference. One may draw a reviewer who tries to follow the canons of scholarship or one who, in effect, praises or condemns your book depending on whether your conclusions match or deviate from his.

I was influenced most by two extraordinary men, Henry Steele Commager and Felix Frankfurter, whose respect for evidence, cogent argument, and disinterestedness outweighed by far their own value judgments. Of Frankfurter I have already written. One can say of Commager, as it was said of his hero, Thomas Jefferson, that he is "a harmonious human multitude," every member of which possesses elegance and eloquence, vividness and vivacity, wit and wisdom. Despite his extraordinary range of knowledge and his fabulous memory steeped in the learning of several disciplines, he did not teach us information, though he taught us how to find and use it. He taught habits of objective thought, a sense of what is important, critical analysis, and a capacity to see our work in our own way, rather than resting on conventional wisdom—or his own. He was a liberating force in the lives of his graduate students at Columbia—awesome, nagging, exhilarating, jolting, and incessantly demanding. He incited us, instigated us, ignited us, and he made us independent of him. A good teacher, he said, makes himself quickly dispensable. Once he was certain that we had looked at all the reliable facts and had considered the various conclusions to which they might lead, he insisted that we reach our own ordering and interpretation of those facts. At least two of my books jarred his preconceptions (and mine), but he generously praised them both.

In 1957 I won a Guggenheim to begin work on a book that sought to explain why "the Framers" included within fundamental law the so-called right against self-incrimination. Thanks to a recommendation from Commager, the Fund for the Republic (later the Center for Democratic Institutions) commissioned me to write a "memorandum" on the original meanings of the First Amendment's clauses. Robert M. Hutchins, who headed the Fund, liked to hold formal conferences with the nation's leading intellectuals on urgent problems of the times. He thought that a scholarly memorandum on historical background would be useful to have at hand in the event that an historical question might arise in the course of a discussion. My opinion was that Zechariah Chafee's *Free Speech in the United States* and Anson Phelps Stokes's *Church and State in the United States* provided all the data that might be needed to resolve a question concerning the intentions of the Framers of the First Amendment. But Hutchins preferred a more convenient packaging of the information based on fresh research into the primary sources. The Guggenheim fellowship paid $4,500 for the year, and Brandeis University paid nothing during my leave because I did not yet hold a tenure appointment. Consequently the offer of $1,000 from the Fund for the best I could do in six weeks was seductive and the task seemed easy. I held very strong "liberal" opinions on the First Amendment, but my training as a scholar required me to forsake all preconceptions, to have no stake in the results of my research, to examine the sources as best I could in the limited time I had, and to give a dispassionate statement of the evidence and conclusions. I wrote a memorandum of about seventy-five pages, two-thirds of which dealt with the clauses on religion and bore out what all liberals knew: The Framers intended a high wall of separation between church and state and guaranteed liberty of conscience even for non-Christians and nonbelievers. But the twenty-five pages on the free-speech, free-press clause flatly contradicted liberal assumptions and their champions, Chafee, Holmes, Brandeis, Black, and Douglas. The Framers, I discovered, had a surprisingly constricted view of the scope of political expression.

The Fund was enthusiastic about my work on the church-state and religious-liberty clauses, but not the rest. I was summoned to New York for discussion. They wanted me to polish the work on the religion clauses, and they would publish it as a handsome pamphlet in their *Basic Issues* series. But Hutchins disapproved of my work on the speech-press clause and made clear to me that the pamphlet would not include that section of my work. Perhaps I was unduly sensitive, but I felt that I was being subjected to a form of censorship—and by one of the nation's foremost strongholds of civil liberties. My fellow liberals seemed to be suppressing scholarship that did not support their presuppositions.

I decided to strike back by giving what I thought would be maximum publicity to the very section that the Fund rejected. I would expand it to a fifty-page article and submit it to the *Harvard Law Review*. Discontinuing my work on the self-incrimination clause, I deepened my research on the speech-press clause and produced the article. Before submitting it for publication, I sent copies to Commager and to Mark Howe, a masterful legal historian at Harvard Law School. Commager was distressed with my findings (so was I), and worried whether I would be providing scholarly ammunition that might be misused by supporters of Joe McCarthy; above all, he thought I should not rush into print on the basis of inadequate research. He argued that if I continued digging into the sources, I would likely find countervailing evidence that supported the Holmes-Chafee position. Howe too believed that I should continue my research; he asked several technical questions on matters that I had not explored and on colonial and English backgrounds that I had slighted.

Instead of producing a law review article, I wrote a book, *Legacy of Suppression: Freedom of Speech and Press in Early American History* (Belknap Press of Harvard University Press, 1960). In my acknowledgments I maliciously thanked the Fund for the Republic for having helped make the book possible, and not till 1972 in a book of my essays did I publish for the first time "No Establishment of Religion: The Original Understanding," the rest of the original memorandum that the Fund had liked. In 1994 it became a book, *The Establishment Clause*. Commager wrote a handsome review of *Legacy of Suppression* for the *New York Times Book Review*, and the book won a couple of journalism awards. It also stirred some controversy. In 1976 Walter Berns devoted a chapter of his book, *The First Amendment and the Future of American Democracy*, to my *Legacy*, mangling the facts of history to fit his conservative prejudices. In a deliciously entitled work,

Willmore Kendall: Contra Mundum, Kendall, a political theorist of
the right, also mauled me and my work from his standpoint.
Berns and Kendall reread my book to yield far more for the cause
of suppression than the facts will support.

Most of my critics, however, came from the liberal camp. The
most powerful and passionate was Justice Hugo Black. Edmond
Cahn of New York University Law School reviewed the book
very favorably and recommended it to Black. As I have re-
counted, Black regretted that I had taken a "completely reactionary view of the First Amendment's purposes." My
conclusions, he believed, would provide an armory of support for
people who want the amendment to mean less than Black and
Cahn thought it meant. As proof, Black wondered if Cahn had
read the favorable review in *The New Republic* by Alexander
Bickel of Yale Law School (who was closely associated with
Frankfurter, Black's antagonist on the Court). Cahn was unable
to disabuse Black of his fixed and naive belief that if only I had
submitted the manuscript to Cahn before publishing it, I would
have reached the conclusion that the evidence showed a "legacy
of liberty." Black disapproved of the people whom I thanked for
having read the book and offered criticism. (They included Max
Lerner, John P. Roche, Henry S. Commager, Paul Freund, and
Mark Howe.)

Black's view of the book showed how selectively and subjec-
tively one can read. My preface concludes with a statement praising the Framers for formulating the amendment in language of
such breadth that we have been able to breathe a liberality of
meaning into it in keeping with the ideals of our expanding
democracy; and the book closes with a paragraph noting that the
amendment's injunction "was boldly stated if narrowly understood. The bold statement, not the narrow understanding, was
written into the fundamental law. . . . It is enough that they [the
Framers] gave constitutional recognition to the principle of freedom of speech and press in unqualified and undefined terms.
That they were Blackstonians does not mean that we cannot be
Brandeisians." If Black had not read with his absolutist convic-

tions dominating his understanding, he would have seen why Cahn and Commager could appreciate the book, though not necessarily agree with all of it, and he would have seen how it was possible for the Kendalls and the Bernses to assault the book from the right. Although the book has been cited in several Supreme Court opinions, not even conservative judges have used it to support the results Black strongly feared.

Legacy of Suppression had led me to a brief examination of Jefferson's opinions and practices on the subject of freedom of the press. I decided to write a book on what I found to be a "darker side" to Jefferson. I really did not write that book with the hope of winning the annual award of the John Birch Society—a plaster statue of Senator Joseph McCarthy. Nor is it true that every July 11 I visit Weehauken, New Jersey, to lay a wreath on the hallowed spot of ground where Hamilton departed this vale of tears. I wrote the book with a pen, not a blunderbuss, a bludgeon, a smearpot, or a muckrake. Jefferson is usually depicted as a noble figure caught in a mythic stance: swearing eternal hostility to every form of tyranny over the mind of man. I focused on only the lesser-known or darker side because Jefferson the apostle of liberty is so familiar a figure. He was a public man for more than half a century and held positions of power at critical moments in our history, when he believed the American experiment in self-government to be surrounded by enemies. Judged by the best standards of his own time, standards that he more than anyone else helped to fix, his career reveals a pattern of antilibertarianism, a fact that should dismay no one familiar with the history of politics.

Among those to whom I sent copies of the manuscript for criticism was Julian P. Boyd of Princeton, the great editor of *The Papers of Thomas Jefferson*. In a letter to me, written, he said, after reading only the last chapter where I give my conclusions (the evidence is in the preceding chapters), Boyd doubted whether he could ever accept my viewpoint. He conceded that he made overly sympathetic and uncritical judgments about Jefferson, but insisted that Jefferson could not properly be gauged any other way. Boyd then declared that in disagreeing with my appraisal he found my premises unacceptable and my yardsticks of judgment often irrelevant and unfair. He ended by declaring that if I was right about Jefferson, he had wasted the best years of his life in the wrong profession. My reply, even more respectful than that of my first letter, stressed that my standards were Jefferson's, that I openly presented only the darker side and thus deceived no one, and that in the book I had recognized Jefferson's achievements on behalf of American freedom. I added that I would correct any errors that Boyd pointed out and entreated him to give me the careful reading he had promised. He did not reply. I sent a copy of Boyd's letter to a distinguished historian, Oscar Handlin, who responded that he found it "a fascinating historical document. That he [Boyd] should have reacted as he did—without actually having read the manuscript—I think is an indication of the importance of bringing this material to light. His last sentence [about wasting the best years of his life] is a classic of its sort." When the book appeared, I sent a copy to Boyd with a letter he described as "generous." Promising to give the book a dispassionate appraisal (he never made it), he momentarily revived my confidence in our profession when he said that the book required all Jefferson scholars to evaluate their own attitudes and be prepared to defend them when challenged. On the whole, though, the reviews showed that the mythic Jefferson is impregnable. Faith outweighs evidence on certain historical subjects as well as in matters of religion. The untarnishable belief of the reviewers in the mythic Jefferson was refreshing in a day when so many people believe in no god at all.

The private letters were mixed. Justice Black, incidentally, refused to read the book because of its subtitle and my track record. I do not know whether Black read the column by our mutual friend, Max Lerner, in which Lerner recommended the book "for its courage in grasping the nettle of Thomas Jefferson's gap between the theory and practice on civil liberties." Chief Justice Earl Warren, by contrast with Black, found the book fascinating and enjoyable. "We sometimes forget," he wrote me, "the complex development of men of history as we accept them, and I was extremely interested in reading this penetrating analysis of one of the greatest. It also reminds us that while they, like the rest of us, have feet of clay, their hearts or minds often take them where their feet would not support them." Frankfurter, who considered himself a Jeffersonian, also took the book in stride.

Three reviews are worth mentioning—the astonishingly inaccurate and deceiving one in the *New York Review of Books* by Cecelia Kenyon, which I felt compelled to answer publicly; the pathetically funny one in the *Washington Post*; and the one by the preeminent Jefferson biographer Dumas Malone. The exchange between Kenyon and me is a matter of record in the pages of the *New York Review*. Alan Barth, the author of several excellent volumes defending civil liberties and an editorial writer for the *Washington Post*, repeated the gist of his review in an editorial in 1967 after President Lyndon Johnson had appointed me a member of the American Revolution Bicentennial Commission. Under the heading, "Subcommittee on Warts," appeared these words:

> There will be, as is always the case, criticism of some of the members, and praise for others. Some will be surprised to find on the commission Dr. Leonard W. Levy whose views of Thomas Jefferson and some other aspects of the period would suggest that he hardly thought the occasion [of the Nation's bicentennial] worth celebrating. Of his book on Jefferson, published in 1963, this newspaper's reviewer said: "The book presents a mass of material, no doubt painstakingly researched, to support these charges. The result is not merely an unbalanced portrait; it is a gargoyle. It is all very well to paint a man, as Cromwell put it, warts and all; but if one paints the warts alone, one has very little picture of the man. . . . The recitation of every misstep in Jefferson's life, including even gossip* about an ama-

---

*The "gossip" was a statement made by Jefferson himself and was relevant to a federal prosecution for seditious libel during Jefferson's presidency.

tory dalliance, is so hostile that one reacts to it as one would to scandalmongering about a friend." Fortunately, Mr. Levy is only one member of a large commission. The chairman might well assign him to the subcommittee on warts and leave the rest of the commission the task of commemorating the constructive side of the statesmen of the revolution.

The most important review should have been by Malone in the pages of the *American Historical Review*. He sent me a copy in advance, remarking that I would find that his main objection to the book, like that of other Jeffersonians, was to the very conception of the book. I replied privately, as follows:

> I am returning the copy of the review of *Jefferson and Civil Liberties: The Darker Side*, that you were considerate enough to send me in advance of its publication. I guess we have reached the Mexican standoff that you anticipated when you remarked in a letter to me, "You did not expect me to like your book and I do not expect you to like my review, but you will understand that there is nothing personal in it." I suspect that what divides us is the question whether personal likes or dislikes would have any bearing on historical scholarship. I think not and feel the same way toward your review; I neither like it nor dislike it, but believe it to be generally lacking in understanding, unfair, and misleading.
>
> The review poorly reports the contents of the book and makes little effort to summarize any of the evidence relating to any of the subject discussed. You do not inform readers, for example, that the book discusses the Josiah Philips' case of attainder-and-outlawry, the problem of search-and-seizure under the Embargo acts, the bowdlerized edition of Hume, or a variety of other matters. To dismiss my seventy pages on the Burr conspiracy and the Embargo simply by remarking that my interpretation echoes that of Jefferson's contemporary political foes is to ignore entirely the specific civil liberties issues to which I address myself. I do not give a rap whether, for example, Burr was guilty. But I do care about the due process of law and

fair trial issue, as well as about the difference between evidence that amounts to treason vs. constructive treason. My point generally is that you do not face up to the book, though you caricature it freely, and you don't explain to readers what I sought to do, however much I may have failed in the effort.

I object to your identification of me with Jefferson's political enemies. I am not now nor have I ever been a member of the Essex Junto, the Quids, the Burrites, or the Hamiltonians. I have much more respect for John Adams than you seem to have, but I regard myself as a "Jeffersonian," though I identify more closely with Madison or Gallatin than with Jefferson himself. In any case, it is quite misleading of you to leave reviewers with the impression that I write from a Federalist bias or judge Jefferson by Federalist criteria. That is simply not so. At other points in your review you seem uncertain about the criteria that I applied in reaching my judgments. I state again and again, and demonstrate, that I use the civil libertarian standards of Jefferson's own time as yardsticks to measure him. For you to argue that Jefferson never set forth a systematic philosophy of free speech (we agree on this) because he "may have" doubted the feasibility of formulating one that would "always work," implies that he had thought through the issue. I challenge you to produce the evidence. Incidentally, if your abstract reasoning stands up, how do you explain the fact that Jefferson did set forth a systematic philosophy in the case of freedom of religion? Surely he was neither doctrinaire nor unrealistic enough to think that his philosophy, more properly his overt-acts test, would "always" work.

Why should you wonder whether I approve of George Hay's proposition that free speech is either an absolute or does not exist? I make my views on that quite clear in *Legacy of Suppression*. More significantly, you evade the real issue, which is whether the concept of seditious libel is consistent with free government. Gallatin and Madison, who were not "minor Republicans" (the validity of Hay's ideas does not depend on whether he was major or minor), repudiated the concept of seditious libel; but Jefferson supported prosecutions for seditious libel by both the federal and state governments.

It simply will not do to evade hard problems by asserting that Jefferson was an absolutist with respect to freedom of mind and spirit. One's thought and feelings raise no issues until they find expression in words and deeds. The question then is where to draw the line between the permissible and impermissible—and why. To speak of absolute freedom of the mind and spirit, unaccompanied by "free exercise," is a dodge and a sham. When in 1651 the Reverend John Clarke was convicted in Massachusetts for preaching Baptist doctrine, contrary to the law's prohibition, he was told, "The Court sentenced you not for your judgment or conscience, but for matter of fact and practice." In other words the court acknowledged Clarke's freedom of mind and spirit. Yet he replied, "Be it so, but I say that matter of fact and practice was but the manifestation of my judgment and conscience and I make account that man is void of judgment and conscience, with respect unto God, that hath not a fact and practice suitable thereunto." Jefferson would have agreed and, accordingly, devised the "overt acts" test to protect the expression of religious opinion. What is significant is his failure to extend that test to political opinion. The "new libertarianism" advocated the overt-acts test for political as well as religious opinions. Your association of the new libertarianism with Hay's absolutist views and exoneration of Jefferson as no absolutist except as to freedom of mind and spirit will fool no one.

It seems to me that you have your cake and eat it too by the proposition that on the one hand Jefferson was a great champion of personal liberties but on the other was a "relativist" deserving our praise. When he defends liberty, you approve; when he doesn't, you approve and praise him for not being doctrinaire, not being absolutist, indeed for being relativist. On what principle do you make the distinction? More important, on what principle did he make the distinction? I cannot accept your standard of judgment, namely that on balance he was more libertarian than his enemies. I should not like to think that Pickering or Ames set the standards by which we judge Jefferson.

I suppose that I may have earned the tinge of sarcasm in your first page, for I probably overstated my case, though some have thought that I am too defensive and apologetic. But you ignore the case altogether, leaving the impression—to me a humorous one—that I have written a faintly dirty book. You make far too much of and distort a reference in the preface to a classic metaphor about the Augean stables. Indeed you give more attention to the first page of my preface than to several chapters of the book. I am mystified why you should regard as dirt indisputable evidence that proves the existence of Jefferson's darker side on questions of civil liberty. Incidentally, the metaphor refers to cleaning, not dirtying, the stables.

My next book was also a controversial subject—*Origins of the Fifth Amendment: The Right against Self-Incrimination* (Oxford University Press, 1968). This time, however, the evidence led me to conclusions that buttressed liberal wisdom. Although there were some predictably hostile notices, like the one in Bill Buckley's *National Review*, the book was widely praised in the newspapers, the law journals, and the historical reviews. To my astonishment, it won the 1969 Pulitzer Prize in History. The Pulitzer is a big-league prize whose award causes giddiness, euphoria, and delusions of grandeur. By chance I happened to be in Manhattan a week after the award and could scarcely contain my eagerness to burst upon Fifth Avenue, where I could walk by Doubleday's, Scribner's, Rizzoli's, and Brentano's, in each of which I expected to see huge pyramids of my book in the window, emblazoned with signs and photos announcing the prizewinner to the passing public. None of the stores had a single copy in the window; only one of the stores, in fact, had a copy, just one, on its shelves. I remembered that Harper and Row had rejected the manuscript of my prizewinner on the calculation, which proved correct, that the book would be a commercial flop. My hapless editor, listening to my outrage on the phone, tried to explain that the editorial department had little to do with the sales department; moreover the publisher could not be responsible for what the stores stocked on the basis of their expectation of what the public would buy. I learned then something I would learn more about later—that "editorial" and "sales" departments in publishing companies may have different values, though today that may no longer be true. In any case, I blamed the publisher for the commercial failure of the book and resolved that the next book would be with a different house.

I like to think that *Origins of the Fifth Amendment* mitigated Justice Black's opinion of me, but I preferred not to send him a copy for fear of receiving a letter welcoming me back to the fold. He would not have understood that I looked at the evidence before forming an opinion and tried not to conceal any of the evidence. Black once joined a 1955 opinion by William O. Douglas in which Douglas discoursed on the historical origins of the Fifth Amendment. Douglas was trying to prove that the Puritans of Massachusetts Bay respected the right against self-incrimination, and he offered as evidence the "typical" remark of a minister who ruled that a magistrate might not exact a confession by any violent means, whether by oath or punishment. On the same page as the source that he cited is the ruling of another minister, Charles Chauncy, which Douglas ignored. Chauncy declared, "But now, if the question be mente of inflicting bodily torments to extract confession from a malefactor, I conceive that in matters of highest consequence, such as doe conceirne the saftie or ruine of states or countries, magistrates may proceede so farr as to bodily torments, as racks and hot-irons to extracte a confession, especially wher presumptions are strounge; but otherwise by no means." I find the concealment and distortion of evidence to be common in judicial opinions, as well as in historical works. Justice Lewis Powell, speaking for the Court on a major issue, quoted and cited my book in an opinion to the effect that the requirements of the Fifth Amendment are met by a statute that requires incriminating testimony but grants less than full immunity against prosecution. My book showed the opposite of what Powell drew from it. The problem is that readers slant what they see on a page. As Rousseau said in *Émile*, facts should not be permitted to stand in the way of truth, and even false facts may serve a useful lesson. Theologians, even more than judges and historians, understand that.

Winning the Pulitzer earned me the chance to serve on Pulitzer juries and learn something about the mysteries of that award in the fields of history and biography. Although the Pulitzer is prestigious, the public, let alone recipients, knows virtually nothing of how the awards in "Letters" are decided. Even publishers, who ought to know better, sometimes fatuously mislead the public by advertising a book as having been "nominated" for a Pulitzer Prize. Oxford University Press, which published my prizewinning book, promoted an author on the dust jacket of his 1974 book by saying that an earlier book of his had been "nominated" for a Pulitzer. Being nominated for a National Book Award is a distinction, because the nominees are the publicly announced finalists; being nominated for a Pulitzer was quite meaningless then. Runners-up were not identified.* All a publisher had to do to "nominate" a book was to fill out a form and send four copies of a book to the Pulitzer Office at Columbia University, along with a photo and biographical sketch of the author. Trashy as well as mediocre books were consistently nominated and dutifully forwarded to members of the appropriate jury.

Since the publication in 1974 of *The Pulitzer Prizes* (Columbia University Press) by John Hohenberg, many "inside" secrets have been made public, but not the most intriguing. Hohenberg, who was a professor of journalism at Columbia, ably served for more than twenty years as secretary to the advisory board and administrator of the Pulitzer Prizes. The trustees of Columbia actually make the awards, ratifying the recommendations of the advisory board, which consists of the secretary, the president of Columbia University, and a dozen preeminent journalism execu-

---

*The policy changed; runners-up are now identified.

tives, such as, over the years, Benjamin C. Bradlee, John Cowles Jr., Robert J. Donovan, and James Reston. The advisory board, notwithstanding its name, is for practical purposes all-powerful: the trustees, with a single exception (Swanberg's *Citizen Hearst*), have followed the board's recommendations, and the board has the authority, which it occasionally exercises, to overrule a recommendation by the jury. The board reversed the History jury in 1960 and 1966. Jurors, who seem to be chosen by the administrator, have for a long time been highly qualified professionals in the fields of history and biography. Hohenberg's book reveals their names up to 1974. What his book does not reveal is the deliberations of the members of the jury. The Pulitzer Office gets merely the end product of a jury's work: its formal letter recommending its choice, much as a court gets a jury's verdict but has no idea of what went on within the jury room. Many a "unanimous choice" was no juror's first choice.

The jury, which consists of three members, has virtually limitless discretion. The advisory committee lays down no rules for procedure or guidance. Jurors, oddly, are not even enjoined to confidentiality. Their deliberations are not revealed to the Pulitzer Office, and their choice for the prize is, as a matter of custom, kept secret until the office announces the prizes after the trustees meet on the first Monday in May. The jurors receive their appointments about a year earlier and begin receiving books about July; the books pour in during September and October; the nomination deadline is November 1. The jury's recommendation is made by a formal letter before New Year's Day. The period for deliberation can be extremely tight, often just the month before reaching a consensus. Even if a jury can unanimously agree on a single choice, it must submit to the board a few alternative titles; juries often indicate several others to which they gave their most serious consideration. "There should be justification of the choices and generally is," I was told in my first letter of appointment. Any member of the jury may request a book that has not been nominated. On my first tour of duty as a juror, a fellow juror (Lou Morton) told me that Harvard University Press had failed to nominate Bernard Bailyn's *Ideological Origins of the American Revolution*, which won the History Prize for 1968. The publisher, so I was told, regarded the book as just an expansion of the long introduction, previously published, by Bailyn to his *Pamphlets of the American Revolution* (1965). Had one juror not requested that the book be nominated, it would not have won the prize. Inasmuch as I am capable of believing that the incompetence of publishers is nearly limitless, during my four stints as a juror I made it a practice to scour *Forthcoming Books* for the purpose of requesting likely titles.

The administrator is shrewd enough to obtain the services on every jury of at least one person who has previously served. During my first tour of duty, Julian Boyd was the chairman of the History jury and Lou Morton, the head of the Dartmouth College Department of History, was the other juror. Both Boyd and Morton had previously served as jurors, twice together. I was soon to learn that their "chemistry" was not harmonious. We received 109 books that year for the 1971 History prize, yet Boyd, the chairman, did not write us until November 30. Before receiving his letter, I wrote him on December 2, with a copy to Morton, saying, "I have received no word from you, no instructions. How do I discharge my duties as a Pulitzer juror. What procedures do we follow?" I then took the initiative of listing in order of preference my selection of the ten best books. Number one was Lawrence Cremin's *American Education: The Colonial Experience*. I observed that James MacGregor Burns's *Roosevelt, the Soldier of Freedom* and David H. Donald's *Charles Sumner and the Rights of Man* were in the same class as Cremin, "but I believe they are properly classified as biographies." I offered my choices and asked, "Where do we go from here, and how?"

Had I waited a day I would have received a remarkable letter from Boyd in which he pointed out that Lawrence Gipson's fifteenth and concluding volume of his great opus, *The British Empire Before the Revolution*, would be published on December 7, Gipson's ninetieth birthday. Gipson had already won the prize for

1962 with one of the volumes in the series, but Boyd thought we ought to consider the fifteen volumes as a whole, though neither the fifteenth nor any of the others had been submitted for our consideration. "If it is to be considered," Boyd wrote, "we shall have to request it. Shall we?" Stressing that the jury could work out its own procedures, Boyd asked, "But how shall we proceed?" He urged that we exchange our lists of choices for the first ten titles, so that we would know whether we were close or far apart, but he did not offer his own list. Gipson's book or his whole series, neither submitted for our consideration, was Boyd's sole recommendation. Two days later Boyd urged us to consider *The Papers of Robert H. Goddard, 1898–1945*, a three-volume edited set that had not been nominated for our consideration either. Boyd soon learned from the Pulitzer Office that the set had been submitted by the publisher for consideration by the Biography jury. (One of the deficiencies in the Pulitzer procedures— if the lack of procedures can be considered a form of procedure—is the sealing off of the Biography and History juries from each other; in any given year, one jury does not know who are the members of the other, or what books the other is considering, though the overlap may be significant; nor do the two juries communicate.) By return mail I replied that I had heard that Gipson's fifteenth volume was merely a bibliography of manuscripts, not meriting our consideration, but that if the book was submitted to us formally we ought to consider backing Gipson for the entirety of his monumental work.

On December 7 Morton wrote us his first letter. It was brusque and incisive. "My first choice for the Pulitzer prize," he began, "is Cremin's *American Education*. So far Leonard and I are in agreement and perhaps it will not be necessary to go any further." That was a warning to Boyd that we could outvote him two-to-one. Morton added that if Burns's *Roosevelt* and Donald's *Sumner* must be considered biography, he and I differed on the second and third choices; but he was not certain that the Roosevelt book needed to be considered biography. He would place it second "and if pushed would agree to giving it first place." The fact that Donald had already won a Pulitzer for his first volume on Sumner persuaded Morton to give priority to Burns.

When Boyd received our letters, he replied without referring to our choice of Cremin, Burns, and the several others under discussion. Boyd spoke only of our uniting behind "Gipson's half-century achievement"—the fifteen-volume set. A few day later Boyd wrote us again. He had a new candidate: Clifford Shipton's *Harvard Graduates*, of which volume 15 had been published in 1970, our year. Boyd had called the Pulitzer Office, discovered that the book had been submitted to the Biography jury, but learned that nothing prevented us from considering it for the History prize. Although the book had not been submitted to us, our libraries surely had copies, he wrote. Did it fall within the category of History, even if it consisted of biographical sketches of Harvard graduates? "In my judgment," Boyd wrote, "it clearly does—all biography is history though not all history is biography." Then, praising Shipton's fifteen-volume set, Boyd concluded that Shipton had never received a Pulitzer. Morton, meanwhile, registered his opposition to considering Gipson, whether the final bibliographical guide or his whole set.

I replied that I was still willing to consider the set but sharply dissented from Boyd's view that Shipton outranked Gipson. I noted that the nomination form provided by the Pulitzer Office included a miscellaneous category: "For a distinguished book by an American which is not eligible for consideration in any other existing category." Could we recommend Gipson's set for that category and proceed to rank the books that were submitted to us? I also observed that if Shipton's biographical sketches fell within our History category, "then we must also reconsider Burns' *FDR*. By Julian's dictum, which I accept, that biography is history, Burns as well as Shipton demands our judgment. So does Donald's *Sumner*," but if one Pulitzer for a given work eliminated David Donald, and Bray Hammond too, we had better start arguing the merits of the other books. I could not choose between Cremin and Burns without further consideration, but I had a tentative winnowing notion based on Morton's and Boyd's principle that all things being equal, award a prize to a person who has not won one. Cremin had previously won a Bancroft; moreover, his book was the first of a projected three-volume set, so he'd have a chance at a Pulitzer later. Burns's book concluded his two-volume study of FDR, and the first volume, to my knowledge, had not won a prize. "Ergo, Burns over Cremin?" After re-ranking my remaining choices, I asked Boyd: "Julian— how do you rank the books. You've discussed Gipson, Goddard, and Shipton, but not the books sent to us."

Next came a telegram from Morton: "I find Leonard's letter of 18 December convincing. I am willing now to cast my vote for Burns. Cremin is second, Bernstein third." Boyd then wrote us an incredible letter. "Now let me give you my choices among the books submitted. I ruled out Burns' *Roosevelt* and Donald's *Sumner* as belonging primarily to biography." He discussed neither book further, but took aim at Cremin and made some telling points. Boyd's first choice was J. Cutler Andrew's *The South Reports the Civil War*, his second Eric Barnouw's *The Image Empire*, the third Charles E. Clark's *The Eastern Frontier*, and his fourth Ann Leighton's *Early American Gardens*, for each of which he supplied a justification. Recognizing that he was outvoted and, amazingly, insisting that Burns should be left to the Biography jury, Boyd offered a compromise. We should submit a divided report, with Morton and me behind the book of our choice and Boyd for Andrews, but in addition I should write a recommendation that a special award be given to Gipson's set while Boyd would write a similar statement on behalf of Shipton's work.

At that point I was fed up with Boyd's inconsistencies and unprofessionalism. Yet I still hoped to win him over to Burns so that we could submit a unanimous choice, thereby diminishing the chance of the advisory board's doing an end run around us. I thought that if Morton and I, without Boyd's support, backed Burns, the board might ignore us because the *Roosevelt* was biographical as well as historical, and that fact might allow Boyd's choices to edge past. I said as much in my next letter and explained why I thought separate statements for books not submitted to us would be a waste of time. Out of courtesy to Boyd, I explained why I could not support any of his four other choices, one of which, Clark's *Eastern Frontier*, I had never heard of. "Julian and I are fated never to agree; happily that does not one whit diminish my immense respect for him and his work, but I just can't respect his choices for the Pulitzer. . . . I'm as 'intransigent' as he confesses to be. So, Lou, speak up. . . . I can't say it's been fun." As I look back I think Morton and I made the mistake of not making a strong argument for the book by Burns. I think Boyd deflected us, exhausting our energies as we responded to his eccentric choices. In any case I had now lost Boyd's support (Morton never tried to engage it). Unable to brook difference of opinion, he drew "unpleasant inferences" from my letter, whose tones and substance he found "astonishing." He also thought I was usurping his role as chairman. In a postscript he conceded that Clark's *Eastern Frontier* had not been submitted to us, and "since it was not, I withdraw it from my list of preferences." The same reasoning applied to Shipton and Gipson.

On January 7 Morton wrote decisively: Burns #1, Cremin #2, and rejection of each of Boyd's choices. In a postscript written by hand to me, Morton repeated what he had told me in a phone conversation. "Let's wind this up. I've been on the jury three times, and this is the first time we've ever taken so long. Also, this is the second time at least that Julian has gone through the Gipson and Shipton routine." I phoned my assent, and the next day Morton wrote a letter to the Pulitzer Office on our behalf, including the amusing line, "Professor Levy and I are unanimous in our choices." He wrote a paragraph for Burns followed by another for Cremin as the also-ran, and he mentioned for third place Irving Bernstein's *History of the American Worker: The Turbulent Years*. A few days later Boyd wrote his own letter, saying that he shared his colleagues' regard for Burns's *Roosevelt* but thought it primarily a biography which should be judged in that category. His first choice, nevertheless, was Shipton's *Harvard Graduates*, his second Gipson's *magnum opus*, his third Barouw's *Image Empire*. Burns won the Pulitzer for History.

I was appointed to the History jury again in 1972. The jury "unanimously" selected Michael Kammen's *People of Paradox: An Inquiry Concerning the Origins of American Civilization*. Hohenberg, in his *The Pulitzer Prizes*, notes that the selection was made by a jury that included Harold C. Syrett of the City University of New York (chairman), Harold M. Hyman of Rice University, and me from the Claremont Graduate School in California: "It was a far cry from the early days of the Pulitzer Prizes when jurors and winners in history and biography often came from a narrow triangle in the northeastern United States." In fact it was an all-Columbia jury; Syrett, who got his Ph.D. from Columbia, was an assistant professor there when Hyman and I were earning our doctorates at Columbia, and we three had been friends for more than twenty years. Unfortunately I have lost or misplaced the records for my jury service in 1972. What I find indicates that I seem to have taken the lead in a letter listing my top ten.

My first choice was Sydney E. Ahlstrom's *A Religious History of the American People*, "incomparably the best book ever written on the subject. Definitive work on a major theme, but too encyclopedic." The last phrase was impolitic: it allowed one who disagreed to use the "encyclopedic" label as an opening wedge, and that is what happened. "A close second," I wrote, "is the dazzlingly learned, brilliant, egocentric, and persnickety book by Michael Kammen. . . . For a long while I thought this would be my first choice, and I wouldn't object if you two ranked it above Ahlstrom. But Kammen ignores too many of his masters—Lerner, Commager, Potter, etc.—and indulges in too many colloquialisms." Hyman, I recall, strongly admired a book not in my top ten, John W. Blassingame's *The Slave Community*. I explained in a lost letter why I disagreed with his choice.

As I recall, Syrett seized on Kammen as a compromise candidate, because Hyman had admired Kammen's book too. Syrett's letter to Hohenberg said that we unanimously considered Kammen's book to be in a class by itself. We ranked Blassingame second (my concession for peace and unanimity on the top choice, the only one that counted). Syrett also reported that the jurors could not agree on their third and fourth choices, which he stated for each of us. Hyman chose David McCullough's *The Great Bridge* and David S. Lovejoy's *The Glorious Revolution in America*; Syrett preferred Pauline Maier's *From Resistance to Revolution* and Lovejoy's book; I voted for Ahlstrom's and Maier's. In addition, Syrett provided a long list of other titles to which we also gave consideration.

No serious disagreements divided the jury; we came to our consensus easily, though neither Hyman nor I saw our differing first choices become the victor. Indeed, I served on four Pulitzer juries, the last two in the manipulative position of chairman, yet I never saw my top choice emerge as the winner. In each case, however, the Pulitzer Office received a letter reporting unanimity. Knowing when to compromise is part of the secret of preventing a book, which you vigorously oppose, from winning. Judging books is based partly on rational evaluation and partly on psychological or emotional presuppositions which are seldom articulated.

Jurors are able to agree on the few most deserving books in a huge batch of nominees. Disagreements may reflect personal taste in much the same way that baseball fans argue the merits of Mays against Mantle, or music experts try to distinguish between Horowitz and Rubinstein. In any given year a book that makes the top five of every juror's list is likely to be as worthy as the one the jury finally agrees upon as the best. The professional training of historians effectively produces a system of judgment that functions creditably over the long haul. In any single case, however, a historian's deepest values and interests sometimes count too heavily. That is probably true in any field of criticism. Historians are not especially culpable and as a group are probably less subjective than appellate judges. How a book is judged can, of course, depend on the luck of the draw. Some jurors unwittingly praise or condemn a book depending on whether the author's conclusions match or deviate from their own. Most jurors try to follow the canons of scholarship.

Being chairman of the Biography jury in 1974 was an exhilarating experience, thanks to the exceptional dedication, marvelous cogency, civility, and scholarship of my co-jurors and the differences of opinion among us. The other two were George Dangerfield, an elder statesman among master historians, who won a Pulitzer in 1953, and Guy Davenport, a brilliant professor of comparative literature at Kentucky who writes short stories, poetry, and criticism, and who had formerly served on the Fiction jury. We began exchanging letters about the books we were reading in early August, not in December as on my earlier tours of duty. In the course of a letter to Dangerfield I remarked on Davenport's "exquisite taste and capacity for incisive, vivid summary of a book, or, rather, his reaction to it. . . . He is a man of immense erudition and style." I felt the same about Dangerfield. In his last letter, when we seemed deadlocked, he wrote: "I can only add that this jury has been such a pleasure to me; our discourse has been so rational and civilized and interesting; and I have been so singularly free of that usual juror's feeling of astral daggers planted between the shoulderblades—that I do hope we can end on a united note. In any case, whatever happens, I feel that I have made two friends." In my last letter, which turned out to be a successful reconciliation of viewpoints, I replied that Dangerfield had expressed my deepest feelings. "I too feel that I have made two friends. . . . We have 'met' and I'm proud of knowing two people whose discourse via letters has earned my highest respect. You two sometimes make me feel like a Philistine or a half-educated technician. Both of you are superb stylists, humane, fair, and powerful in argument. Working with you has been very gratifying. I've served twice before and . . . found it all so different. I give thanks to you two. Each of you has my utmost admiration." I think that the quality of our letters merits their publication, and I treasure them. I doubt that any Pulitzer jury could have worked so hard, so conscientiously, and so scrappily, nor could any jury have consisted of three such discrepant personalities. The experience also confirmed my conviction that subjectivity in judgment, even among cooperative and harmonious scholars, is overwhelming. We finally managed to agree, but it was a near miss.

After many letters, and with many books still to be sent to us, on October 19, 1974, I listed my first five choices among the books I had read so far. My squibs summarized former discussions. I ranked Bernard Bailyn's *Ordeal of Thomas Hutchinson* first. ("This one stands out above all others. For me it has no faults.") Then came Wallace Stegner's *Uneasy Chair* ("Love it as I do, DeVoto seems not important enough"); Dumas Malone's *Jefferson the President* ("Apologetics"); Laura Roper's *FLO* [*Frederick Law Olmsted*] ("If not so plodding and unimaginative, would rank higher"); and Justin Kaplan's *Lincoln Steffens* ("Weak on Ideas"). Dangerfield replied that Bailyn's book was "a most distinguished work of scholarship and a work of art, elegant and austere," but disagreed with Bailyn's approach. Malone's fifth volume caused us much soul-searching. Dangerfield agreed that it was "apologetics and dense at that." We did not know that the History jury was also considering Malone's work, and we debated at length whether to recommend the five-volume work, which had been submitted to us, for a Special Citation. I got the impression from the Pulitzer Office that the advisory board might not welcome a Special Citation, though clearly we could have made the recommendation if we chose, and we were deeply tempted. The five-volume set, which the publisher submitted to both the History and Biography juries, won the History prize; we did not think the fifth volume, the one published in our year of decision, deserved a prize from us.

Dangerfield, as early as October, called our attention to Robert A. Caro's *The Power Broker: Robert Moses and the Fall of New York*, the book behind which we finally united. Dangerfield thought that for sheer readability, nothing was like it. Caro, he said, "deals with the grand theme of 'power tends to corrupt.' Robert Moses was a brilliant man, but as he seized power his brilliance turned phosphorescent. . . ." Davenport read it next. Early in November he wrote that it was thus far the book he found "most impressive in sheer labor, vision, and interpretation. . . . I think the real subject is the modern city and how it is torn by conflicting ideals, big short-sighted ideas, political power, deals, etc., in which case it is a very important book. It is beautifully written for what it is." Davenport also liked Bailyn's book but agreed with Dangerfield that Bailyn "pretty much writes his own context. It is indeed a model biography; I also think that if we give it the prize, the Big Committee (the Advisory Board) will countermand our choice on the grounds that the press and public will say 'Thomas Who?'" Near the end of November I read Caro and in a lengthy letter wrote, "Left alone, I would choose Bailyn's *Hutchinson*." I gave half a page defending Bailyn against the criticism he had encountered, but knew I was outvoted; I devoted the rest of my letter to a critical analysis of Caro. What attracted me to *The Power Broker*, apart from the fact that it was an enormously vital, important, and fascinating story, was Caro's superb dissection of the role of the politically unaccountable urban planner using the "public authority" device as a force for good or evil in the growth and management of our cities. Berle and Means, forty years earlier, had described the rise of a new elite, the corporate managers who run the business enterprises that others own; Caro, in effect, I wrote, "extended that analysis from the corporation to the contemporary city." Although I also had a great deal to say against the book, I suggested that it seemed to be the book we could rally around. Despite my last-ditch defense of Bailyn, neither Dangerfield nor Davenport supported me. That was no surprise.

But on December 1, Davenport suddenly discovered and fell in love with David Wooldridge's *From the Steeples and Mountains*, an idiosyncratic life of Charles Ives (Charles Who?). For one who tended to be terse in expression, Davenport's two letters in succession on behalf of Wooldridge's book seemed expansive, but his plaintive comment, "I hope I'm not being impossibly quixotic," hit the mark. As for my decision to recognize reality and go for Caro, Davenport merely said that he wished he could write as good a critique of Wooldridge "pro and contra as Len does of the Caro."

Next came the surprise from Dangerfield. He was glad I would go along with the Caro; reading my letter on Caro, he wrote, "was rather as if a fortress had been battered by an expert artillerist and had happily survived." Next he devoted considerable space to Wooldridge. I thought it was a devastating critique yet framed to appease as well as dissuade Davenport. Still, Dangerfield too "loved" the book and said that if I agreed with Davenport, Dangerfield would go along. The surprise came in the remainder of the extremely long letter: "Now for my contender." It turned out to be *All God's Dangers: The Life of Nate Shaw* (Nate Who?) by Theodore Rosengarten. I think that if the advisory board had read Dangerfield's assessment of *All God's Dangers*, the book would have won the prize. Davenport wrote, "George's defense of *All God's Dangers* should win some kind of prize in itself." Davenport's letter got in some subtle digs at *All God's Dangers*, even as he eloquently praised its merits, and included a sentence that turned out to be decisive: "I can live with the decision to give the prize to Caro." Yet he made a last-ditch defense of Wooldridge, whose book he believed to be "the most original."

The day before Davenport wrote that letter which was en route, I wrote a gloomy one. "We are now badly split, though I had anticipated a unanimous jury. I'm still for Caro, *Power Broker.*" I conceded to Dangerfield all the virtues in *All God's Dangers* that he so vividly described, but lamely concluded, "I just honestly think that Caro's *Power Broker* is a better, more deserving book." I did not concede to Wooldridge the virtues that Davenport found. I thought it was not a biography as I understand that art form, and I explained why. Dangerfield, for his own reasons, had compelling doubts about Davenport's choice, so I ruled that the two-to-one vote disqualified Wooldridge as first choice. I thought we were at a state where Davenport would support Wooldridge, Dangerfield would stand fast for Rosengarten, and I would favor Caro—or go back to Bailyn. Then came Dangerfield's next and final letter. He again agreed with me on Wooldridge and handsomely found my objections to *All God's Dangers* "pretty forceful." He wrote, "I would consider any strong and rational objection [to Rosengarten] from either of you quite sufficient for me to surrender in favor of Caro's *Power Broker.*" The book was worthy of the Pulitzer, he said, and therefore he could not concur with my judgment that we were badly split. Indeed, each of us had expressed genuine and high respect for Caro's work.

In my final letter to my fellow jurors, I summarized our viewpoints on the three books that had so exactingly demanded our attention at the end, and I concluded that a consensus existed for Caro. Unless I heard differently within a week, I would write the letter to the Pulitzer Office on behalf of a unanimous jury. Hearing no dissent, I wrote the letter, as follows:

The Biography Jury for 1975 unanimously recommends Robert A. Caro's *The Power Broker: Robert Moses and the Fall of New York* (Alfred A. Knopf, 1974).

The Power Broker is gargantuan in theme and impact as well as size. It is shattering, enormously vital, and original in a sense that no other book is. There were several conventional biographies this year that the jury seriously considered. The best of these were Roper's *FLO*, Bailyn's *Ordeal of Thomas Hutchinson*, Kaplan's *Lincoln Steffens*, Stegner's *Uneasy Chair*, and Malone's fifth volume of his *Jefferson*. Each may be "definitive," yet each is original only in the usual scholarly sense of being based on research in the primary sources. Although a journalist writing on a man who is alive, Caro has also done everything a scholar should to get at his subject; his research exhausted virginal manuscript collections, municipal records, personal files of political leaders, and other rarely used sources, and he conducted over 500 interviews. The research is as impressive, prodigious, and thorough as it could be.

Caro's achievement goes well beyond that of the comparatively conventional biographies: he has excelled at the interpretative level by brilliantly analyzing the role of a master urban planner-and-builder who worked outside the normal democratic process and used the "public authority" device as a force in the growth and management of the city.

About forty years ago, Adolf Berle and Gardiner Means described the rise of a new elite, the corporate managers who run the great business enterprises that others own. Berle and Means analyzed the separation of ownership and management, and the consequences of that separation. Caro has in effect extended that analysis from the modern corporation to the contemporary city, an accomplishment without rival from any of the contending books this year.

Moses was the greatest builder of public works in American history. Caro describes how he developed the "public authority" as a means of achieving enormous power and influence without being accountable to the electorate. The public authority is a self-perpetuating, self-governing public corporation whose records, unlike those of other public agencies, are as private as those of a private corporation, yet whose activities are founded on sovereign powers lubricated by public tolls amounting to hundreds and hundreds of millions of dollars. Moses's mastery of the public authority was the lever by which he shaped New York and made himself a political czar who could manipulate and compete with elected officials; by his power to award contracts, commissions, and fees, he exercised a behind-the-scene control over unions, contractors, banks, insurance companies, investment firms, real estate companies, great retail merchandisers, public relations companies, and politicians.

The book has many faults. It is too long; its use of information obtained by interviews is questionable; it has a pugnacious and prosecutorial tone; it is filled with righteous indignation, scorn, and bitterness. Still more important, it seeks to prove too much: though Moses did not lead New York City and its environs to the promised land, as Caro demonstrates by techniques of overkill, almost everything wrong with the City is probably the result of forces well beyond Moses's ability to have controlled. Other cities suffer from the ills of New York and have managed to decay without a Moses. Caro makes too much of the devil theory of history, with Moses cast in the role of the devil. Nevertheless his book is alive; it throbs and screams and clutches, and it tells a tremendously fascinating and crucially important story, never before revealed. Its achievement is so monumental in its vivid depiction of Moses and his city that there is no better illustration in all our literature of the theme that power tends to corrupt. Moses was a genius of the most formidable accomplishments, but as he seized power, his ideals flagged and his brilliance turned phosphorescent. The real subject of the book is the modern city and how it is torn by conflicting ideals, huge but short-sighted ideas, political power struggles, vast deals, and the decline in the quality of urban life. And it is all knit together by Caro's devastating revelations of how Moses operated in the interstices of the political system, using the power of money that he controlled through his public authorities; they vested him with an almost irresponsible or nonaccountable but quite legal power in urban planning, management, and development. For Caro's unique achievement, the jury believes that despite extravagances, he deserves the Pulitzer Prize for Biography. Unanimous verdict.

The jurors voted, as their *second* choice, in favor of Theodore Rosengarten's *All God's Dangers: The Life of Nate Shaw*. This too is an exceptional book. It is about a poor black farmer of the deep South and is based on his taped recollections, in old age. Shaw's storytelling has an almost Homeric quality; the book has a special kind of eloquence, dramatic power, and heroism, and undoubtedly will long endure as a significant American document.

One juror was utterly captivated by Wooldridge's *From the Steeples and Mountains: A Study of Charles Ives*. He regards it as an important breakthrough in American cultural history, the opening of a vista, that for the first time places Ives as America's greatest composer and as the last great composer in the Western Tradition.

Both *All God's Dangers* and *From the Steeples* ran into very serious objections. Each had deficiencies that seemed to thrust it toward the edges of our category. The one is a documentary that may in some respects be fictitious without rivaling Faulkner, while the other is less the life of the man than a depiction of his work. Both are beautiful and unconventional major works. We do not mean to detract from them when concluding that Caro's *Power Broker* is the best book of the year.

I like to think that my long statement recommending *The Power Broker*, yet paying dutiful respect to *All God's Dangers* and to Wooldridge's book, matched in eloquence and forcefulness the letters my fellow jurors had written earlier, when they briefly strayed from the path of ultimate truth. Compared to other letters I had seen on behalf of Pulitzer juries—and I had seen more than the ones written by Morton, Syrett, and Boyd—my letter was a pamphlet of strong and reasoned judgment.

The History jury that I chaired in 1975 seemed especially important because we were choosing the book that would win the award for 1976, the bicentennial year. My colleagues were Kathryn Kish Sklar of UCLA and Michael Kammen of Cornell, both of whom had strong convictions and, like me, some sympathies that were hard to down. Kammen matched me in aggressiveness and in detailed analysis of the books he liked. Early in August, when there were still perhaps a hundred books yet to be received, he took the lead by writing us that of those he had so far read, James McPherson's *Abolitionist Legacy* and David Potter's *Impending Crisis* seemed best; and he had the uncanny discernment to say he was looking forward to three books that would prove to be the basis of considerable discussion: Henry May's *Enlightenment in America*, Herbert Gutman's *Black Family*, and Alex Haley's *Roots*. A month later I wrote that Potter's book was "easily the best" of those that we had received to date; I ranked

Robert A. Gross's *The Minutemen and Their World* and McPherson next in order but clearly inferior. "I must warn you," I enjoined, "about my personal tastes. I like brilliant, stylish, unorthodox books, even if stubborn and wrong (like Michael's *Paradox*). That means I'll dump Potter as my first choice if I get the chance." I thought Irving Howe's *World of Our Fathers* met my conditions; it was an exceptionally vivid recreation of the nearly dead but unique and influential world of Yiddish culture. I urged the jurors to consider it along with Potter and May.

Kammen rated Potter, May, and Howe among his favorites but declared that he was also taking the Gutman and Haley books very seriously and, in fact, inclined to favor Gutman above all. Sklar, reporting in for the first time, wrote that she, like Kammen, accepted my dictum about "brilliant, stylish, and unorthodox" books, and she agreed that those we had discussed were the top contenders. May, Potter, and Howe, in that order, were her favorites, yet like Kammen, she was attracted to the books by Haley and Gutman. Sklar was the first to point to a monumental infirmity in *Roots*: what is the difference between it, she wondered, and a historical novel? The book moved and impressed her. She thought it the best book she had read to date in terms of authentic content and moral perspective, but she also thought it was fictive. Although she disliked the prose style of Gutman's book, she praised it highly. I had skimmed but not studied Gutman's *Black Family*. Haley's *Roots*, I replied, was a book I had dismissed as excessively emotional and semifictitious at many points. I even called it a "novel" and asserted that it did not fit our History category. I recommended that my colleagues give serious consideration to a book I had just read—Richard Kluger's *Simple Justice*. I sensed that the other two jurors were likely to push Gutman, whose book I had begun and disliked. I pointed out that we still had many books yet to come, as of November 8, and that the three of us agreed on Potter, Howe, and May as among the leading contenders. I asked Sklar to justify her rank-order. "Reasons, please."

Kammen replied with a brace of letters. He agreed with us

that, notwithstanding the many admirable qualities of *Roots*, it was not history; it belonged in a new category: "semi-fiction." But it was so good that Kammen thought we might consider recommending it for a Special Citation. He strongly disagreed with my reaction to Gutman, whose book he thought the most original and innovative among all the books he had read so far; concisely and powerfully he stated why. In his next letter, having finished Gutman, he said I had wanted "reasons," and he supplied them—in detail.

At that point I realized that I was outvoted; the other two favored Gutman, forcing me to study his book very carefully. On November 17, I wrote the following letter, addressing myself to Kammen with a copy to Sklar:

> Your letter recommending Gutman's book as our first choice kept me up most of the night. Your argument is strong, challenging, yet reasonable. It is also surprising. I don't share your opinions. I have read the book and have re-read parts of it, especially the historiographical stuff (fascinating, provocative, repetitive, but belongs in an appendix), stuff I found stupefying or unclear the first time around, and the stuff you focused on. Our disagreement about this book is irreconcilable. I might rank it in the top ten, but never #1.
>
> For me style is very much a matter of substance. Gutman writes so badly that I could not recommend him for a Pulitzer for reasons of style alone.
>
> I do not trust any book that relies heavily on a single-factor explanation, whether it be an "economic interpretation," "the frontier," or class, party, religion, etc. In ROLL, JORDAN, ROLL, Genovese had the blacks overcoming because of their religion. For Gutman their humanity prevails because of family and kinship relationships. For him that explains it all. I am deeply skeptical. Someone who has talents in the quantitative field and cares deeply about Gutman's subject is going to come along and do unto him as he and others did unto Fogel & Engerman. The depth and variety of Gutman's research seems impressive, but I

don't need to be told so ponderously and with such overkill that blacks are people capable of loving and caring and wanting to stay together if at all possible. But I am strongly suspicious of generalizations based on samples not proved to be representative (more on that when I get to ch. 10). Much of what Gutman says is obvious; the lion labored and brought forth a mouse. Much of it is dressed in sociological jargon. Some of it may be wrong, or is not proved by his evidence. I don't have the patience to study all his charts and graphs and tables; I have tried in some instances and I have read the lengthy prose (?) summaries that seem interminable. With my very inadequate quantitative talents, I have found enough to be suspicious. An expert might murder Gutman.

Gutman's kind of history is heavily quantitative, analytical, and sociological; I prefer more movement and drama. Still I recognize the place of the new sociometric history. I've given Gutman far, far more time than any other book. I see the diversity and depth of his materials, his prodigious research, and his multidisciplinary approach; I grasp his main themes, and I can place his book historiographically. But I see lousy rhetoric; I see the obvious being inflated into jargon that putatively gives us novelty; and, I see generalizations based on insufficient data and/or generalizations that overreach.

Take, for example, ch. 10 which you praise as "very powerful" and as representing "an incredible compression of massive amounts of highly significant information." I find the chapter worthy of distrust. It is extremely spotty, though it purports to cover the 50 years between 1880 and 1930. Its theme (p. 433) is: "But at all times—and in all settings—the typical black household (always a lower-class household) had in it two parents and was not 'unorganized and disorganized.'" Read that again: *all* places, always. Personally I prefer to allow for exceptions. The next few pages tell me that there were exceptions; indeed, they seem to be frequent, though tragic and the result of circumstances beyond black control. At 442 I learn that the generalizations that follow will be based on entire communities, urban and rural, not just samples. Two cities, two towns, and six rural areas provide the data. Why these places and not others? Aren't they "samples"? But never mind that. What is the character of the generalizations that emerge? Adult black males are poor and unskilled! On farms they are share-croppers and tenants, while in the cities they are the unskilled laborers. The women are field-hands or servants. Still, "the typical black household everywhere contained only the members of a core nuclear family" (p. 443). But in the next line, despite the "only," I learn that there are also lodgers and relatives, so that my nuclear family, which is typical and everywhere, no longer contains only the core members (parents and children). So I learn that a lot of families contain "subfamilies" vs. "father absent. . . ." There are a lot of the latter, a fact "partly" explained by a "surplus" of black women. But the section concludes (p. 445) with some generalizations that are either tricky (few young mothers with kids live alone— thus hiding the fact that they are not living with *their* husbands; *both* parents are *not* present), or obvious (when the father isn't there, the family has fewer kids than when he is there), or suspect ("As a result, between 66 percent and 75 percent of black children under the age of six everywhere lived with a mother and a father"). That last is not only suspect; it is tricky. The evidence is supposed to be in Tables A12 through A18. So I examined those tables, carefully (pp. 489–94). They tell me about 8 places in the South, not about "everywhere." None of the tables mention children under six. None of the tables show *both* mother and father being present with children. A10, however, is pertinent—but is it reliable, does it bear out all the generalizations in the paragraph on 445, and would the evidence change with eight other communities???

Continuing with this supposedly powerful and significant chapter, I next find that poor whites are better off than poor blacks. I then learn that within the eight communities, there are significant differences even among the rural ones. For example, male-absent households are twice as common in one place's black female-headed household and four times as common among another's than among white female-headed or male-absent household in still another of the communities being studied. Not only does that raise the possibility that white and black families differ; it means that the eight communities (or, rather, some of the rural ones) differ substantially, raising, again, the possibility that the choice of different communities, rural and urban, might really alter the main conclusions of the book. Similarly, on 446, I also learn that the male-absent households among blacks in the two cities chosen for study are more common than male-absent white families somewhere else. But, I am reassured, there are reasons—as if reasons alter the facts. The fact at this point seems to be that both parents are *not* present *all* times *everywhere*; also, maybe white and black families do differ after all. At 448 I learn that as time goes by (1900) the kin-related household is still the norm; was I supposed to have believed that household consisted of unrelated people? I never thought that. Even so, at the end of p. 448, I discover that the nuclear household is yielding a bit to extended and augmented households (relatives—of course!, and lodgers), and I am treated to "speculations." Immediately, however, I am reassured: as of 1900 the southern black household still is headed by a husband or father—proof for which consists in Tables A22–26. I look at the tables. A22 is about occupations in just three (not even eight) places. Indeed A22 through A26 generally show only the same three. A23 has a cop-out proving nothing: "Percent including husband and wife or *parent-child*." (My emphasis.) A24 does tell me how many families had fathers present—or does it? There is a doubt because 1) I do not know whether the mothers were also present, and 2) because "sub-families" are included and they do not have both parents present. A26 is more convincing, but when it tells me about black families in *two* rural places and *one* urban place, can I assume that I have the basis for generalizations about black families everywhere, or even in the other communities present on other pages in the study? Is it the black family in the South? In the U.S.? If so, why just Richmond and those selected rural places? And what am I to make of the fact that the nuclear family is 65% of black families in Richmond in 1880 but only 41% in a black ward of that city in 1900? Does 41% justify all and every? At A24 I am reassured by learning that in 1900 in three areas the figure for the nuclear family ranged from 41% to 70%—but what a variation among just three places! What *is* "typical"?

I'm tiring. I meant to continue this sort of thing to the end of that powerful and significant chapter. But, of course, I don't find it powerful and significant. I find it dull, trite, and suspect. Perhaps I very much exaggerate (as does Gutman). The point is that in my view the book is not good enough to merit a Pulitzer. Incidentally, one might argue at length about the validity of his having stopped at 1925 and inferences that might be drawn from the fact.

As of now, my first choice is Irving Howe; I think I like Potter for second place. But we ought not prejudge: there are a lot of books still to come in, though the November 1st deadline has long since passed. I haven't received Cappon's *Atlas* and two more boxes of books are still en route. Of those received, Silverman looks worthy of consideration and perhaps others.

A special citation for Haley? Let me reserve judgment about that.

I am really sorry we disagree so deeply about Gutman. The extensiveness of my reply suggests the respect I have for your opinion; if I didn't take you so seriously, I would have dismissed Gutman with one line. Even now, I am disturbed by our profound differences, so much so that I distrust my own judgment. But, the issue boils down to this: should Gutman rank #1? I could be 75% wrong about him, but even if I'm partly right, the answer to my question is a resounding "no." In the top ten for innovation, etc., yes. The winner? No.

Before Sklar received my letter on Gutman, she finally replied to my request for "reasons." She agreed with Kammen that *The Black Family* should rank as number one and did an effective job of explaining why. She placed May second, Potter third, and Lester Cappon's *Atlas of Early American History* fourth, a book deserving "some kind of honorable mention if that is possible." Kammen too wrote another letter before receiving mine about *The Black Family.* He had just finished Potter's book, "the only other" that he deemed prize-worthy, and at length he brilliantly explained why. (Later I would use his letter as a point of departure for the ultimate letter to the Pulitzer Office recommending Potter.) My problem at that time was that I did not know how Kammen would react to my letter against Gutman or how Kammen would rank Gutman against Potter when it came to a necessary choice. To stop the book by Gutman, my best tactic at that point was to sacrifice Howe and support Potter. I wrote a low-key letter explaining that though I really preferred Howe, his book had deficiencies (some oppressive detail and a failure to cover business, Zionism, and religion). I could not put Kluger's book or May's in the same league as Potter's. Since Sklar preferred May's *Enlightenment,* I felt obligated to say why it could not qualify as the best book, though I thought it splendid. May saw the Enlightenment mainly in terms of religion, but it was as much scientific, philosophical, political, and literary as religious; while the categories overlapped and May did not ignore the overlaps, his angle of vision was too limited. Desperately I suggested that maybe we ought to turn to Cappon's *Atlas*—anything to head off Gutman at the pass.

Growing more desperate, I wrote again hoping that Kammen preferred Potter to Gutman but recognizing that if he finally voted for Gutman, I was outvoted. "If you two choose him over my dissent, you act within your right and I within mine when I go to war." (I thought a copy of my strong November 17 letter against Gutman might scare off the advisory board.) But I was seeking a unanimous recommendation. To Skar's contention that Howe's book, though excellent, was on a "fairly narrow topic," I replied that Howe had a broader canvas than Gutman. I pushed Potter, however, as the most likely basis for a unanimous decision. I added, "I'm for a citation for Cappon."

Sklar by now had received what Kammen later called my "articulate and well-reasoned tirade against Gutman." She also had Kammen's statement on behalf of Potter. The two letters, she conceded, prompted her to reconsider. She decided to favor Potter as our top choice. Since I had still urged Howe's book, for the first time she gave a reasoned judgment against it. To me her argument sounded like a professional feminist's; Howe somehow had portrayed the role of the mother in Jewish family life as giving substance to the origin of Portnoy's complaint. I could not disagree, however, with Sklar's judgment that Howe's historical skills were narrower than Potter's. Our discussions led her to downgrade May. She now ranked his book fifth, behind Potter, Gutman, Howe, and Cappon in that order. But she had second thoughts. A few days later she praised Cappon's *Atlas* and concluded that she would be willing to award the prize to Cappon with only an honorable mention for Potter, because his book had appeared posthumously.

Kammen, before receiving her last letter, wrote to endorse Potter. He too wanted a unanimous jury to prevent hanky-panky from the advisory board. With a split decision from us, the board might do what it wanted. Two years earlier, Kammen said, they had given the prize to Malone's *Jefferson*, which was not the jury's first choice. Therefore we had better unite. Respecting my persistent support for *The World of Our Fathers*, Kammen explained why he could not back my judgment. He argued that Howe's book lacked "comparative perspective" in the sense that the New York experience was not necessarily typical of the lives of eastern European Jews in America. Out of consideration for Sklar's feelings, Kammen also explained why he could not support May's book: it said too little of the reception and impact of European science, especially scientific agriculture, in America. Finally, Kammen cast his vote in favor of a Special Citation for Cappon, though he feared that the *Atlas* would get the advisory board's award unless we all supported *The Impending Crisis*.

The struggle was over: Potter's book, after all, was superb, and Gutman as an also-ran would not get the advisory board's nod over a unanimous choice. But Sklar's second thought about preferring Cappon over Potter needed an answer. I seriously studied the *Atlas*, which previously I merely had admired, and found to my surprise that the beautiful cartographical work was based on too many secondary sources that were questionable. For Sklar's benefit I rejoined that we should recommend the best book, the book not the author: that Potter was dead was irrelevant. When Kammen next reported in, he too had done his homework on the *Atlas* and found it wanting; he had also located an expert cartographer's review supporting our suspicions. Kammen voted, in the end, for Potter, Gutman, and Kluger, in that order. Sklar's final verdict was for Potter, Gutman, and Howe. I would have placed Howe second but felt obligated to defer to my fellow jurors. Coming in second for the Pulitzer is not coming in at all if the jury is united and the letter of recommendation is overpowering. I wrote that kind of letter for the three of us nominating *The Impending Crisis*, while paying appropriate respect to Gutman, Cappon, and Howe as also-rans. The Pulitzer Office thought I had written "a great report," Kammen found my letter "elegant," and Sklar believed it "eloquent and effective."

Our work was over on December 23, but early in March I received an extraordinary phone call from Richard T. Baker, Hohenberg's successor as secretary to the advisory board and administrator of the Pulitzer Prizes. Because *Roots* had been sent to the History jury, Baker wanted to know what we thought of the book. I was alarmed, thinking that the advisory board might slip in Haley over our choice of Potter. Assuring me, however, that Potter would win the prize, Baker said that influential members of the advisory board wanted somehow to give a Pulitzer to Haley. Relieved, I spoke glowingly of Haley. Having bashed his book as nonhistory, I praised it as a moving, original, and significant work of art, even if semifictive. Baker then asked what I thought of the idea of awarding *Roots* the Pulitzer for Fiction. That struck me as hilarious but stupid, but I did not say so. I told Baker that the idea was a very bad one for several reasons. First, it would be an insult to the book which purported to be history, or at least nonfiction, certainly not fiction. Second, it would make the Pulitzer Prizes look silly to the public. Third, it might cause a lot of trouble for Columbia University by provoking a sensitive black community. Baker asked if I had any suggestions. I thought I had a great one: the Pulitzer Plan of Award had long had a category for a "distinguished book . . . which is not eligible for consideration in any other existing category." The most recent rewording of that category called it "nonfiction" for a work of "high literary quality and originality." That, I thought, sounded as if invented for *Roots*. No, Baker replied, the nonfiction prize that year was going to make it "a Jewish year, not a black year." Howe's *World of Our Fathers*, Baker told me, was going to win the award in that category. I was delighted, of course, but where did that leave *Roots*? I remembered that Kammen had once suggested that we recommend it for a Special Citation; he had pointed out that James Flexner's four-volume life of Washington had once received such a citation, and we had also discussed Cappon's *Atlas* for a Special Citation. Accordingly I recommended a Special Citation for *Roots*. Baker remarked that that might be the best way out of the dilemma. The advisory board agreed.

The news that the advisory board had decided to accept Potter for the History prize and Howe for the Nonfiction prize, and had considered Haley for the Fiction prize, was too good to keep private. I passed the information to Kammen and Sklar, and I also did something foolish and wrong. I was so pleased to learn that Howe was going to get the Pulitzer that I convinced myself that notwithstanding unwritten custom, the Pulitzer Office had never cautioned me about confidentiality. So I breached it. Howe had long been a colleague of mine at Brandeis, so I happily sent him a note encouraging him to look forward to early May when the Pulitzers would be announced. On that Monday in May I was appalled to learn that the Nonfiction prize went to a book I had never heard of, Robert N. Butler's *Why Survive? Being Old in America*. Unable to admit that I had innocently deceived Howe, and having no jurisdiction concerning the Nonfiction prize (Was there a Nonfiction jury? What did they recommend?), I could not ask the Pulitzer Office to tell me what had gone wrong. Four stints as a juror is about as much as anyone is called upon to serve; and after writing this essay, I knew that I would never hear from the Pulitzer Office again.

While judging the books of others, I continue to write my own and to marvel at the opinions of others and the chanciness of being reviewed in the right places by the right people. I read somewhere the clever line that in the reviews, as in the toilet, all men are peers. Not necessarily. Literary tongs, like theological ones, do exist, and it is far better for one's reputation to draw a like-minded ally than a member of a rival tong. Still better for the ego is a complimentary review, even if a little cutting, from an unexpected source or from that rare bird, the disinterested scholar who understands that his first obligation to an author and to readers is to explain what a book purports to do, before evaluating it. *Judgments: Essays in American Constitutional History* (Quadrangle, 1972), a slight effort on my part, drew some reviews that make one's head, like a doorknob, easily turned. One man whose work I admired wrote, "Levy's brand is skeptical and liberal, and just now he dominates the field of constitutional historians." In one review, under some editor's heading, "Contentious Brilliance Redeemed: Levy at the Bar of Judgment," Alfred H. Kelly, then the dean of constitutional historians, passed the laurel wreath when he wrote "that for penetrating originality of thought, sharpness of analysis, and brilliance of style the author stands forth as preeminent in his field." Almost twenty years earlier Kelly had dismissed me from his staff of researchers who were gathering data for the NAACP's brief in *Brown v. Board of Education*. After a few weeks of research I had told Kelly that no responsible historian could conclude that the authors of the Fourteenth Amendment specifically intended to ban compulsory racial segregation in the public schools.

Against the Law: The Nixon Court and Criminal Justice (Harper and Row, 1974) was, I thought, a major effort and a powerful book. On the whole, it bombed. For example, in the same journal that gave me Kelly's review, I drew a very able academic lawyer, Edward White, who subordinated his Kelly-like compliments to elaborate and unplumbable stupidities. He condemned me for being judicious. I admired the efforts of justices to produce well-reasoned, convincing arguments while at the same time I recognized that as long as mere mortals sit on the Supreme Court, we will get opinions that tend to be subjective and result-oriented. What most nettled me was White's calling *Against the Law* "a popular book . . . a frolic." It could be a bad book, but five hundred pages of microanalysis of a few years of the Court's work in the field of criminal procedure is scarcely a frolic for a mass audience. The reviewer's wit seemed like nature's way of filling a vacuum. (He later had the gall to ask me to write an introduction for a book of his essays, on the theory, he said, that they deserved a send-off by the best legal historian in the country. I declined the honor.) Except for the *New York Times Book Review*, which rated *Against the Law* so-so, the mass media pretty much ignored my book, and so even did most of the law reviews.

The publisher also slighted *Against the Law*. I had switched to the trade department of Harper and Row, thinking that a big commercial house sells books the way Heinz sells pickles or Goodyear sells tires. I have a conviction, probably wrong, that a trade publisher can "hype" even a scholarly book and make a modest profit. According to my editor, however, the "sales" department decided, during the season of the impeachment hearings that ended in Nixon's resignation, that the last thing the book-buying public wanted to read was that tricky Dick had a long-range contaminating influence on our great and impartial Supreme Court. "Sales" decided to downplay *Against the Law* and cut the press run to seven thousand copies. The cloth edition sold out, almost unadvertised, went out of print, and disappeared with scarcely a ripple. Harper and Row was not better for me than Harvard University Press. Years earlier, I remembered, when *Time* magazine gave my book on Jefferson the lead review, I had discovered that only one bookstore in Cambridge, Massachusetts, the Harvard Coop, had copies of the book. When I complained to the director of Harvard University Press, he replied, "We publish fine books; we don't sell hotcakes." But Harvard University Press does look for hotcakes, long hoping that I had a potential one in a book it wanted me to write on the trials of Jesus.

Harvard University Press, et al.,
v. A Book

> We are about to speak of very ugly matters,
> concerning which, for more than one reason, we
> should like to keep silent; but we are obligated to
> mention events which come within our province,
> since they have for their theatre the hearts of
> actors in our story.
> —Stendhal, *The Charterhouse of Parma*

*I*N A WORLD whose absurdity increases daily, I should not have
been surprised when Harvard University Press (HUP) rejected a book that I did under contract to HUP and that my editor, Aida Donald, had praised. Rejection was not a new
experience. I had written a different book, which won the
Pulitzer Prize for History, with the understanding that Harper
and Row would publish it, but that company rejected the book
on the basis of a decision that it would not be a commercial success. I can understand that sort of decision from a commercial
publisher—not respect it but understand it. To a commercial
publisher books are a commodity, like bicycles, pocket calcula-
tors, and jockstraps to their manufacturers. Harvard University
Press, however, is not a commercial publisher. It has an obligation to publish excellent scholarly books. Like all publishers,
though, it properly reserves for itself the decision whether a manuscript is "acceptable," even when written under contract by an

author who had published three books with HUP. Like all university presses, HUP does not rely wholly on in-house judgment. It requires approval of the manuscript from at least one outside reviewer, a reasonable rule that protects the press from the importunities of local faculty authors.

The book that HUP rejected was *Treason Against God: A History of the Offense of Blasphemy* (Schocken, 1981). I had been collecting materials on that subject for many years and in 1975 was getting close to the writing state. HUP was under new management, and the editor for social sciences was Aida D. Donald, an old friend of mine, who had solicited my work. Disillusioned by my experiences with trade publishers, I decided to "go home" and signed contracts for two books with HUP, one on blasphemy, the other on the trials of Jesus. I had no idea what I might write on the trials of Jesus or, for that matter, on blasphemy. Most historians tend to become specialists; they write books on subjects with which they have become familiar, if not expert. I write a book as the best way to learn about a subject, just as I find that teaching others is the best way for me to master my own course. The most famous blasphemy trial in history having been the one depicted in the Gospels of Mark and Matthew, I assumed that the book on Jesus would grow out of the broader one on blasphemy, might require some reuse of the same material, and ought therefore to be published by the same house to avoid permissions problems.

I do not compose from a prospectus or outline, I told HUP, so I never know what I'm going to write till I do so. I knew only that I would start *Treason Against God* with the Old Testament origins of the crime of blasphemy and trace its history down the ages to the present. "Most of the book," I said, as we negotiated the contracts, "will be on England and America, much more on the former than the latter." When I finished the first chapter on the origins of the concept of blasphemy in ancient Jewish law, my editor suggested that I might be spending too much time on background before getting to the American scene. The American scene, I replied, is "minor compared to the English. Most of the book will be about blasphemy in England," because the crime has been more frequently prosecuted in England. I was planning a book that would, implicitly, be a study of the evolution of freedom of opinion on religious matters from ancient times to the present, using "blasphemy" as a litmus test of what society will tolerate. As I completed each chapter, I sent a copy to my editor. Of one she wrote, "In both its structure and presentation it is near perfect and the material intellectually exciting. I couldn't be happier with it. . . ." "A superb chapter," she said of another. "It is clear, has intellectual verve, and reader interest." The next chapter was "delightful . . . I find it both scholarly and lively and congratulate you on presenting difficult material so flawlessly and easily." Another chapter she found to be "a high point. . . . You have written about the Quakers with authority and sensitivity. I . . . found myself moved time and again by your story. It is a rare experience to read something like your rendition of Nayler's trial and tortures and be genuinely touched . . . such empathy."

By August 1977 I believed that the book would grow beyond the confines of one volume. I suggested two separate books, the first to end at 1700, a natural breaking point in the history of this particular subject. A book covering three thousand years to 1700 struck me as having enough sweep, and I thought HUP would welcome two books for the price of one. But my editor ridiculed a book on just the "roots" of the subject; HUP's interest, she replied, was in the history of blasphemy in the United States—a subject I preferred to cover in the sequel. To my astonishment I learned for the first time that Harvard regarded the book on Jesus as "an exciting trade book" that had made the press want the book on blasphemy. The trade book would have "a wide audience to balance things." I wondered why a distinguished university press denigrated a mere "scholarly monograph," whored after a best-seller, and thought I could write it. I also wondered why, contrary to my initial descriptions of *Treason Against God* and the chapters I had submitted, my editor persisted in thinking I was writing a history of blasphemy in the United States. HUP was firm. I could make *Treason Against God* as big as I wanted: it would have a Belknap imprint to subsidize it and keep down the price; but HUP would not publish the book until I brought the story up to the present. I reluctantly agreed.

Several months later, as a sabbatical semester came to a close, I was nearly finished with the book—to 1700. I deplored having to sit on some six hundred pages of finished material for several years before getting into print with the whole history of the subject. My editor ignored the letters in which I tried to reopen the possibility of publishing what I had finished; I argued vainly that it constituted an independent volume. After my editor had received all the chapters to 1700, she gushed, "How proud I am to have an author of such authority and brilliance." I decided to add an epilogue to the book, rounding it off as a freestanding volume by concisely bringing the story from 1700 to the present so that a reader would not be left stranded in the past. I had resolved that if Harvard would not publish the book I had finished, I'd return the advances and cancel our contracts. This time I was firm. My editor told me I could not cancel the contracts. They wanted my books; after all, I was "one of the six most distinguished historians HUP has ever published!" We reached an odd compromise, approved by Arthur Rosenthal, the director of HUP. They would publish *Treason Against God* (up to 1700) on the condition that I changed my writing plans. Instead of continuing with the sequel, which I planned on calling *Blasphemy! An Anglo-American History*, I must first write the book on the trials of Jesus. I agreed. We drew up and signed new contracts for three books. By July 1978 we had agreed on the design of *Treason Against God*, which was slotted for publication in the early fall of 1979.

I spent the summer of 1978 intensively studying the New Testament and NT scholarship, while Harvard sent *Treason Against God* to a reader, the reader of my choice. My editor had asked me to recommend someone. My first choice was Jaroslav Pelikan, the Sterling Professor of History at Yale and dean of the graduate school there. As an amateur in the field of religious history, I had belatedly discovered Pelikan's *The Christian Tradition*, a work scheduled for five volumes when completed. The outstanding historian of Christianity, Pelikan seemed the best-qualified American to assess my work. My editor agreed and got him. I had also recommended Martin Marty as a second reader, if a second were necessary. Marty had been associate dean of the Divinity School at the University of Chicago, where he held an endowed professorship. His work ranged from a short survey of Christian history to an interpretive volume on Protestantism in America.

In July I asked my editor a question about Pelikan which turned out to be prescient: "Will he be offended?" I had not cited Pelikan's books in my notes; that he might be offended for any other reason did not occur to me. In the same letter I wrote:

> The literature about Jesus is unique: it is massive, scholarly, erudite, technical, and in the form of nonfiction, yet it is all fictive. Never have so many written so much so seriously in such detail about something of which we know so little, so little that all is conjecture. A professional historian can't or should not write about Jesus. To do so violates the very canons of the profession; there is no evidence in the usual sense. History can't be written from theology. Whatever I write ought to be labeled fiction. . . .

The more I read about Jesus the more inexplicable I found HUP's interest in a book by me on his trials. As I reminded my editor, I had never indicated what sort of a book I'd write or what its theme might be. The subject intrigued me as no other had, but why in the world, I asked, did HUP want such a book from "a gross amateur in the field?" I'm learning, I wrote my editor, "that the historian cannot reconstruct a life of Jesus. . . . We know too little about him to write even an obituary." I received no reply but continued intensively my course of reading. When I finished Bultmann and the post-Bultmannians, I wrote that I was beginning to understand the German-influenced New Testament scholars for whom all that counts is the kerygma of the eschatological Christ—faint echoes from the historical Jesus who lived. They were really theologians who "demythologize Jesus and recreate a Heideggerian Christ; anyone not on the same wavelength (Christian existentialist) is unkosher." As a medium for intellectual gymnastics, I told my editor, the New Testament (and the Old) had the Constitution beat a mile. "I'm advancing tediously but feverishly from form criticism to redaction criticism. Each of the four Gospels has a different theology and purpose, an amazing number of meanings and levels of meanings, like playing chess in three dimensions. . . ." I had had the benefit of critical readings of my chapter on "The Jewish Trial of Jesus," in *Treason Against God*, by several distinguished New Testament scholars in Claremont. They had found some minor errors, I warned, but I could easily make the corrections on the copyedited manuscript.

On August 1, 1978, my editor, having belatedly read the chapter on "The Jewish Trial of Jesus," wrote that she could accept it fully for *Treason Against God*, but not as the basis of a trade book on Jesus and his trials. I had never intended to write the "trade" book the same way, but she was now asking me to write a "story." In early August I wrote two elaborate letters on the impossibilities of writing either a life or a straight narrative. The New Testament scholars in Claremont, I reported, had tried to make me understand that I had to depict separately what each evangelist meant in his own time and place. I now understood them and sought to make my editor understand. I would try to write an historical account of the trials of Jesus in the context of his ministry. "You sound as if you want it done à la Jim Bishop for a commercial press. If I had the talent for such a task and the disposition, I think I might write under an assumed name. Otherwise scholars would think me an idiot. A fixed tenet of modern NT scholarship," I explained, "is that a life of Jesus cannot be written. I didn't propose a life, but his ministry cannot be separated from the trials, and the ministry puts me into the life, which is unrecoverable. I could use some counsel from you. I've asked, 'what do you expect of me?' If you want a story, a narrative, it's impossible." Again I tried to explain, in considerable detail, that the New Testament, our only source, tells us what later Christians thought about Jesus, and they differ crucially on details, even in theology and Christology. HUP wanted a vivid narrative with a novel and attractive theme, a book that would sell, not a monographic, analytical work. Yet no responsible scholar would write the book HUP wanted. Such a book, if written, I insisted, ought not be published by a great university press. "Why," I asked, "are you acting as if Harvard is Doubleday?" One thing sustained me, I added. "People who keep saying that a book on Jesus can't be done write books on Jesus. But we can't prove what may have happened. We can't know what happened." Everything we think we "know" about Jesus is speculative and unprovable. I also explained that when I wrote my third chapter for *Treason Against God*, covering the subject of blasphemy from the Gospels through the fourth century in early Christian thought, I had mischaracterized some early Christian writings. I had revised a few pages, I wrote, and would substitute them for the old pages when I got the copyedited version back.

"The Jesus book," I reported in another letter, "has become an obsession with me, though for reasons I cannot explain; maybe it's my Everest, the nearly insuperable, the most difficult subject I could pick. . . . I can't explain why I want to do the Jesus book; I just know I must, though I go through torments about my inadequacies. All reason tells me, don't do it. That, maybe, is why I must prove to myself that I can." I returned again to an old theme in my letters: "HUP's desire for me to do the book is beyond my comprehension. 1) I'm not qualified, and 2) HUP wants a trade book, in itself a paradox: why does a university press want a trade book on the most sacred subject from an unqualified, Talmudic agnostic? Had I given you a smashing prospectus with a striking new thesis, however inspired, your decision might make sense. But I didn't. If you wanted a trade book or any book on Jesus, why not go to a major NT scholar? If not that narrow a specialist, why not to someone like Pelikan? Getting me to do even the trials of Jesus . . . makes as much sense as getting [James M.] Robinson or Pelikan to do a new study of the Sacco-Vanzetti case or a Civil War expert to write a life of Socrates."

At last my editor answered me about the book on Jesus. "You are probably the only scholar now (or you will be the only scholar when you complete your research) who will be able to say with a degree of certainty what happened more than 2000 years ago just before a Messiah was crucified by the Romans." In the margin I impulsively wrote, "Bullshit. She just doesn't understand. All my letters wasted." I tried once more, knowing the attempt would also be a waste. By then I was studying Paul and Acts of the Apostles, and I pointed out how the Paul of Acts was utterly unlike the Paul of the Epistles. I reminded my editor to tell my reader that I had rewritten several pages of chapter 3 of *Treason Against God* and that she should pay no attention to the errors. I had also learned that several NT letters attributed to Paul were now regarded as "deutero-Pauline" letters. "The changes that I will have to make in my text are all minor and can be handled when I get the copyedited manuscript back." I warned my editor to expect a blunderbuss against me on the third chapter, because the ribbon copy, in the hands of the reader, had none of the corrections.

At the end of September 1978 my editor sent me Jaroslav Pelikan's report, with his name deleted to preserve anonymity. Being a providential person, she said, she had had the foresight to arrange for two readings, and she advised suspending judgment until the second report was in. She was "calm" and knew that I would remain "cool" too. I exploded and wrote an angry critique of Pelikan's report. He was clearly offended by the first half of my book, which carried the story through the Reformation. In effect he thought I had blasphemed. He also maximized a few factual errors—very few. Privately I thought that he overflowed with pedantry. He had the ability to read and write in many languages but could not stanch his religious prejudices in any of them. Two weeks later the second reader's report arrived. My editor had not revealed his identity, but the style and allusions to his own work were as good as a signature: Martin Marty's. After many months of delay, he had lost little time in reading my manuscript—very little time. He didn't know which side of the fence to straddle, but finally decided, he said, "51 to 49" against publication. His letter was full of contradictions, mischaracterizations, and irrelevancies that in my opinion constituted a disgrace to scholarship.

My editor tried to soothe me by saying, "You can see that by being a polymath you have stirred the feelings and intelligence of scholars. Neither scholar feels at home with a manuscript with majestic sweep and our second scholar wants us to call in some help on a few chapters"—that is, he thought each questionable chapter should be farmed out to a specialist. Enjoining me to be of "good cheer," she asked me to write a formal reply to my readers for the benefit of HUP's board of syndics. I was to compose one letter, here reprinted, but it was never presented to the syndics.

October 16, 1978

Aida D. Donald
Editor of Social Sciences
Harvard University Press
79 Garden Street
Cambridge, Mass. 02138

Dear Aida:

I now have the second reader's report, so different in tone from the first one. I owe it to myself to answer both.

The first is the one that is double-spaced. This report saddened me because I offended the writers' religious beliefs. In effect he is saying that I am blasphemous. The irony aside, I did not mean to affront anyone and regret having done so. I would make amends, consonant with the canons of scholarship, if only my reader gave specific examples. He does not. He says that my account of the patristic and medieval periods is written "with a deep animus against orthodox Christianity, expressed in gratuitous digs about Christian beliefs such as the Trinity and about Christian theologians." His only proof consists in a reference to a line in a footnote, which I deleted, where I say that unlike the

Christian scholars whose works I relied on for factual information, I have no animosity toward Arius. The words I lined out say
that if I had to choose between Arianism and Athanasianism, I'd
prefer the former. I thought at first that a statement like that
would candidly reveal to my readers my unitarianism; I finally
decided that was superfluous because obvious. I am as entitled
to my unitarianism as my reader is to his trinitarianism. I am not
entitled to "digs" or quips; if they are pointed out to me, I will
soften or eliminate them. I really don't wish to offend anyone's
religious beliefs unnecessarily. That is why I asked colleagues
here to read the chapters on the trial of Jesus and on the rise of
Christianity. I asked all my readers to be especially on the lookout for errors of fact or offensive comments. I got caught in a
number of errors, including errors of interpretation of the
Gospels, in chapter 3; I got a lot of disagreement; but no one was
offended by anything I said. Only my first reader is offended.
My readers here included James M. Robinson, Hans Dieter
Betz, and Burton Mack, who are among the foremost New Testament scholars in the nation. I also had the benefit of a reading
by a Roman Catholic priest who is one of my graduate students.
He found nothing offensive. Moreover, all my readers here believe that I proved my point in the chapter on Jesus; that is, they
agree that the Mark/Matthew depiction of the trial of Jesus by
the Sanhedrin probably never happened. My readers here also
set me straight on a number of points that your readers missed.
You will remember that I told you early in the summer that I had
rewritten pp. 5–8 of chapter 3 on the conflicting theologies
within the New Testament. I wish I had sent those revised
pages to you then; I include them now. My readers here also set
me straight on a number of Pauline points. Before I received
your readers' reports, I wrote to you to say that I had made some
minor errors of attribution, all of which could easily be corrected
at the copyediting stage. Your first reader's report caught the
misattribution of *Hebrews* to Paul; your second caught the misattribution to *Timothy*. I had already caught those errors myself and
corrected them on my copy, plus others of a similar nature that

your readers did not catch. Incidentally, I do not think errors of that sort are very important, but I want to avoid them if possible. The first reader says that when I cross the English Channel my book is "for the first time, fun to read, a good yarn." Whether that's true may depend on what gives one kicks. Personally I see no fun in the burning of Kett, Legate, and Wightman, or the jailing of Biddle and Penn, or the brutal treatment of the Quakers. The first reader seems excessively sensitive to my depiction of persecutory theories and actual persecution during the middle ages and Reformation. The ferocity of his attack seems to derive from his having been affronted by my treatment of the period from Athanasius and Augustine to Luther and Calvin. Although I am evenhanded and do not change my attitude or style when depicting English persecutions (Catholic and Protestant), the English materials appeal to the reader. No accounting for some people's tastes. I think the reader wrote a damaging report because he was upset with my viewpoint on some matters concerning which he strongly disagrees. Anyone can be emotional and disparaging when confronted by a view that cuts deeply across fixed assumptions.

Let's look carefully at the first reader's report. He levels two heavy charges—that I am prejudiced and incompetent. But he provides no bill of particulars on important matters relating to those charges. He nitpicks a lot; "nitpick" is his word. He finds trivial errors that do not support his major charges. All of us make mistakes; it's impossible to write a big book covering such a span of history and not make some. My reader wrote only a bit over five pages, yet he made mistakes. He correctly pointed out that I misspelled Gwatkin and Lietzmann, but at p. 5 of his letter he refers to me as "Lewy." Those things happen. Some mistakes should not be made. I did misdate the year of Augustine's birth. (Not that we really know that the correct date is 354 rather than 340.) But that is the only criticism the first reader has of my handling of Augustine. I elaborately define the theory of persecution that Augustine devised (based on his understanding of blasphemy and heresy); that theory served the Church for over

1,200 years. If I made a mistake on other Augustianian points my reader would have seized the opportunity to reveal them. His silence on my handling of Augustine in general and his focusing on just the wrong date-of-birth suggests to me that my stuff on Augustine is impregnable.

I did mistakenly spell the names of Gwatkin and Lietzmann. My bibliographical cards on them have the correct spelling. I shall have to double check the spellings of all names in the copyediting stage. Lapses like that and typos ought to be forgiven. I forgive "Lewy." I'm not sure I forgive the first reader's mistaken assertion that I cite St. Thomas Aquinas's *Summa* wrongly. He says I refer the reader to "any edition" of Aquinas "as though the matter could be found without any specification of the parts of the *Summa*." But I do not do that, and the footnote to which the reader refers for proof is my proof that I cited the work correctly and fully, giving very explicitly the volume and pages of the particular edition that I used of the *Summa*; only then did I add that the reader can find the quotation in any other edition "under Question XI, 'Of Heresy,' articles 1–2." That is the correct way to cite the *Summa*. Your reader is wrong in saying that I am wrong.*

Your reader also misleads you on the Septuagint. That Greek version of the Old Testament (translated about 250 B.C.) offers no usage of the word or concept of blasphemy that differs from my treatment of blasphemy in the Old Testament. Indeed your reader does not say that I am wrong. I don't even understand why he dragged in the Septuagint. I also went through a huge intertestamental literature (200 B.C.–100 A.D.) trying to discover whether I might find a Jewish source that had a different meaning of blasphemy from that which I depict. I did not find it, and so I did not cite the intertestamental sources. Mark's depiction of the Sanhedrin's trial of Jesus is the first time we got a different meaning of blasphemy. As the final pages of my chapter on the trial show, scholars have gone crazy trying to find the blas-

---

*I was wrong. Pelikan later informed me that I had omitted "Part II, Second Part."

phemy at that trial from the standpoint of Caiaphas. There was none, of course; Jesus did not blaspheme and the Sanhedrin saw no blasphemy from the standpoint of Jewish law at that time. The real point in Mark is that Mark is trying to make us understand that the Jewish rejection of Jesus was blasphemy—in a new sense of the word. The Septuagint helps not at all. I committed some errors; I don't want to be convicted for those I did not make.

The first reader also accuses me of having a more precise definition of blasphemy than my sources do. I have no definitions of blasphemy; I present only what my sources show. I also show that Aquinas "bollixed" the relationship of blasphemy to heresy or confused their meanings. The reader doesn't dispute that. I suppose his real point is that if Aquinas (like Athanasius and Augustine and so many others) used heresy and blasphemy as if they were interchangeable, then the Church did not differentiate between blasphemy and heresy. But that is my point. I'm not using my own yardstick to measure the correctness of definitions I find in Paul or Luther or whomever. I start by showing what the definition was in the Old Testament and then show how it enormously broadened thereafter and how the word "blasphemy" was promiscuously used to condemn deviance of religious opinion.

I am struck by the discrepancy between my first reader's gross charges and the triviality of his specific corrections. I plead guilty to having read Lietzmann's four volumes in English rather than German. I have no reason to believe that the English translation is faulty. True, I did not read Harnack's *Marcion*, though I read him on Marcion in his *Dogma*. Your reader notes that I did not read German and French secondary accounts. He is correct. But he does not say how Grundmann on heresy would teach me something different, new, and important that I did not find in Leff, Cohn, and all the other accounts that I used. Ditto on Borst's work on the Cathars. I didn't use it; what would it have taught me of relevance? How would it alter what I wrote on that subject from other sources? The reader does not say. True,

I did not rely on Leclercq's revision of Hefele. Frankly, at the time I wrote ch. 3 on the church councils, I did not know that Hefele had been updated. I did find that out later, and I did look at the revision: I found no reason to alter my viewpoint or citations, because the revision does not alter the facts that I used from the older version of Hefele. Why doesn't my reader point out mistakes that I made on medieval heresies or on the Cathars or on the church councils? He doesn't. He rests on my failure to have used foreign-language monographs, because he has revealed all my mistakes that he found—a wrong date for Augustine's birth, a misattribution of *Hebrews*, plus some typos on a couple of names. On that evidence he concludes that I am prejudiced and incompetent, except for all that "fun" stuff on the English persecutions of Anabaptists, Socinians, Quakers, *et al.* I will not follow the first reader's suggestion that I scrap or quickly summarize the first half of the book, leaving only the English materials that he found "fun to read." (I wonder why he didn't find the burning of Servetus as much fun as the torture of Nayler.)

The first reader claims that my book "meanders through the centuries." He finds long stretches in which blasphemy is not the focus. I disagree. Unfortunately I cannot follow the reader's specific page references; you have the only consecutively paginated copy of the book. My Xerox copy was made when I started each chapter with page one. But the reference to Luther (pp. 186–88) allows me to find the place the reader thinks is in focus and therefore to look at the surrounding pages. I am dealing with blasphemy in the context of Luther's views on religious toleration or persecution. I'm trying to explain Luther's position, what it was, how and why it changed. Every word is pertinent. Nothing is out of focus. Nor does the reader show error.

I don't know how to answer the accusation on p. 3 of the reader's report that my "exegesis" is "altogether amateurish." I wish he had given an illustration or two. On the other hand, he is right: I am an amateur. I have no professional training for anything I wrote in this book. I have no training in Old and New

Testament, in ancient history, in medieval history, in English history, or in religious history. I am known, I suppose, as a legal historian, but I have no legal training. Harvard published my first book 21 years ago in the field of legal history. I was as self-taught in that as I am in the subjects I touch in this book on blasphemy. My reader commends the second half of the book. He hears an "audible click" when I pass the reformation and cross the English Channel. I never had a course on English history. I am an amateur, but I do not think I'm incompetent. Nor do I believe that I am unfair or prejudiced. I suspect that my reader is unfair to me. But I'm used to that sort of reaction. Most of my books have been controversial. You will remember that I once wrote to you about Justice Hugo Black having called *Legacy of Suppression* one of the worst blows against American liberty in years. Dumas Malone and Julian Boyd reacted very emotionally to my book on Jefferson. HUP published those books. This book on blasphemy may also be provocative, enough to make the first reader (and perhaps others) react emotionally and aim overbroad and unsubstantiated charges. To me, the one thing that stands out so much in the first reader's report is his failure, other than the nitpicks, to prove his charges by giving a batch of illustrations. For example, I gather that he doesn't like the way I treat my subject in the time of the Reformation, but you will notice that he does not offer one single piece of evidence showing mistakes of fact or interpretation. He does not even say I am mistaken. I cannot respect the reader's estimate of my work.

The second reader's report is quite different in tone and substance. I would not take it very seriously but for the fact that it is a second adverse report. That is, after the first report I find that I must face another that decides against me, though not by much. Indeed, reader #2 is not quite certain of much. He raises questions about his own competence as well as mine, delicately: "Who can be an expert on both the trial of Jesus, and say, the Ranters?" If what follows seems like meandering, the reason is that I am following the sequence of #2.

OK, I guess I say "the Mass" rather than just "Mass." And I

say "Waldensee" instead of Waldensian. (I also say Cathari rather than Cathars.) Waldensee is NOT wrong, but I can change it to Waldensian. I do NOT credit Luther for "patenting freedom of conscience." Ridiculous. I point out that he passed through an early stage in which he advocated freedom of conscience even for Catholics, and I explain the extenuating circumstances, and I show how Luther's position changed—and why. I do say that despite his intolerance, he had an advanced position at a time when the Inquisition was employing torture. I have 8 typed pages on Luther's thought on blasphemy and toleration. #2 oversimplifies me. At p. 2 he says I credit Luther with patenting freedom of conscience; but at p. 3 he says "in this work Luther is nothing but the persecutor of heretics and blasphemers. . . ." Am I really guilty, simultaneously, of both these accusations? I do not depict Luther as "nothing but" a persecutor because I do show the strain of toleration in his thinking. I do not show his "life of gentle fatherhood, ballsy sermonizing, composing of tender music, etc." because I'm writing about Luther only in the context of my subject, which is not ballsy sermonizing.

At p. 1 reader #2 says you ought to farm out the chapters to four or five different people. Not a bad idea, except that another five months will go down the drain. #2's recommendations of people include a mixed bag. I do not know of Robert Handy, but I do NOT need the advice of someone who guided a dissertation by someone else on Ranters, Muggletonians, and sundry sorts of Quakers. I have read all the Ranter tracts in the British Museum. I have read the Muggletonian and Quaker sources, too, as well as the principal secondary accounts. Bainton at Yale does have the savvy about Castellio and Servetus; that's why I relied on Bainton for Castellio and Servetus—and for Luther. J. Pelikan is also at Yale; ask him whether I made any mistakes in my coverage of Luther: Pelikan is the editor of Luther's *Works* in 55 vols. which I used. (Reader #1* would probably censure me for using Pelikan's translations instead of the German.) #2 recommends

*Pelikan.

Morton Smith, Robert Grant, Krister Stendahl, and Samuel Sandmel for the trial-of-Jesus chapter, "the stickiest." I have already had the benefit of readings by J. J. Robinson, Dieter Betz, and B. Mack. I don't need Smith's critique: I have read his far-fetched book, *Jesus and Magician*: it's a book that might give reader #1 a heart attack—it's wild, sneering and disrespectful. See Kermode's review of the book in the current *New York Review of Books*. I read and used R. M. Grant's book on the Gnostics; I have also read his *Historical Introduction to the New Testament*, in which he concedes that he changed his mind on essential points between the first printing and the reprinting 10 years later. He's an honest man. I don't agree with him, but I respect him. Krister Stendahl is first-rate. So is Sam Sandmel, every one of whose many, many books I have read. No, don't get Sandmel's opinion on my chapter on the trial of Jesus. Sandmel says that he doesn't know what happened and that no one can know what happened, because the Gospels are unreliable evidence. Sandmel is right. I don't know what happened. But I do think the evidence is against the Gospel depiction of the trial by the Sanhedrin, and Sandmel would agree, without doubt. (Come to think of it, get Sandmel's opinion.)

At p. 2, reader #2 admires my industry and then says that my book is "more on the order of an encyclopedia or a catalogue," following which he makes a remark that I gather is damning but which I take to be a great compliment: "The book for all its backnotes, borders on trade book style." That fits #2's remarks on my treatment of Luther: he's a tolerationist, no, he's a persecutor. I wrote a catalogue, not a trade book. But it "is a curiously old-fashioned book, like Lea on Inquisition or Foxe on Martyrs." I don't mind being like Lea. The Foxe remark is silly in some respects, correct in another: I've written, at least in part, a martyrology. But it's accurate. I handle evidence much better than Foxe did.

In the same para. at the bottom of p. 2, reader #2 destroys me when he says that by page 200 he no longer cares very much why people persecuted as they did. I have failed, then, in this book:

I was trying to explain how and why religious beliefs connected with eternal salvation could lead people to persecute those who dissented from those beliefs. But, then, I think I did explain that quite clearly, and that #2 read a bit quickly. As a matter of fact I don't rely on large mathematical reckonings of the number of victims, which is exactly why I felt now and then that I ought to mention in passing that there were a lot of victims, though I am telling individual stories. I did say that the Duke of Alva killed a lot of people, and I don't give much help in sorting out who were blasphemers and who were the victims of war; I give little help of this sort because to Alva, all Protestants were blasphemers. He killed as many as he could because they were Protestant. #2 is quite wrong. My overwhelming stress is on individual case histories. I rarely give gross figures, but on the few occasions that I do, I think they are important. If I left them out, #2 might complain that I have only individual case histories. #2 is frequently inconsistent.

If calling Beza "bloodthirsty" is too strong, I'll delete the word. I read Beza and think he was bloodthirsty for Castellio. However, the brunt of #2's point is that I take Beza and Luther out of context, which brings us back to my failure to mention that Luther loved music and that Beza loved flowers. Bunk. So is #2's analogy. I see nothing wrong in a book reporting racism in the verbal expressions of presidents, even though such a book would not give us the presidents in their fullness. I didn't pretend to give fullness when I wrote and HUP published my book on Jefferson: it openly said in the subtitle, "The Darker Side." In this book I do Beza, Luther, Calvin, etc., in the context of theories and practices of persecution for religious reasons, more specifically in the context of ideas about what a particular offense against religion (blasphemy) means . . . what is justification of persecution, and at appropriate points I indicate as much, but I let others define it.

At p. 3 reader #2 raises the question of balance. The first half of the book is not on England; the second half is. Does that mean England was the worst persecutor, he asks. No. This book is the first half of a two-volume study of the history of blasphemy. The rest of it will cover only England and America, from where I leave off in this volume up to the present time. #1 says I meander. #2 says I hop, skip, and jump. I do neither. Blasphemy was originally an Old Testament concept. I show it. The trial of Jesus as depicted in the Gospels changed our understanding. I show that. Blasphemy as an offense against religion came to be the basis of a theory of persecution and got confused with heresy. But #2 wants to know why I give the Ranters as much space as the trial of Jesus and why small Puritan sects get more space than Aquinas and Augustine. Because once I do cross the channel, I am beginning to burrow in, in great detail. England becomes my subject, as America will become the subject along with England, when I do the volume covering from 1700 to present. #2 is right when he says I am writing about "our" history in the main. My preface, not yet written, will explain that a second volume will follow and that my main interest is "our" history, Anglo-American history. #2 thinks I have some personal concept of blasphemy. Ridiculous. In the first chapter, early off, I give the current Anglo-American legal definition plus some illustrations. Then I give the Old Testament definition. Then I start the Christian definitions. I do talk a lot about heresy and sometimes (especially in Restoration England) about seditiousness. I also plead guilty to using the terms "blasphemous heresy" and "heretical blasphemy," because my sources do. I mean the primary sources. The admixture is fascinating and revealing, and I explain why. Heresy and blasphemy were different facets of the same crime in Christian thought, though there was movement from heresy to blasphemy as we move from Catholic to Protestant thought. #2 reads too fast. I do not write without clarity, yet #2 says on p. 4 that I do not make out my case that blasphemy is right now a threat in our culture. #2 says I say that it is a threat in my opening and my final pages. That is simply not so. Indeed, it is contrary to what I say. I'm beginning to get angry at the misuse and abuse from both #1 and #2. I shall shorten my comments from here on.

I am a "Whig." I plead guilty. I sympathize more with the victims than with the persecutors. But I do not depict the persecuted as lovable. #2 has a jazzy style and gets carried away with his own enthusiasm in scoring a point. Sometimes the victims were "out of power knaves" and other times, they were NOT. Biddle was no knave. Nor Penn, nor Nayler, nor Servetus, nor Bruno, nor the Anabaptists. The Ranters were knaves. Who else, #2?

P. 4: "lack of comparative models." Right, in part. I do not do Islam. I have enough problems as an amateur in doing what #2 cannot do—covering the subject from Jesus to the Ranters, which he thinks is a bit much for one man. Now he wants me to do Islam too. Why not the whole Orient and Africa? I can't. #2 is right: "There is a Christian provincialism to the story." (Worse, it will become—as it has, halfway through this book—Anglo-American provincialism.) If I wrote the full story of all the presidents, #2 would assault me for not covering English prime ministers; we must have comparative models. Indeed we must. That's why I devote a hunk of chapter 1 to Periclean Athens—to show that blasphemy can exist in a non-Christian culture. That's why I give some continental examples—to show that what happened in England was not without precedents. I have comparative models.

P. 4. My "tone." My editor can help me catch my moralizing or my cuteness. I'd rather not moralize or be cute. The one example #2 offers is not to his point—he refers to my remark about the name of Pope Innocent III. A bad pun (I'll kill it), but nothing cute. Yes, I suppose I do lose my "cool" at times. I retched when I first read the hideous account of Servetus's execution at the stake, and I deliberately left out the more gory sections of the story. But I probably do reveal a certain disgust. Let someone else write a book about the bright side of the Inquisition.

P. 4. Ashtorath is a typo, nothing more. Baals is correct; the *Interpreters Dictionary of the Bible* says "baalim" is the plural of "baal" meaning "baals." Baalim is not English; baals is English. Ananus: #2 is right; I should use the more familiar "Annas," and in fact in my copy of the manuscript I had already changed the spelling and intended to catch it in the copyediting stage. (But Ananus was not wrong.)

I'm fed up with this. I am right about Pilate. I do not at all sound like Schonfeld and resent the comparison; I don't mind sounding a bit like Brandon. Sandmel has written that he thinks Brandon was probably right, but that no one can prove it. But I don't mind throwing in a few more "possibly's" and "probably's" as #2 suggests. (He's back on the trial of Jesus). Finally, p. 5. #2 says I make more redactor errors than I need to. My local New Testament experts—Robinson and Betz—made the same points, so I modified the first draft. My suggestion of alteration of the Gospels by very early churches seems to disturb NT experts. They will allow that one evangelist freely rewrote earlier ones; they will allow that Mark has been given a brand-new ending not in the original; they will allow that John went through a couple of editions and was finally redacted by someone else who supplied a new beginning and a new ending; but they will not allow me to surmise that we don't know for sure what the original Passion stories were. Robinson directed me to Epp's study comparing 4th and 5th century texts, in which Epp concluded that the anti-Judaics got more severe as time passed and that the exoneration of the Romans became more pronounced. I buried Epp in a footnote, because my surmise referred to the 2nd and 3rd centuries. I don't make much about the point, but I think it is true: we really do not know what the original (1st century) manuscripts said. Our first surviving texts on the trial of Jesus are from the 4th century.

#2 concludes that I've given you a grand-scale work that is a stumper. I think it's a book with unusual sweep, covering about three thousand years from Moses to 1700; it's a feisty, controversial book that is vividly written—some of the chapters include the best work I've ever done or at least as good as I've ever done. The research is pretty deep as well as enormously varied. It's a very monographic book, yet so broad that few people seem to be able to cope with and judge it: witness #1 reader's unmitigated approval of the second half and #2 reader's bedazzlement at one man daring to cover from Jesus to the Ranters (really from Moses to the Restoration). It is a book with a viewpoint which I see as unitarian, Whiggish, and liberal. The book has old-fashioned virtues. It is well written, very comprehensive, and aims big. I see this book, together with its successor (covering 1700 to the present) as falling directly within a field I have staked out—odd though the book is, it is a study of the origins of the freedom of religion clause of the 1st Amendment. It probably is an idiosyncratic book, something personal and different; that adds to its appeal. HUP is right for it: Harvard used to be a Unitarian stronghold. It is a unique book—the first book on the history of blasphemy, even though neglecting Islam and the Orient. Even if #2 is right and it's only a book that has rare scope and is a well-written encyclopedia, that's a big plus. It has breadth, despite the monographic focus on something far-out like blasphemy. Even should it have bad luck in the critical reviews, it might trigger a squabble. Better to try too much and fail than to write on the family in Andover or on the Boston police. Even a hostile reviewer can admire my chutzpah. At age 55, I'm not interested in "safe" books. This is a "fling" book. Be bold and daring with me. Take a chance on an amateur maverick.

I owed it to myself—and to you, who have given me encouragement and support—to defend myself from the disagreements and criticisms of men of little scope and overmuch specialization. HUP's record has earned it the duty of joining me in an unorthodox fling.

The next day I wrote again, informally, to my editor. I had neglected to defend my use of "the Mass" instead of just "Mass," one of the "thousand nuances" that disconcerted Reader #2 (Martin Marty). I found that where I had said "the Mass" in the page noted by the reader, I was directly quoting Martin Luther. If there was a mistake, Luther made it. I also proved, from books on religion that surrounded me in my study, that "the Mass" could be correct usage. But that was not the point of my letter.

"How," I asked, "can you credit your readers, when #1 is a vehement trinitarian who can't stand a difference of opinion, and #2, who accuses me of a thousand tonal boo-boos, is unreliable?" I could not understand why HUP was taking so seriously "these criticisms that are either trivial, misguided, wrong, or biased." I conceded that I had not written an impeccable book but contended that it was preposterous to say that the book did not deserve to be published. HUP had published many controversial books, including my earlier three. "Read Stuart Hampshire on Wilson's *Humane Nature* (HUP, 1978). If Hampshire, who has appropriate credentials, gave you the report he published in the *New York Review of Books*, would you have stopped publication?" In my own field, Harvard had recently published a mediocre book by Raoul Berger, *Government by Judiciary*; if any one of dozens of adverse critics of Berger's book had submitted a reader's report, would HUP have failed to publish Berger? "HUP lost its virginity long ago. Why apply to me standards of perfection rarely if ever achieved by others?" I wanted to know when the syndics met, and I insisted, in several letters, on getting judgment by the syndics, as promised—and as I thought was my right.

In a phone call my editor told me that she had shown two of the syndics the readers' report and my reply. They said that the subject of my book was not in their field. They knew me as an historian of the American Constitution; the readers were experts in the field of religion. Accordingly, my editor said, the two syndics felt that doubt must be resolved on the side of the readers. She predicted that the board of syndics would react the same way, and she asked that I withdraw the book to save myself the embarrassment of rejection. "But I won't be embarrassed," I reiterated in writing. "I'll be mad as hell and feeling very much that I'm a victim of injustice and prejudice and cowardice." In that letter and succeeding ones I stressed that I wanted to see the issue through to a final decision by the syndics. I believed, though, that my editor was shaken by the readers' reports and did not feel that she could champion my cause with the syndics.

Regretfully I realized that a third reader might be necessary. The second reader had mentioned Krister Stendahl, whose writings I admired. I thought of Stendahl as a counterpart of Jaroslav Pelikan, whom we had discussed anonymously as Reader #1. The second reader's report could be ignored as contemptible and lacking in competence, but not Pelikan's. A good report from Stendahl—like Pelikan, an ordained minister of the Lutheran church, a senior scholar, and an academic dean—might cancel out the adverse report from Dean Pelikan of Yale, especially because Stendahl was dean of the Divinity School of Harvard. I suggested that Stendahl be asked to read the few chapters in question. My editor agreed, as did Stendahl.

By the end of November 1978 I had his report, and though it was not what I had hoped for, I thought it a favorable report by someone whose judgment I could live with. He didn't make a federal case out of a typographical error or get uptight with my Whiggish unitarianism. He found a half-dozen errors in the third chapter. I had miscited a statement by Irenaeus, misdated the canonization of the books of the NT, confused Clement I with Clement II, and the like. Stendahl also thought I garbled the point I had quoted from Clement, but I disagreed; even in the differing translation that he provided, Clement had said that blasphemy consists "in that you do not do what I [Clement] want." That, I replied, was exactly the point: "those who disagree with me are blasphemers . . . that's all I am trying to show and it is a crucial point." I cleaned up the errors in my copy of the manuscript within ten minutes. Stendahl, like Pelikan, thought my chapter on Jesus' trial by the Sanhedrin was too discursive and needed tightening, though he found the "nucleus of the chapter sound." In my reply to the editor, I stressed that I was willing to revise along the lines suggested by Stendahl. I thought he was flat wrong, however, on a point he made about the "Greek Jewish texts" on the meaning of blasphemy. I was also amazed that he called Chronicles a Greek-Jewish text. That was a mistake worse, I thought, than my having confused Clement I and Clement II. But I decided that because Pelikan, like Stendahl, had also complained about my omission of the Septuagint, I had better consider adding a few pages covering the intertestamental literature on the subject of blasphemy. Stendahl would not pass judgment on chapters 4 and 5, covering Augstine to the Reformation: "outside my field of competence." He believed that "rather serious questions can be raised" about the first three chapters. "My advice," he concluded, "is simple: minimalistic approach with only such material as bears directly on the issue of blasphemy as a crime." I did not take that as advising against publication. I emphasized my willingness to make the few factual corrections, dealing with the Greek-Jewish texts, and shorten the chapter on Jesus by omitting the discursive material.

My editor did not respond to a word of my letter. I had mis-read the third report, she wrote; it was intended as a "negative" report. The syndics, according to my editor, who had just had a conference with the director, would not approve publication of my book. Because there were twelve syndics, she reminded me, their decision would be "a bit public." Wisdom, she advised, dic-tated my withdrawal of the book. Since I was willing to revise and the minor errors were correctable, I refused to withdraw. On December 13 my editor formally rejected the manuscript as un-worthy of the syndics' consideration. "We must judge the manu-script is unsatisfactory in content to Harvard University Press. We cannot publish it and you are released from any obligation to us contractually for this book."

I could not believe that I had a bright future behind me. My manuscript, I kept telling myself, was a success; only the readers were failures. But reason told me that not everyone zeal-ously attached to an opinion I did not hold is necessarily wrong. Holmes said somewhere that the first task of a civilized man is to make generalizations, bearing always in mind that no generaliza-tion is worth a damn. My impulse was to fight and defend my work; but my mind told me that I might have something to learn from my critics. They did not know that I knew their iden-tities. University presses, not their manuscript readers, fix the rule of anonymity, though in this case it had not been observed. Nor should it have been. Reading a book for a press is an easy way to be formidable with the least risk: like a masked highwayman, the reader can destroy and slink away. But only geese, snakes, and fools hiss, not scholars. My antagonists were scholars. The differences between us did not outweigh the values we shared in common. I was sure of that, as sure as I was that scholarship is incompatible with secrecy and ex parte argument. My loyalty was to rational discourse, to the open production of proofs, and to the right of each to interpret evidence as long as he adhered to the facts and faced the best argument his opponents could muster.

I decided, therefore, to write directly to my readers, starting with Stendahl. To prove to him that I had nothing to hide and did not at all resent his evaluation of my work, I enclosed a copy of the three-page letter I had written to my editor when reacting to his report. I wrote to Stendahl on the premise that he might have something to teach me about the meaning of blasphemy in the Greek-Jewish texts—the Septuagint, the Jewish Apocrypha, and the Pseudepigrapha. Stendahl had referred to specific texts which, he thought, threw doubt on the sharp distinction I had found between the ancient Jewish concept of blasphemy and the Christian concept. I had not discussed those texts in my book because I thought them to be redundant, on all fours with the original Scriptures. Stendahl seemed to think those texts seriously obscured the distinction I had found. Accordingly, I reviewed each text in my letter to him, giving chapter and verse, and I sought to explain why I thought I was right. Where had I gone wrong? I expressed my gratitude to Stendahl for the corrections he had made; he had written his report for HUP, but I benefited from his exposure of certain errors. "I really would appreciate your telling me what you think I have missed or misunderstood," I said. Anyone might err; he had said Chronicles was a Greek-Jewish text.

Stendahl had also said that my viewpoint on the trial of Jesus by the Sanhedrin had been well established by Paul Winter,

Joseph Blinzler, and Haim Cohn. I objected to his saying that, I told him. I had explicitly rejected Blinzler and Cohn. In his *Trial and Execution of Jesus*, Cohn argued that the Sanhedrin convened to save Jesus, "a preposterous conjecture," I thought. My argument was that the Sanhedrin had not met to try Jesus or consider his case. Blinzler's *Trial of Jesus* presented the pre–Vatican II Catholic position on Jewish guilt for deicide; my chapter was, in part, a refutation of Blinzler's acceptance of the Gospel account of a formal trial and condemnation of Jesus by the Sanhedrin. My letter to Stendahl was reasoned and civil. Before he replied, I composed a few pages on the subject of blasphemy in the Greek-Jewish texts, to be added to my manuscript. I sent Stendahl a copy of those pages, which also covered Philo.

Stendahl's reply disappointed me. He thanked me for my "gracious letter" which he said he "appreciated," but he pleaded that pressing diaconal duties allowed him no opportunity to consider my points. "So I ask for time." I wrote him again a few months later, but he never replied. His silence seemed to me to be out of character with everything I had heard about the man. In the end all I got from Stendahl was a polite brush-off, though I had sought to engage his interest on a scholarly issue that he seemed to care about, indeed, an issue he had raised.

Having failed with my editor at HUP, I wrote directly to Arthur Rosenthal, the director. I called his attention to the fact that HUP rejected my book after I had offered to make revisions suggested by Stendahl. That HUP would not allow me to revise "means that HUP thinks the manuscript is hopeless; it cannot be remedied; nothing can make it worthy of publication." Such an opinion must rest on the authority of the readers. HUP, I said, simply buckled in deference to authority without considering my reasoned responses and revision. That HUP acted pusillanimously or did not consider my rejoinders on their merits was not the burden of my letter. "It is, rather, that I must conclude that Harvard rejected the book in the belief that I cannot write a book on religion that you wish to publish." That raised a problem. We had two more books under contract, one a sequel to the book rejected, the other a book on Jesus. I was willing to write those books, but logic dictated the conclusion that Harvard didn't want them and by canceling the first contract had in effect voided the others. I wanted from Rosenthal a statement on where we stood, because he had signed the contract with HUP.

Meanwhile I wrote to Pelikan, enclosing a copy of my letter of October 16, 1978, the reply to my readers written for the benefit of the syndics at my editor's request. I told Pelikan how I knew he was my reader. I was writing, I said, because he was in the best position to assist me on the one point in his critique that really disturbed me, his assertion that passages of my book were anti-Christian. I wanted his help in pinpointing the offensive passages. I asked him to reread the first half of the book, from the first chapter through the one on the Reformation, and make marginal comments on the pages or red-pencil the anti-Christian or blasphemous remarks. I added: "I am no more anti-Christian than you are anti-Semitic, but sometimes we say things without realizing their impact on others. Take, for example, your remark that if the manuscript were a history of the Cabbala written by a Christian and contained 'such statements, I would have denounced it as anti-Semitic.' That's not a comment you would have made if my name were Jones. I read your comment to mean that because my name is Levy, you found certain statements to be anti-Christian. Those are the sort of statements I'd like you to pinpoint so that I can expunge them or modify them." Pelikan replied that "the least" he owed me was to make suggestions about changing the phrases in the early chapters that struck him as offensive; he would be willing to reread the first five chapters with that in mind. He also explained the Cabbala remark. I mailed the five chapters.

Having had no reply from Rosenthal at HUP, I wrote him again, bringing him up to date on developments. "It may interest you to know that I have been in touch with Stendahl and Pelikan, very amicably in both cases. I think I have proved to Stendahl's satisfaction that he was wrong about the Greek-Jewish texts." Pelikan, I reported, had agreed to review the first five chapters for the purpose of explicitly noting in the margins my intolerable and offensive judgments. I reported too that I had queried Pelikan about his damaging Cabbala remark which, in its context, could be construed as anti-Semitic, though not intended as such. I told Rosenthal what Pelikan had replied: "I should explain my comment about the Cabbala; just a month earlier I had read a MS for another publisher in which there was a chapter on the interest of Renaissance figures like Reuchlin in the Cabbala, and I objected to the tone of the chapter. That was still in my mind when I was reading your book." To Rosenthal I put a query: Did he and my editor, when reading Pelikan's savaging of my book as anti-Christian, realize that Pelikan had been thinking, at least in part, of some other manuscript? I asked Rosenthal for the second time whether he had read my formal reply of October 16, and I wanted to know whether the book was rejected because it contained mistakes, even though all my critics also made mistakes. Did evidence and reasons matter or just the say-so of an authority? If the authorities, in HUP's understanding, were saying that I could not write a book on religious history worthy of HUP's imprint, why would HUP want the other two books from me, especially the book on Jesus? Alternatively, if HUP thought I could write the other books, the issue was just one of expression and mistakes, which were correctable and HUP should publish *Treason Against God.* If it wouldn't publish that book, how could I be expected to work with HUP on the other books?

Rosenthal, in a polite and unresponsive reply, expressed regret that HUP could not publish my work on blasphemy to 1700. The readers' reports would have created an insurmountable problem for the syndics. During the "trying period," Rosenthal wrote, both he and my editor were definitely on my side, but my request for a quick yes or no "doomed our hopes for a favorable solution." He saw "no reason whatever" why we could not work together amicably in the future. I thanked him for his gracious but evasive reply, which did not address the problems I had defined in my letters to him. Yet his reference to a "favorable solution" mystified me, because I had insistently stressed my willingness to revise. I really did not understand the basis of the rejection, I responded. Either my book was rejected because it was beyond repair, or it could be revised. If it was beyond repair, in effect HUP was telling me I couldn't write for it a book on Jesus or a sequel to the rejected book. Yet HUP was saying that the contracts were in force. "Fine," I concluded. "Then revisions and publication are in order."

More than a month later, on March 20, 1979, Rosenthal had not replied, so I wrote again and a week later got an answer of sorts. Nothing was to be gained, he said, by an effort on his part to refute point by point the matters raised in my letters. HUP's position was unchanged: though publication by HUP of my first book on blasphemy was impossible, Rosenthal saw no impediment to HUP's publication of the other two titles. He added that he was surprised to learn that I had communicated directly with Stendahl and Pelikan on the "assumption" that they were the reviewers. Rosenthal had never known such a thing to have happened before and hoped that Pelikan and Stendahl did not hold "this breach of publishing propriety against us."

When I later got Martin Marty's "Dear Len" letter, confirming that he was the second reader for HUP, he wrote to be helpful, though I found him bumbling; the point is that he did not for a moment think I breached proprieties. Indeed, he congratulated me on my "good taste in referees." That was no longer an opinion I shared. Marty could not remember what I had written when he first read it, let alone remember his critique months later. He didn't even recall that it was an adverse report. He conceded that "the Mass" could be correct, given the context, and dismissed my "disembodied" Luther as nothing but a "nuance, not a structural problem." His letter to me had the same surrealistic quality as his report to HUP on my book.

On March 7, 1979, Pelikan had returned my five chapters with a note saying that the glosses on the pages covered not only the matter of offensiveness but also the pace of the book, which he thought would benefit if tightened. He was referring to the chapter on "The Jewish Trial of Jesus," which Stendahl had also found discursive and which I had been willing to revise immediately on getting his report. In my letter thanking Pelikan, I expressed puzzlement. "I had expected something like an onslaught, given your extremely negative report to the Harvard University Press and given my request, to which you acceded, that you offer substantiation and be as critical and candid as possible. What puzzles me is that you found so little to comment upon and that the differences between us are so few and minor." I would put the axe to everything he labeled a "cheap shot" and rewrite the Jesus chapter in order to delete the extraneous matter. I promised Pelikan a point-by-point summation of how I would treat every one of his comments.

On the day that Rosenthal wrote to me, March 17, 1979, I wrote a letter to my editor, informing her that I had received from Pelikan the five chapters with his annotations. "All of a sudden he's a pussycat. I wonder what all the fuss was about and why he's changed his tune so drastically. I can meet his criticisms easily." I reminded my editor that I had offered to meet Stendahl's criticisms immediately on receiving a copy of his report. I sent her a copy of my last letter to Pelikan. To Rosenthal I replied that the letters I had received from Stendahl and Pelikan showed that they did not hold HUP responsible for any breach of propriety. As if Rosenthal did not know, I explained to him as I had explained to Stendahl and Pelikan how I knew that they had been my readers. They were the readers of my choice. "Both," I wrote, "respect scholarly candor, truth, and evidence; my correspondence with them has been civil and cordial, and they have been quite cooperative." (At that time I was still expecting that Stendahl would, as he had promised, respond in full to my communications.) Pelikan, I reported to Rosenthal, had given me a page-by-page private reading. "Some of his remarks are complimentary; some raise questions; others raise questions of taste in expression. As I told Aida, I can easily cope with all his marginal comments. . . . I think he overstated his case originally and knows it. In any case he, who offends easily on religious points, did not remotely take offense at my writing him or think that proprieties had been breached. The proprieties issue is not real."

I intended, I told Rosenthal, to revise in accordance with the suggestions made by Pelikan and Stendahl. I then intended to resubmit the book to HUP for judgment by critics and a decision by the syndics, which I had never received. Rosenthal had expressed himself to be on the side of a favorable solution. If he was now telling me that HUP would not under any circumstances reconsider the book, I asked him to say so. At the same time I wrote my editor, briefing her on the developments, asking why Rosenthal was in a snit, and requesting from her a civil and rational response. She had not written me since she sent the rejection letter, nor did she answer my later letters. On April 19, 1979, Rosenthal replied tersely by quoting a statement in his preceding letter: HUP found it impossible to publish *Treason Against God* but saw no impediment to publishing the other two titles under contract.

I ceased correspondence with Harvard, but in mid-June 1979 I suddenly received a copy of HUP's catalogue of forthcoming books, with a note sent by my editor "with all good wishes" and ending "Faithfully." It was the catalogue in which notice of my book should have appeared. "Faithfully?" "Alice's Wonderland," I replied, "seems saner than my relationship with HUP." I sent her a copy of my last letter to her, dated April 2, which had gone unanswered. "Indeed your note today is the first I've heard from you since you rejected my book early last December without having responded to my explicit statement that I was prepared to revise the manuscript." I reported that I had completed the revision after reaching a rapprochement with Pelikan. I sent her a copy of my final letter to him, in which I systematically enumerated every one of his comments and explained how I meant to deal with each. The book, I told my editor, ought now be acceptable. "But Rosenthal has somehow turned the whole affair into something personal, though I haven't the vaguest idea why." The situation was ridiculous. I had tightened the Jesus chapter, added the material on the Greek-Jewish texts, corrected all errors, and expunged or modified most remarks deemed offensive by Pelikan. "Now Harvard won't let me submit the book to determine whether readers, old or new, think the book acceptable! This is the same book most of whose chapters you praised, and this is the same publisher that tells me that the remaining contracts are in force, and this is the same editor who writes me a 'Dear Len' letter without ever acknowledging my letters since last December in which I offered to revise. . . . I found dealing with my critics quite easy and dealing with HUP quite impossible, that is, irrational and arbitrary."

My editor sent me a copy of an expensive new book published by HUP and a note saying that she was willing to recommend my book to a friend of hers who was an editor at another university press. She expressed hopes for "a new beginning" between us. I replied that the only publisher I wanted her to help me with was HUP. Her evasiveness, I wrote, was absurd. She never wrote again.

After the rejection by HUP in early December 1978, I did not expect a reversal of the judgment. My editor had never wanted that book on three thousand years of the "roots" of the history of the offense of blasphemy; she had always wanted its American history, because it would sell better. I had pursued the correspondence with my editor and with Rosenthal in an effort to draw them out but failed. I regarded HUP as untrustworthy, our relationship irremediably poisoned, and our contracts breached and void.

> On the whole, at any rate, I have achieved what I set out to achieve. But do not tell me that I was not worth the trouble. In any case, I am not appealing for any man's verdict, I am only imparting knowledge, I am only making a report. To you also, honored Members of the Academy, I have only made a report.
>
> —Kafka, *A Report to an Academy*

Origins of the Fourth Amendment

*B*EFORE the American Revolution the right to be secure against unreasonable searches and seizures had slight existence. British policies assaulted the privacy of dwellings and places of business, particularly when royal revenues were at stake. The right to be taxed only by the consent of representatives of one's choice was the great right whose violation helped cause the Revolution. But British attempts to enforce tax measures by general searches also occasioned deeply felt resentments that damaged relations between England and the American colonies, and provoked anxious concerns which later sought expression in the Fourth Amendment. That amendment repudiates general warrants by recognizing a "right of the people to be secured in their persons, houses, papers, and effects, against unreasonable searches and seizures." Any warrant that is vague about the persons, places, or things to be searched violates the specificity required by the command of the amendment that warrants shall issue only "upon probably cause, supported by oath or affirmation, and particularly describing the place to be searched, and the persons or things to be seized."

The Fourth Amendment would not have been possible but for British legal theory which Britons of North America inherited and cherished as their own. The Fourth Amendment emerged not only from the American Revolution; it was a constitutional embodiment of the extraordinary coupling of Magna Carta to the appealing fiction that a man's home is his castle. That is, the amendment resulted from embellishments on the insistence, which was rhetorically compelling though historically without foundation, that government cannot encroach on the private premises of the individual subject. What mattered was not what Magna Carta actually said but what people thought it said or, rather, what it had come to mean. What also mattered was the inspiring imagery that swelled the sense of freedom in the ordinary subject. William Pitt expressed it best in a speech in Parliament in 1763, when he declaimed: "The poorest man may, in his cottage, bid defiance to all the forces of the Crown. It may be frail; its roof may shake; the wind may blow through it; the storm may enter, the rain may enter, but the King of England may not enter; all his force dares not cross the threshold of the ruined tenement."[1] The assertion that "a man's house is his castle" goes back at least to the early sixteenth century, and it was repeated with such frequency that it became a cliché.[2]

The first person to link the privacy of one's home to a right secured by Magna Carta seems to have been Robert Beale, clerk of the Privy Council, in 1589. Beale asked rhetorically what had happened to chapter 39 of the great charter when agents of a prerogative court, acting under its warrant, could "enter into men's houses, break up their chests and chambers," and carry off as evidence whatever they pleased.[3] That Beale's statement was historically unsound is unimportant compared to the fact that he took a feudal document, which protected the barons, and converted it into a constitution for everyone. Creative glosses like Beale's would make Magna Carta a talismanic symbol of freedom, subjecting all authority, including the royal prerogative, to the rule of law. Construing chapter 39 to be a ban on general warrants helped make a myth that would transform American thinking about privacy rights against government.

[1]Quoted in Nelson B. Lasson, *The History and Development of the Fourth Amendment to the United States Constitution* (Baltimore, 1937), pp. 49–50. Variations of the statement exist, and its date is not certain.

[2]1505 opinion of Chief Justice John Fineux in a King's Bench case reported in the Year Books.

[3]Leonard W. Levy, *Origins of the Fifth Amendment* (New York, 1968), pp. 170–171, 466.

One of the most strategically significant places for the belief that a legal writ authorizing a legitimate search must be specific as to persons and places was Sir Edward Coke's *Institutes of the Laws of England*.[4] From the Puritans of Massachusetts Bay, who studied Coke, to Jefferson, who admiringly said of him that "a sounder Whig never wrote" nor one more learned "in the orthodox doctrines of British liberties," Americans regarded Coke as the foremost authority on English law.[5] Coke's authority legitimated the belief that Magna Carta outlawed general warrants based on mere surmise.

Sir Matthew Hale, another seventeenth-century legal luminary, more systematically analyzed the problem of search and seizure in his book *History of Pleas of the Crown*.[6] Hale criticized warrants that failed to name the persons sought for crime or the places to be searched for evidence of theft. He even laid a basis for the concept of probable cause by maintaining that the person seeking a warrant should be examined judicially under oath so that the magistrate could determine whether he had grounds for his suspicions. Hale also asserted that an officer who made an illegal search and arrest was liable to a civil suit for false arrest.[7]

Beale, Coke, and Hale did not stand alone. They invented a rhetorical tradition against general searches, which Sergeant William Hawkins and Sir William Blackstone continued.[8] But the rhetoric was empty; the tradition had almost no practical effect. Beale's views leaked out through officially licensed publications that sought to refute him, but he did not dare publish his manuscript.[9] Coke's own report of *Semayne's Case* of 1604 refuted the

[4]Sir Edward Coke, *Institutes of the Laws of England* (London, 1628–1644, 4 vols.), vol. 4, pp. 176–177.

[5]Francis R. Aumann, *The Changing American Legal System* (Columbus, Ohio, 1940), pp. 46–47, and Charles Warren, *A History of the American Bar* (Boston, 1911), p. 174.

[6]Sir Matthew Hale, *History of Pleas of the Crown*, ed. Solom Emlyn (London, 2 vols., 1st ed., 1736), vol. 1, pp. 577–583; vol. 2, pp. 107–111, 149–152.

[7]See Lasson, *History of the Fourth*, pp. 35–36, for discussion of Hale.

[8]Serjeant William Hawkins, *A Treatise of the Pleas of the Crown* (London, 1724, 2nd ed., 2 vols.), vol. 2, pp. 81–82, and William Blackstone, *Commentaries on the Laws of England* (Oxford, 1766–1769, 4 vols.) vol. 1, pp. 288, 308.

[9]Levy, *Origins*, p. 171.

accuracy of the propositions that he advanced in his *Institutes*, for in that case the court had held that although a man's house is his castle, his privacy did not extend to his guests or to "cases where the King is the party."[10] Coke's own experience shows best that the maxim represented only the frailest aspiration, not the law in cases involving the crown. In 1634, when Coke lay dying, the Privy Council's agents searched his home and law chambers for seditious papers and seized not only the manuscripts of his voluminous legal writings but also his personal valuables, including his money, keys, jewelry, will, and a poem addressed to his children.[11] Hale's book was not even published until sixty years after his death. Pitt spoke in a losing cause; Parliament enacted the excise bill whose passage he so eloquently opposed as dangerous to the liberty of the subject. Blackstone made only a passing remark against general searches; his target, rather, was the general arrest warrant.

In fact, English law was honeycombed with parliamentary enactments that relied on warrantless general searches and on general warrants for their enforcement, including sumptuary legislation and measures aimed at punishing theft, at governing crafts and guilds, bankruptcy, and military recruitment, as well as measures preventing illegal imports, manufactures, poaching, counterfeiting, unlicensed printing, seditious, heretical, or lewd publications, and nonpayment of taxes. Taxes extended to hearths and stoves, to estates, to intoxicating drinks, to a variety of consumer goods such as salt, candles, soap, glass, and paper, and to foreign goods. The king's customs office and his exchequer depended on both the general warrant and warrantless searches as ordinary means of collecting royal revenues, and Parliament passed dozens of pieces of legislation to provide the taxes and authorize general searches. Promiscuously broad warrants allowed officers to search wherever they wanted and to seize whatever they wanted, with few exceptions. An

---

[10] 5 Coke's Reports 91a, 91b, 93a, 78 English Reports 194–195, 198.

[11] Lasson, *History of the Fourth*, pp. 31–32, and Catherine Drinker Bowen, *The Lion and the Throne: The Life and Times of Sir Edward Coke* (Boston, 1956), pp. 533–534.

eighteenth-century collection of warrants contains 108 authorized by secretaries of state or by the King's Bench for the period 1700–1763, all but two of which were general warrants.[12] With time, the use of general warrants substantially increased.

General searches pervaded colonial law as well as Great Britain's. Colonial legislation on search and seizure either copied Britain's or derived from it; until 1750 all handbooks for justices of the peace, who issued warrants, contained or described only general warrants. Until the 1760s a man's house was actually less of a legal castle in American than in England, because the Americans, when adapting English models, ignored exceptions. As a result, warrants in America tended to give their enforcers every discretion. The Fourth Amendment would not emerge from colonial precedents; rather, it would repudiate them.

Officers or their informants in colonial America merely reported that an infraction of the law had occurred or that they had a suspicion, not that a particular person was suspected or that a particular place contained evidence of a crime; on the basis of such an assertion, a magistrate issued a warrant. Neither custom, judicial precedent, nor statutory law provided that he should interrogate the seeker of the warrant to determine the credibility of the suspicion or of his informant. The magistrate made no independent determination of his own whether a basis existed for the warrant other than the assertion that a crime had occurred or that a basis existed for suspicion. Magistrates had an obligation to provide the warrant rather than deny one or limit one to a particular person or place that was suspected. Probable cause in a modern sense did not exist; not even a reasonable basis for suspicion existed. Although an officer seeking a warrant more than likely would designate a particular person or place if known to him in advance, he need not do so to get a warrant.

Colonial documents contain no suggestion of a right against general warrants. Recommendations for them were common in

---

[12]Philip Carteret Webb, ed., *Copies of Warrants Taken from the Records Office Books of the Kings Bench at Westminster; The Original Office Books of the Secretaries of State . . .* (London, 1763), pp. 10–72.

the manuals that had been published in the colonies before 1763 for the use of justices of the peace. American legal writers even relied on the great authority of Coke and Hale as proof that an officer could forcibly enter a person's house.

In 1756, however, the province of Massachusetts enacted extraordinary legislation that reversed the tide of practice by abandoning general warrants in favor of warrants founded on some elements of particularity. The legislation of 1756 marked a watershed in Massachusetts law, indeed in Anglo-American law. Beginning in 1756 Massachusetts revised the statutory precursors of the Fourth Amendment. The new legislation resulted mainly from a vehement public clamor against provincial legislation of 1754. The excise act of that year authorized tax collectors to interrogate any subject, under oath, on the amount of rum, wine, and other spirits he had consumed in his private premises in the past year, and taxed it by the gallon. Pamphleteers condemned the measure in hyperbolic language. John Lovell, a Boston schoolmaster whose pupils had included John Hancock and Samuel Adams, called it "the most pernicious attack upon *English Liberty* that was ever attempted," and the minister of the Brattle Church imagined that he saw a revival of the Inquisition, requiring people to incriminate themselves. One pamphlet, *The Monster of Monsters* (the excise act), so savagely attacked the legislature that it condemned the tract as a seditious libel and imprisoned its seller and the suspected author.[13] That author warned of the danger of the tax collector having power to break chains, doors, locks, and bolts, and invade bedchambers and wine cellars.[14] In the torrent of tracts against the excise, it was described as a violation of Magna Carta, of the sanctity of one's home as his castle, and of natural rights.

The provincial impost laws, which employed general warrants for enforcement, provoked such animosity that mobs threatened impost officers who tried to collect duties on uncus-

---

[13]Levy, *Origins*, pp. 386–387. See Paul S. Boyer, "Borrowed Rhetoric: The Massachusetts Excise Controversy of 1754," *William and Mary Quarterly*, 3rd ser., 21 (1964), 328–351.

[14]M. H. Smith, *The Writs of Assistance Case* (Berkeley, 1978), pp. 113–114.

tomed imports—foreign goods on which the duties had not been paid. The hostility to general searches further intensified as the result of two other practices. In 1755 the royal governor of Massachusetts issued ex officio writs of assistance, a type of general warrant that became enormously controversial. And, since 1745, British impressment gangs, operating under a general warrant provided by the governor, had been invading private premises as well as taverns and inns seeking to kidnap able-bodied men for service in the royal navy.[15]

Enforcement of the excise and impost acts by general searches, the introduction into the province of writs of assistance, and the general warrants for impressment gangs produced a hullabaloo which the enactments of 1756 sought to allay. The excise and impost acts of that year required an element of probable cause only in the sense that the informant had the obligation to swear on oath that he knew that an infraction of the law had occurred in the place specified. The justices of the peace, who issued the warrants, had no discretion to deny a petition for one; magistrates made no independent judgment whether adequate grounds for the issuance of the warrant existed. But the informant had to swear that he had "just cause" for his sworn statement. The officer conduced his search during the daytime, only in the designated location, and could seize only things or objects regulated by the statute that he enforced by his search and seizure. The statutes of 1756 also authorized warrants of arrest for named individuals.[16] "The British, in short," Cuddihy and Hardy stated, "introduced writs of assistance into Massachusetts just as the colony itself was rejecting the legal assumptions on which they were based."[17]

The writ of assistance was a type of general warrant deriving its name from the fact that a crown official possessed the legal au-

---

[15]William Cuddihy and B. Carmon Hardy, "A Man's House Was Not His Castle: Origins of the Fourth Amendment," *William and Mary Quarterly*, 3rd ser., 38 (July 1980), 396–397.

[16]Act of Feb. 28, 1756, chap. 31, sect. 24, *Acts and Resolves . . . of the Province of Massachusetts Bay* (Boston, 1869–1922, 21 vols.), vol. 3, p. 109. Ibid., vol. 3, pp. 936–937, for the impost act of April 20, 1756.

[17]Cuddihy and Hardy, "A Man's House," p. 397.

thority to command the assistance of a peace officer and, if necessary, of all nearby subjects, in his execution of the writ. Parliament authorized writs of assistance by an act of 1662 which empowered the Court of Exchequer to issue a writ to a customs official who, with the aid of a constable, could enter "any House, shop, Cellar, Warehouse or Room or other Place, and in Case of Resistance to break open Doors, Chests, Trunks and other packages, there to seize" any uncustomed goods.[18] The writ, once issued, lasted for the life of the sovereign and therefore constituted a long-term hunting license for customs officers on the lookout for smugglers and articles imported in violation of the customs laws. In 1696 Parliament extended the act of 1662 to the colonies, but because the Court of Exchequer did not operate in America, no way existed to enforce it. Massachusetts, however, had extended the jurisdiction of its own high court to include the jurisdiction of the Court of Exchequer, thus opening the possibility of enforcement in that colony and in New Hampshire, which copied Massachusetts.[19]

When George II died, the high court of Massachusetts, presided over by Chief Justice Thomas Hutchinson, heard *Paxton's Case*, a petition by a customs officer for a new writ of assistance.[20] James Otis, Jr., appeared, he said, on behalf of the inhabitants of Boston to oppose issuance of the writ. Any fastidious legal historian must acknowledge that Otis's argument compounded mistakes and misinterpretations. In effect he reconstructed the fragmentary evidence buttressing the rhetorical tradition against general searches. He advocated that any warrant other than a specific one violated the British constitution. That Otis distorted history is pedantic; he was making history. By an

[18] 13 & 14 Car. 2, chap. 11, sect. 5, as quoted by the crown attorney Jeremiah Gridley in Paxton's Case, reported in L. Kinvin Wroth and Hiller B. Zobel, eds., *Legal Papers of John Adams* (Cambridge, Mass., 1965, 3 vols.), vol. 2, p. 131; Smith, *Writs of Assistance Case*, pp. 17–50, contains a detailed account of the originating legislation. On the writs, see also the documents and annotations by Justice Horace Gray, Jr., in Josiah Quincy, Jr., ed., *Reports of Cases Argued and Adjudged in the Superior Court of Judicature of the Massachusetts Bay Between 1761 and 1772* (Boston, 1865), Appendix I, pp. 395–540.

[19] Wroth and Zobel, eds., *Legal Papers of Adams*, vol. 2, p. 132.

[20] Smith, *Writs of Assistance Case*, is a massive study of Paxton's Case.

old British technique, which Coke himself had practiced, Otis sought the creation of new rights while asserting strenuously that they had existed nearly from time immemorial. His speech electrified young John Adams, who was present in the courtroom and took notes. As an old man, fifty-six years later, Adams declared, "Otis was a flame of Fire! . . . Then and there was the first scene of the first Act of Opposition to the arbitrary Claims of Great Britain. Then and there the child Independance [sic] was born." On the night before the Declaration of Independence, Adams asserted that he considered "the Argument concerning Writs of Assistance . . . as the Commencement of the Controversy, between Great Britain and America."[21] Adams's reaction to Otis's speech is so important because a straight line of progression runs from Otis's argument in 1761 to Adams's framing of Article XIV of the Massachusetts Declaration of Rights of 1780 to Madison's introduction of the proposal that became the Fourth Amendment.[22]

We have Adams's brief notes of Otis's speech made at the time of the speech and the fuller version made by Adams not long after. The fuller version takes about twenty minutes to read by comparison with the original, which took Otis four to five hours to deliver.[23] He denounced the writ of assistance as an in-

---

[21]Both statements by Adams quoted in Wroth and Zobel, eds., *Legal Papers of Adams*, vol. 2, p. 107.

[22]For the Massachusetts Declaration, see Bernard Schwartz, ed., *The Bill of Rights: A Documentary History* (New York, 1971, 2 vols.), vol. 1, p. 342, sect. XIV. Madison's proposal in his speech of June 8, 1789, in the First Congress is in ibid., vol. 2, p. 1027.

[23]Wroth and Zobel, eds., *Legal Papers of Adams*, reprinted both versions of the speech, vol. 2, pp. 125–129, 139–144, with elaborate annotations. The longer version was first published by the *Massachusetts Spy* (Boston), April 29, 1773, p. 3. In John Kukla, ed., *The Bill of Rights: A Lively Heritage* (Richmond, 1978), pp. 85–97. William Cuddihy, "From General to Specific Search Warrants," at p. 93, alleges that Otis "cited Sir Edward Coke's exaggeration of Magna Carta, incorrectly asserted that Coke required all search warrants to be specific, and appealed to 'higher law.'" Cuddihy cites Wroth and Zobel as his source for Otis's remarks, but that source does not show any reference by Otis to Coke's use of Magna Carta to condemn general warrants or to any reliance by Otis on Coke as an authority for specific warrants. Quincy, ed., *Reports of Cases*, pp. 51–57, includes a fourteen-line extract from Otis, in which Otis's claim that a writ of assistance is illegal is backed by these citations: "1 Inst. 464.29M." Vol. I of Coke's *Institutes* is on feudal tenures. "29M," a reference to the famous judgment-of-peers or by-law-of-the-land clause, seems to support the point. But Gray's discussion of Otis's quotations from Coke on Magna Carta, cap. XXIX, in Quincy's *Reports*, pp. 483–485, has nothing to do with search and seizure.

strument of "slavery," of "villainy," of "arbitrary power, the most destructive of English liberty and [of] the fundamental principles of the constitution. . . ." The writ reminded him of the kind of power that had cost one English king his head and another his throne. The only legal writ, Otis asserted, was a "special warrant directed to specific officers, and to search certain houses &c. especially set forth in the writ may be granted . . . upon oath made . . . by the person, who asks [for the warrant], that he suspects such goods to be concealed in those very places he desires to search."[24] In the recent past, Otis alleged, only special warrants existed, authorizing search of particularly named houses, and they were issued only after the complainant had taken an oath to support his suspicion; "special warrants only are legal," he concluded. He condemned writs of assistance because they were perpetual, universal (addressed to every officer and subject in the realm), and allowed anyone to conduct a search in violation of the essential principle of English liberty that a peaceable man's house is his castle. A writ that allowed a customs officer to enter private homes when he pleased, on bare suspicion, and even to break locks to enter, was void. An act of Parliament authorizing such writs was void because it violated the British constitution, and courts should not issue an unconstitutional writ.[25]

Otis lost his case. The writs issued, but Americans found a cause and a constitutional argument. In 1762 the Massachusetts legislature passed a bill that would have required all writs to be as specific as the warrants used by provincial officers to enforce the excise and impost acts, but the royal governor vetoed the bill. Thereafter crowds frequently prevented enforcement or "rescued" goods seized by customs agents. In a 1766 case a Boston merchant, believing that in "Whig Boston Whig furies made Whig law," used force to barricade his home as a crowd gathered.

---

[24]Wroth and Zobel, eds., *Legal Papers of Adams*, vol. 2, p. 141; I have not followed the capitalization of the original.
[25]Ibid., p. 144. Curiously, in the briefer version of the speech Otis relied more fully on Coke's decision in Dr. Bonham's Case, 8 Coke's Reports 113b, 118a (C.P. 1610), and more clearly asked the court to hold the act unconstitutional, Wroth and Zobel, eds., *Legal Papers of Adams*, vol. 2, pp. 127–128.

Officers prudently decided that calling on bystanders to assist as a *posse comitatus* might result in a loss of life—their own—and abandoned efforts to enforce the writ. After a rescue in Falmouth (Portland), Maine, the governor conceded that public opposition had effectively paralyzed the use of writs to conduct searches and seizures. Britain's attorney general William DeGrey decided that the act of Parliament that authorized the writ allowed them to issue only from the Court of Exchequer, whose writ did not run in America.[26] In London, far more than DeGrey's technical opinion damaged the principle of general warrants.

John Wilkes's studied insult of the king's speech in 1763, in the forty-fifth number of his journal *North Britain*, provoked massive retaliation by the government. One of the secretaries of state issued general search warrants for the arrest of everyone connected with *North Britain* #45. Crown agents enforcing the warrants had unfettered discretion to search, seize, and arrest anyone as they pleased. They ransacked printers' shops and houses and arrested forty-nine persons including Wilkes, a member of Parliament, his printer, publisher, and booksellers. The officers seized his private papers for incriminating evidence after a thorough search; thousands of pages and scores of books belonging to persons associated with him were also seized. The House of Commons voted that *North Britain* #45 was a seditious libel and expelled Wilkes, and he was eventually convicted and jailed. The government found, however, that it had mounted a tiger; no one since the time of John Lilburne, more than a century earlier, had proved to be such a resourceful and pugnacious antagonist. Wilkes had quickly filed suits for trespass against everyone, from flunky to minister, connected with the warrant that had resulted in his undoing; others who had suffered searches and arrest filed similar suits. A legal donnybrook ensued. On the one hand, the government, based on about two hundred informations, had engaged in mass arrests and searches, and on the other, the victims

[26]Smith, *Writs of Assistance Case*, pp. 442–447, 542–543; Quincy, ed., *Reports of Cases*, pp. 437–438, 446, 495–499; John Phillip Reid, *In Rebellious Spirit* (University Park, Pa., 1979), pp. 1–35.

filed a couple of dozen suits for trespass and false imprisonment. The Wilkes case became the subject of sensational controversies, angry tracts, and confusing trials. Wilkes would emerge from his prosecution a popular idol, the personification of constitutional liberty to Englishmen on both sides of the Atlantic. Although he focused mainly on the dangers of general warrants and the seizures of private papers, some of his supporters also championed freedom of the press and the right against self-incrimination.[27]

In the colonies, "Wilkes and Liberty" became a slogan that patriot leaders exploited in the service of American causes. In New York, for example, Alexander McDougall, a leader of the Sons of Liberty who had censured a bill to provision the king's troops, posed as an American Wilkes and turned his imprisonment into a theatrical triumph, as had Wilkes, while his supporters used the number 45, the seditious issue of *North Britain*, as a symbol of their cause. On the forty-fifth day of the year, for example, forty-five Liberty Boys dined on forty-five pounds of beef from a forty-five-month-old bull, drank forty-five toasts to liberty—liberty of the press, liberty from general warrants, liberty from compulsory self-accusation, liberty from seizure of private papers—and after dinner marched to the jail to salute McDougall with forty-five cheers. On another festive liberty day, forty-five songs were sung to him by forty-five virgins, every one of whom, according to some damned Tory, was forty-five years old.[28] The Fourth Amendment, as well as the First and Fifth, owes something to the Wilkes cases. Unlike *Paxton's Case*, the Wilkes cases

[27]See Robert R. Rea, *The English Press in Politics, 1760–1774* (Lincoln, Nebr., 1963), pp. 40–85; Raymond Postgate, *That Devil Wilkes* (New York, 1929); George Nobbe, *The North Briton: A Study in Political Propaganda* (New York, 1939), chap. 16; and George Rude, *Wilkes and Liberty* (Oxford, 1962).

[28]Leonard W. Levy, *Emergence of a Free Press,* (New York, 1985), p. 79. For the fallout of the Wilkes cases in America, see Patricia Bonomi, *A Factious People: Politics and Society in Colonial New York* (New York, 1971), pp. 267–276; Pauline Maier, *From Resistance to Revolution* (New York, 1972), pp. 162–177; Jack P. Greene, "Bridge to Revolution: The Wilkes Fund Controversy in South Carolina 1769–1775," *Journal of Southern History* 27 (1963), 19–52.

filled the columns of American newspapers from Boston to Charleston.

The first of these cases, *Huckle v. Money*, established the doctrine, traceable at least to Hale, that crown officers are liable to damage suits for trespass and false imprisonment resulting from unlawful search. Chief Justice Charles Pratt said, when charging the jury: "To enter a man's house by virtue of a nameless warrant, in order to procure evidence, is worse than the Spanish Inquisition, a law under which no Englishman would wish to live an hour." The jury awarded 300 pounds in damages, an excessive sum for the deprivation of a journeyman printer's liberty for six hours, but on appeal Pratt ruled that the small injury done to one of low rank meant nothing compared to the "great point of the law touching the liberty of the subject" invaded by a magistrate of the king in an exercise of arbitrary power "violating Magna Carta, and attempting to destroy the liberty of the kingdom, by insisting on the legality of this general warrant. . . ."[29] In *Wilkes v. Wood* (1763), Pratt presided over a similar trial and engaged in similar rhetoric ("totally subversive of the liberty of the subject"); the jury awarded damages of 1,000 pounds to Wilkes, who later won an award of 4,000 pounds against the secretary of state who had issued the warrant.[30] In fact the government paid a total of about 100,000 pounds in costs and judgments.[31]

In one of the Wilkes cases the government appealed to England's highest criminal court, the King's Bench, and Lord Mansfield, the chief justice, agreed that the warrants in the Wilkes cases were illegal. Although the common law, he observed, authorized arrests without warrant, and Parliament had often authorized searches and arrests on the basis of general warrants, in this case no circumstance existed justifying warrantless searches

[29]*Huckle v. Money*, 95 Eng. Rep. 768 (C.P. 1763), in Philip B. Kurland and Ralph Lerner, eds., *The Founders' Constitution* (Chicago, 1987, 5 vols.), vol. 5, p. 230.

[30]98 Eng. Rep. 489 (C.P. 1763), in ibid., pp. 230–231.

[31]Thomas Erskine May, *Constitutional History of England Since the Accession of George III* (New York, 1880, 2 vols.), p. 249. May is the source of the earlier statement that the government filed two hundred informations in these cases; ibid., vol. 2, p. 112.

or arrests, and no act of Parliament was involved. Accordingly a secretarial warrant, based on executive authority, leaving discretion to the endorsing officer, "is not fit." Mansfield thought that the "magistrate ought to judge; and should give certain directions to the officer"—a foundation for what later emerged as probable cause.[32]

The victories of the Wilkesites encouraged other victims of secretarial warrants in seditious libel cases to bring suits for damages. The most important of those cases, *Entick v. Carrington* (1765), resulted in an opinion by Chief Justice Pratt, now Lord Camden, which the Supreme Court of the United States would describe as "one of the landmarks of English liberty."[33] Victory for the government, Camden declared, would open the secret cabinets of every subject whenever the secretary of state suspected someone of seditious libel. The law required no one to incriminate himself, for that would be "cruel and unjust" to the innocent and guilty alike, "and it would seem, that search for evidence is disallowed upon the same principle." Camden held that neither arrests nor general warrants could issue on executive discretion, and he implied that evidence seized on the authority of such a warrant could not be used without violating the right against self-incrimination. Similarly the Supreme Court in 1886 ruled that the Fourth and Fifth Amendments have an "intimate relation" and "throw great light on each other."[34]

In 1764 and 1765 the House of Commons irresolutely debated whether general warrants should be regarded as illegal, and in 1766 it repeated the debate. The upshot was the passage of three resolutions, not statutes, that revealed a victory for the narrow position of Mansfield rather than the broader one of Camden. The Commons condemned general warrants in all cases

[32]*Money v. Leach*, 97 Eng. Rep. 1075 (K.B. 1765), in Kurland and Lerner, eds., *Founders' Constitution*, vol. 5, p. 235.
[33]*Boyd v. United States*, 116 U.S. 616, 626 (1886), citing *Entick v. Carrington*, 95 Eng. Rep. 807 (K.B.), most easily available in Kurland and Lerner, eds., *Founders' Constitution*, vol. 5, pp. 233–235.
[34]19 Howell's *State Trials* at pp. 1038, 1041, 1063, 1073. *Boyd v. United States*, 116 U.S. 616, 633 (1886).

involving arrests but condemned general warrants for searches only in cases where the warrants issued from the executive branch in connection with the crime of seditious libel. Secretarial search warrants in treason cases remained legal. The resolutions of 1766 left in place the elaborate system of warrantless searches when authorized by Parliament, and of general searches when undergirded by statutory authority. The House of Lords rejected a proposal from the Commons that would have restricted general search warrants to cases of treason and felony. Thus the reforms resulting from the judicial decisions and parliamentary resolves of 1763 to 1766 conformed to the prime directive of England's law of search and seizure: even promiscuously general searches did not violate the liberty of the subject or infringe the maxim about a man's home as long as Parliament had laid down the law.[35]

On the other hand, the Wilkes case and the parliamentary debates unleashed a lot of rhetoric that went far beyond the reality of actual judicial holdings and legislative resolves. Americans were practiced in making a highly selective use of authorities and other sources that suited their needs. They could even turn Blackstone, that spokesman for parliamentary supremacy, into an advocate of constitutional restraints. In Britain, Englishmen often spoke thunderously but thrashed about with a frail stick; in America they threw the stick away, contenting themselves with the thunder. They found a lot of it in Pitt, Camden, Wilkes, and in "Father of Candor," all of whom they knew well. Father of Candor was the author of a little book of 1764, "on libels, warrants, and the seizure of papers," which by 1771 had gone through seven editions. He condemned general warrants as "excruciating torture,"[36] and he urged that search warrants be specific as to persons, places, and things, and be sworn on oath.[37]

---

[35]Robert Bisset, *History of the Reign of George III* (London, 1782–1783, 2 vols.) vol. 1, pp. 182–188, and John Adolphus, *History of England* (London, 1802, 3 vols.), vol. 1, pp. 152–154, 191–192, and 235–236.

[36]Father of Candor, *An Enquiry Into the Doctrine Lately Propagated Concerning Libels, Warrants, and the Seizure of Papers* (London, 1765, reprinted New York, 1970), p. 55.

[37]Ibid., pp. 55–56.

That was the sort of thing Americans could exploit when confronted by Parliament's determination to impose writs of assistance on the colonies.

Twenty years after the Townshend Acts of 1767, James Madison, speaking in the First Congress on the occasion of recommending the amendments to the Constitution that became the Bill of Rights, recalled that the legislative power constituted a great danger to liberty; the British, he noted, "have gone no farther than to raise a barrier against the power of the Crown; the power of the Legislature is left altogether indefinite."[38] Notwithstanding grandiose rhetoric against general warrants, Parliament in 1767 superseded its act of 1696, which had extended writs of assistance to America without providing a mechanism for granting them under the seal of the Court of Exchequer. The Townshend Acts of 1767 provided that the highest court in each colony possessed authority to issue writs of assistance to customs officers to search where they pleased for prohibited or uncustomed goods and to seize them.

The Townshend Acts therefore expanded the controversy over writs of assistance. What had been a local controversy, centering mainly in Boston, spread to all of the thirteen colonies. Only the two colonies, Massachusetts and New Hampshire, that had previously experienced the writs continued to issue them, although the mobs "liberated" seized goods as often as not. Elsewhere the provincial high courts stalled, compromised, or declined the writ. The New York court issued the writ but deviated from the exact language authorized by Parliament, with the result that the customs officers refused to execute the deviant writ and sought one in the correct form. It was not forthcoming; indeed, applications kept getting lost or mislaid. In 1773, five years after the first application, the New York court held that "it did not appear to them that such Writs according to the form now

---

[38]Speech by Madison, June 8, 1789, in Schwartz, ed., *Bill of Rights*, vol. 2, p. 1028.

produced are warranted by law and therefore they could not grant the motion."[39]

Something like that happened in several colonies. In Connecticut, Chief Justice Jonathan Trumbull and Judge Roger Sherman refused to be rushed into making a decision on the application for a writ. Trumbull remarked privately that he and his associates were not clear "the thing was in itself constitutional."[40] Chief Justice William Allen of Pennsylvania was more forthcoming. In 1768 he declared that he had no legal authority to issue the writ. Customs officials sent Allen's statement to Attorney General William DeGrey in London for his opinion. He thought that Allen would see the error of his ways if confronted by a copy of the writ, a copy of the act of Parliament, and a copy of the opinion of England's attorney general.[41] On a new application for the writ backed by English legal artillery, Allen replied that he would grant "particular [not general] writs whenever they are applied for on oath." The customs agent must swear he knew or had reason to believe that prohibited or uncustomed goods were located in a particular place. Allen's groping toward a concept of probable cause as well as specific warrants became clearer as customs officials vainly persisted to engage his cooperation.[42]

In South Carolina a judge, explaining his court's refusal to issue the writ, stated that it "trenched too severely and unnecessarily upon the safety of the subject secured by Magna Charta." After five years of persistence, however, the customs officials got a writ of assistance in South Carolina.[43] In Georgia, where the judges declined to issue the writ, they said they would authorize

[39]Oliver Dickerson, "Writs of Assistance as a Cause of the American Revolution," in Richard B. Morris, ed., *Era of the American Revolution* (New York, 1939), pp. 54–58.

[40]Ibid., pp. 52–54.

[41]Quincy, ed., *Reports*, pp. 453–454, for DeGrey's opinion, dated Aug. 20, 1768.

[42]Dickerson, "Writs of Assistance," pp. 59–60.

[43]William Henry Drayton, *A Letter from Freeman of South-Carolina* (Charles Town, 1774), pp. 19–20; Dickerson, "Writs of Assistance," p. 67.

a search warrant for a specific occasion if supported by an affidavit.[44]

Virginia issued writs of assistance in 1769 but undermined the process by annexing a degree of specificity obnoxious to the customs office. Its agent had to swear an oath in support of his suspicion and could obtain a writ only for a special occasion and for a limited duration of time. The Virginia judges alleged that the writ sought by the customs office under the Townshend Acts was "unconstitutional" because it allowed the officer "to act under it according to his own arbitrary discretion." The customs office appealed to England for support against the Virginia court. Attorney General DeGrey had to acknowledge that he knew of "no direct and effective means" to compel a provincial court to award a writ of assistance. He asserted that judges might be impeached for contumacious refusal to execute an act of Parliament, but he did not know how to proceed in such a case. He preferred to believe that Virginia's judges had acted out of a mistaken understanding of the law. Virginia's court, however, remained contumacious.[45]

Between 1761 and 1776 a glacial drift in American legal opinion can be discerned toward increased reliance on specific warrants. Law books, including manuals of the justices of the peace, began to recommend specific warrants in some cases; most, however, relied on general warrants, as did American judges in actual practice. American rhetoric and reality diverged. John Dickinson's *Letters of a Pennsylvania Farmer*, which circulated in every colony, censured general warrants and repeated the cliché about a man's home being his castle; but Dickinson did not recommend specific warrants in their place or condemn any warrantless searches. Americans never spoke of a right to privacy as such, although they understood the concept and, like their British counterparts, expressed outrage over the possibility that customs agents might ransack houses and "enter private cabinets" or "se-

---

[44]Dickerson, "Writs of Assistance," p. 66.
[45]Ibid., pp. 68–71.

cret repositories." The best known of such remarks, which received considerable publicity in the colonies, was that of the Boston Town Meeting of 1772, which complained:

> Thus our houses and even our bed chambers, are exposed to be ransacked, our boxes chests & trunks broke open ravaged and plundered by wretches, whom no prudent man would venture to employ even as menial servants; whenever they are pleased to say they suspect there are in the house wares &c for which the dutys have not been paid. Flagrant instances of the wanton exercise of his power, have frequently happened in this and other sea port Towns. *By* this we are cut off from that domestick security which renders the lives of the most unhappy in some measure agreeable. Those Officers may under colour of law and the cloak of a general warrant break thro' the sacred rights of the domicil, ransack mens houses, destroy their securities, carry off their property, and with little danger to themselves commit the most horred murders.[46]

In all the American rhetoric, only one writer seems to have urged special warrants in place of warrantless searches and general warrants. Some writers revealed that their objection lay against a parliamentary empowerment, rather than one of their own assemblies.[47] General searches continued in the colonies as the prevailing standard, not the specific warrants used in Massachusetts. Nevertheless, some colonies became more familiar with specific warrants and even used them in various kinds of cases. One need only add that Otis's extraordinary forensic effort of 1761 on behalf of specific warrants, which a Boston newspaper printed in 1773, bore scarce fruit elsewhere, at least not until well after the Revolution.

The Declaration of Independence, however, spurred the definition of American ideals. Although that document, which itemized the king's perfidies, failed to say anything about search and

---

[46]"The Rights of the Colonies," 1772, in Schwartz, ed., *Bill of Rights*, vol. 1, p. 206.
[47]William Henry Drayton, cited above, n. 43, seems to have been the exception.

seizure or even about general warrants, it inspired the making of the first state constitutions. In the midst of war, Americans engaged in the most important, creative, and dynamic constitutional achievements in history, among them the first written constitutions and the first bills of rights against all branches of government. Their provisions on search and seizure are significant because they distilled the best American thinking on the subject, constituted benchmarks to show the standard by which practice should be measured, and provided models for the Fourth Amendment.

Virginia, the oldest, largest, and most influential of the new states, anticipated the Declaration of Independence by adopting a Declaration of Rights on June 12, 1776, and completed its constitution before the month ended. Article 10 of the Declaration of Rights provided: "That general warrants, whereby any officer or messenger may be commanded to search suspected places without evidence of a fact committed, or to seize any person or persons not named, or whose offence is not particularly described and supported by evidence, are grievous and oppressive, and ought not to be granted."[48] Obviously this provision is a substantial step in the direction of specific warrants. Its force is weakened by the wishy-washy climax: certain warrants are grievous, not illegal, and "ought" not be granted, but the language imposes no prohibition against them. The concept of probable cause is stunted with respect to searches but considerably broader with respect to arrests. The search may be conducted, presumably under warrant, if the fact of a crime has been established, though no need exists to show a connection between the crime and the place to be searched, and there is no reference to a need for specificity with respect to the things to be seized. Moreover, the warrant need not be based on a sworn statement. Probable cause must be shown for the criminal involvement of the persons to be arrested; far more than mere suspicion is required for an arrest.

[48]Schwartz, ed., *Bill of Rights*, vol. 1, p. 235.

As the first search and seizure provision in any American constitution, Virginia's had egregious deficiencies as well as pioneering attainments. That the attainments might have been better still is evident from the fact that in a committee draft of May 27, the property to be seized had to be "particularly described." We do not know why that clause was omitted in the final draft.[49] We do know that the provision could have been far worse or altogether nonexistent. George Mason, who provided the original draft of the Declaration of Rights, had omitted a search-and-seizure provision, and Thomas Jefferson's draft of a state constitution omitted one too.[50] Edmund Randolph may have been right in recalling that his state's search-and-seizure provision "was dictated by the remembrance of the seizure of Wilkes's paper under a warrant from a Secretary of State,"[51] but Virginia went well beyond a condemnation of general warrants issued under executive authority.

In August 1776 Pennsylvania adopted its extraordinary constitution preceded by a Declaration of Rights influenced by Virginia yet original in major respects. Its tenth article provided:

> That the people have a right to hold themselves, their houses, papers, and possessions free from search and seizure, and therefore warrants without oaths or affirmations first made, affording a sufficient foundation for them, and whereby any officer or messenger may be commanded or required to search suspected places, or to seize any person or persons, his or their property, not particularly described are contrary to that right, and ought not to be granted.[52]

That provision is memorable because it recognizes a right of the people in affirmative terms rather than merely declaring against general warrants or grievous searches. And, the right of the peo-

---

[49]Ibid., p. 238, Article 12.
[50]Ibid., pp. 232, 243–246.
[51]Ibid., p. 248.
[52]Ibid., p. 265.

ple is broad, promiscuously so. There is no such thing as an absolute right to be free from search and seizure; the provision meant, rather, that searches and seizures made without specific warrants "ought"—that weak word again—not to be granted. Even that proposition had to be subject to exceptions, because no evidence suggests that Pennsylvania intended to depart from common-law exceptions to the need for a warrant if a peace officer was in hot pursuit of a felon or had reason to believe that the felon might escape if the officer called time out to obtain a warrant. Exigent circumstances of various kinds always allowed warrantless arrests and even warrantless searches and seizures of evidence of crime, of weapons, or of contraband. The Pennsylvania provision had the virtue of including a requirement for specificity with respect to the things seized when a warrant was attainable. It was also the first to require that the warrant be available only if the informant swore or affirmed that he had "sufficient foundation" for specific information about the person, place, or things described. Probable cause, attested to on oath, derives partly from Pennsylvania's contribution to the constitutional law of search and seizure.

Delaware's Declaration of Rights of 1776 derived its search-and-seizure provision partly from Maryland and partly from Pennsylvania, though the Delaware variant was truncated; it omitted the clause recognizing the right of the people. It also omitted a requirement for specificity respecting the property to be seized under a warrant, yet deplored as grievous any warrant for the seizure of property not based on a sworn statement. Delaware's contribution consisted, rather, in the fact that its provision was the first to declare "illegal" any warrants not meeting the constitutional requirement of specificity.[53] In this respect the Delaware provision was based on a draft of the Maryland Declaration of Rights, not yet adopted.[54] The texts of the search-and-seizure provisions of these two states were nearly the same. As

[53]Ibid, p. 278, Article 17.
[54]Ibid, pp. 279, 283, Article 23.

Delaware copied Maryland, North Carolina copied Virginia, and Vermont copied Pennsylvania.[55]

Similarly, New Hampshire in 1784 would copy Massachusetts, which did not adopt its Declaration of Rights and constitution until 1780. As a source of the Fourth Amendment, the Massachusetts provision on search and seizure was the most important of all the state models, because it was the one that the Fourth Amendment most resembles. The Massachusetts provision was the work of John Adams, the witness to and recorder of Otis's monumental speech in *Paxton's Case* about twenty years earlier. Through Adams and Article XIV of the Massachusetts Declaration of Rights, Otis's influence at last bore triumphant fruits. Article XIV declared:

> Every subject has a right to be secure from all unreasonable searches, and seizures of his person, his houses, his papers, and all his possessions. All warrants, therefore, are contrary to this right, if the cause or foundation of them be not previously supported by oath or affirmation; and if the order in the warrant to the civil officer, to make search in suspected places, to arrest one or more suspected persons, or to seize their property, be not accompanied with a special designation of the persons or objects of search, arrest, or seizure and no warrant ought to be issued but in cases and with the formalities, prescribed by the laws.[56]

The detail of the provision is striking. No other right received such particularity in the Massachusetts constitution, and, like the provision of Pennsylvania, which Adams borrowed, it is a "right" that is protected. The right is to be secure against "unreasonable search, and seizures," the first use of the phrase that would become the prime principle of the Fourth Amendment. The warrant must be based on sworn statement providing "case or foundation" for the warrant—but the provision omits, amazingly,

[55]Ibid, pp. 287, 323.
[56]Ibid., p. 342.

a requirement that the search, arrest, or seizure occur within specifically designated premises.[57]

The war years were the worst possible for testing whether American practices matched American ideals or constitutional provisions. Search and seizure was a method of fighting the enemy and those suspected of adhering to his cause. Perhaps the grossest violation of a constitutional provision occurred in 1777 in Pennsylvania. Three years earlier Congress had complained about customs officials breaking and entering without authority. In 1777, though, Congress urged Pennsylvania's executive council to search the homes of Philadelphians, mostly Quakers, whose loyalty to the American cause was suspect. Congress wanted to disarm such persons and to seize their political papers. Pennsylvania's executive council authorized a search of the homes of anyone who had not taken an oath of allegiance to the United States. The searches of at least six Quaker homes were conducted cruelly and violently, and all sorts of books, papers, and records were confiscated; more than forty people were arrested and deported without trial, let alone conviction, to Virginia, where they were detained until the next year.[58] Nothing that the British had done equaled the violation of privacy rights inflicted by Pennsylvania on its "Virginia Exiles," in defiance of the state constitution and a writ of habeas corpus by the state chief justice, but with the support of Congress.

American adherence to professed principles stands up far better and is more fairly tested after the shooting stopped. Between 1782 and the ratification of the Constitution, five states—Maryland, New York, North and South Carolina, and Georgia—employed general searches. The Southern states conventionally employed warrantless searches without restriction against slaves, especially to detect vagrants and fugitives. But all five states used general warrants to enforce their impost laws. Al-

---

[57]For New Hampshire, see ibid., p. 377, Article 19.
[58]Isaac Sharpless, *A History of Quaker Government in Pennsylvania* (Philadelphia, 1900, 2 vols.), vol. 2, pp. 151–168.

though Maryland's constitution banned general warrants, Maryland used them to enforce excise laws and laws regulating bakers. Such laws, however, derived from past experience. More significant, perhaps, is the fact that the laws of Massachusetts kept faith with its commitment to specific warrants. Moreover, Rhode Island, which had no constitution, and New Jersey, which had one but did not include a search-and-seizure clause, enacted legislation that required the use of specific warrants. In the remaining states, general warrants continued to be used, but specific warrants were becoming more common, especially in cases of theft. In Virginia the trend toward specificity was pronounced, if belated.

In Connecticut, which, like Rhode Island, had no constitution, the state supreme court delivered an opinion of major consequence that voided a general warrant directed against every person and place suspected by the victim of a theft. The state chief justice ruled that a justice of the peace, in granting a warrant, had an obligation "to limit the search to such particular place or places, as he, from the circumstances, shall judge there is reason to suspect," and he must limit the arrests under the warrant to those persons found with the stolen goods. The warrant before the court, the chief justice concluded, "is clearly illegal" because not specific. The case, *Frisbie v. Butler* (1787), shows that probable cause as determined independently by a magistrate was not an unknown concept.[59]

The failure of the Framers to include in the Constitution a bill of rights exposed it to the withering criticism of those who opposed ratification for any reason. Ten days after the Constitutional Convention adjourned, Richard Henry Lee of Virginia, a member of Congress, sought to wreck the ratification process by moving that Congress adopt a bill of rights. Acting out of genuine fear of the proposed national government, Lee had troubled to frame his own bill of rights rather than simply urging the famous

---

[59] 1 Kirby (Conn.) 231–235 (1787), excerpted in Kurland and Lerner, eds., *Founders' Constitution*, vol. 5, p. 237.

one of his own state. He omitted numerous liberties of importance but included a search-and-seizure clause of significance: "... the Citizens shall not be exposed to unreasonable searches, seizures of their papers, houses, persons, or property." Lee had constructed the clause from the Massachusetts Constitution of 1780. It was the broadest on the subject.

Lee's colleague from Virginia, James Madison, led the fight against Lee's motion. Madison observed that the Articles of Confederation required that all thirteen state legislatures would have to approve the Lee proposals if endorsed by Congress. That would cause confusion because of the Convention's rule that ratification by nine state conventions would put the Constitution into operation.[60] Lee's motion lost, but he did not quit. He wrote his *Federal Farmer* letters, the best of the Anti-Federalist tracts.[61]

In an early letter, Lee discoursed on the rights omitted from the proposed Constitution. The second one he mentioned was the right against unreasonable warrants, those not founded on oath or on cause for searching and seizing papers, property, and persons.[62] In another letter he included the term "effects," which would become part of the Fourth Amendment.[63] In his final word on the subject, he urged a constitutional provision "that all persons shall have a right to be secure from all unreasonable searches and seizures of their persons, houses, papers, or possessions; and that all warrants shall be deemed contrary to this right, if the foundation of them be not previously supported by oath, and there be not in them a special designation of persons or objects of search, arrest, or seizure."[64]

[60]Lee's Proposed Amendments, Sept. 27, 1787, in Merrill Jensen, ed., *The Documentary History of the Ratification of the Constitution. Constitutional Documents and Records, 1776–1787* (Madison, Wisc., 1976), vol. 1, pp. 325–340; the quotation from Lee is at p. 338.

[61]*Observations . . . in a Number of Letters from the Federal Farmer* (New York, 1787), a tract that sold several thousand copies in a few months. Reprinted in Herbert J. Storing, ed., *The Complete Anti-Federalist* (Chicago, 1981, 7 vols.), vol. 2, pp. 214–357. Lee's authorship is not certain, but the author's remarks on search and seizure accord with Lee's motion in Congress and with his letter of Dec. 22, 1787, in ibid., vol. 5, p. 117.

[62]Storing, ed., vol. 2, p. 249, Letter IV, Oct. 12, 1787.

[63]Ibid., vol. 2, p. 262, Letter VI, Dec. 25, 1787.

[64]Ibid., vol. 2, Letter XVI, Jan. 20, 1788.

Other Anti-Federalists also popularized the demand for a provision on searches and seizures, and some used significant language. "Centinel" employed an extract from the Pennsylvania constitution. The "Dissent" of the Pennsylvania convention's Anti-Federalists, which also circulated throughout the country in newspapers and pamphlet form, used a truncated form of the same provision. "Brutus," another whose writings were reprinted almost everywhere, used his own formulation against warrants that were not specific.[65] Anti-Federalists who addressed the issue usually opposed general warrants in purple language, either reflecting fear or calculated to inspire it. Newspapers in the four largest states reprinted the rant of "A Son of Liberty," who depicted federal officers dragging people off to prison after brutal searches and confiscations that shocked "the most delicate part of our families."[66] No one could compete with the florid fears expressed by that first-rate demagogue, Patrick Henry.[67]

Virginia's convention ratified the Constitution with recommendations for amendments to be considered by the First Congress. Among them was a detailed provision on the right of every free person "to be secure from all unreasonable searches and seizures"; the provision also required sworn warrants to be based on "legal and sufficient cause." The Virginia recommendation of 1788, of unknown authorship, was moved by George Wythe on behalf of a powerful bipartisan committee which included James Madison.[68] The committee blended the precedents of the Penn-

---

[65]Ibid., vol. 2, pp. 136 and 153 for Centinel (Samuel Bryan of Pennsylvania); ibid., vol. 3, p. 151, for the Pennsylvania minority; and ibid., vol. 2, p. 375, for Brutus (Robert Yates of New York).

[66]Ibid., vol. 6, p. 35. See also John DeWitt, in ibid., vol. 4, p. 33, and Mercy Otis Warren, in ibid., p. 279.

[67]Jonathan Elliot, ed., *The Debates in the Several State Conventions* (Philadelphia, 1836–1845, 5 vols.), vol. 3, pp. 58, 412, 448–449, and 588, for Henry's oratory on the despoliations of hearth and home by tyrannical federal agents unrestricted by a requirement of specific warrants.

[68]Lee was not a member of the Virginia convention. Mason, a member of the Wythe committee, had omitted from his draft of the Virginia Declaration of Rights a search-and-seizure provision. The Wythe committee ignored the weak provision in their own state's constitution. See Robert A. Rutland, ed., *The Papers of George Mason* (Chapel Hill, 1979, 3 vols.), vol. 3, note on p. 1071.

sylvania and Massachusetts state constitutions and the recommendations of Richard Henry Lee. Virginia was the first state to ratify with a search-and-seizure recommendation. North Carolina copied it in her recommended amendments; New York and Rhode Island did so also, with slight changes.[69]

Without a single supporter when he began his fight in the House for amendments safeguarding personal liberties, Madison struggled to overcome apathy and opposition from members of his own party as well as the Anti-Federalists. He meant to win over the great body of people who withheld their support of the new government in the sincere belief that the Constitution should secure them against the abuse of powers by the United States. And he meant to isolate the leaders of the opposition by depriving them of their supporters. But Madison could have achieved his goals and redeemed his campaign pledge by taking the least troublesome route. On the issue of search and seizure, for example, he might have shown up the Anti-Federalists by proposing that the United States would not enforce its laws by searches and seizures that violated the laws of the states, most of which still allowed general warrants. That would have put the burden on the states to bring about reforms securing the rights of citizens against unreasonable searches and seizures. Or, Madison might have simply proposed that the United States would not employ general warrants.[70] Or, he might have recommended the weak formulation of his own state's constitution, with its omission of specificity for the things to be seized, its failure to require a sworn statement, and its flabby assertion that "grievous" warrants "ought" not to be granted. Even Virginia's excellent 1788 recommendation for a search-and-seizure provi-

---

[69]Charles Tansill, ed., *Documents Illustrative of the Formation of the Union of the American States* (Washington, D.C., 1927), pp. 1030, 1036, 1046, and 1054. The recommendations of North Carolina and Rhode Island were made too late to be of influence; Congress had already recommended the Bill of Rights.

[70]In his speech of June 8, 1789, urging amendments, Madison took note of the fact that one argument against the Constitution was that the government, under the necessary and proper clause, might enforce the collection of its revenue laws by issuing general warrants. Schwartz, ed., *Bill of Rights*, vol. 2, pp. 1030–1031.

sion to be added to the federal Constitution employed the same "ought."

If Madison had chosen a formulation narrower than the one he offered, only the citizens of Massachusetts could consistently have criticized him. Facing a variety of minimal options, any of which would have been politically adequate, Madison chose the maximum protection conceivable at the time. He recommended:

> The rights of the people to be secured in their persons, their houses, and their other property, from all unreasonable searches and seizures, shall not be violated by warrants issued without probable cause, supported by oath or affirmation, or not particularly describing the places to be searched, or the persons or things to be seized.[71]

No one previously had proposed the imperative voice, "shall not be violated," rather than the wishful "ought not," which allowed for exceptions. "Probable cause" was also a significant contribution, or became so; it required more than mere suspicion or even reasonable suspicion, as had its antecedents such as "just cause" and "sufficient foundation." Above all, Madison used the positive assertion drawn from Pennsylvania and Massachusetts that the people have rights against "unreasonable searches and seizures"—John Adams's formulation for the Massachusetts constitution.

A House Committee of Eleven, composed of one member from each state, deleted the crucial phrase that establishes the general principle of the Fourth: no "unreasonable searches and seizures." Specificity in warrants is the lesser half of the amendment, because it provides the standard of reasonableness only when a search or seizure is conducted with a warrant. But the standard of reasonableness must also apply to warrantless searches according to the Fourth Amendment. The committee version initially declared that the "rights of the people to be secured in their persons, houses, papers, and effects, shall not be

[71]Ibid., p. 1027.

violated by warrants issuing without probable cause, supported by oath or affirmation, and not particularly describing the places to be searched, and the persons or things to be seized."[72] During the debate by the House acting as the Committee of the Whole, Elbridge Gerry of Massachusetts moved the restoration of "unreasonable seizures and searches." Oddly, he said he did so on the presumption that a "mistake" had been made in the wording of the clause, which he corrected by changing "rights" to "right" and "secured" to "secure." The effect, he argued, was to provide security, or, as we might say, privacy to the people; Gerry's motion changed the meaning from a protection of the right to a protection of the individuals in their persons, homes, papers, and effects. The Committee of the Whole adopted his motion but defeated others that were also important.[73] According to the House Journal, the defeated motions of August 17 were reported as agreed upon by the Committee of the Whole. Thus the provision recommended to the House, in the articles arranged by a special committee of three, read:

> The right of the people to be secure in their persons, houses, papers, and effects, against unreasonable searches and seizures, shall not be violated; and no warrants shall issue, but upon probable cause, supported by oath or affirmation, and particularly describing the place to be searched, and the persons or things to be seized.[74]

The changes that seem to have been sneaked in did more than eliminate a double negative. The entire provision was split into two parts separated by a semicolon. The first part fixed the right of the people and laid down the standard against unreasonable searches and seizures. The second part required probable cause for the issue of a specific warrant. No other changes were made except in the number of the article. Its text remained the same as adopted by the House and accepted by the Senate. Thus Otis

[72]Ibid., p. 1061 and p. 1112, Aug. 17.
[73]Ibid., p. 1112, Aug. 17.
[74]Ibid., p. 1123.

and Adams finally had a belated but cardinal impact on the making of the Fourth Amendment, even though Madison was immediately influenced by Lee and Virginia's recommendation. Lee, whom Virginia's legislature had elected to the United States Senate instead of Madison, bitterly complained to Patrick Henry that the idea of recommending amendments to the Constitution turned out to be political suicide; the Bill of Rights made impossible the amendments most desired by the Anti-Federalists limiting national powers concerning taxes, treaties, and commerce.[75]

When Madison had first recommended to the House that it consider amendments to the Constitution, some Anti-Federalists thought the House should not neglect the more important business of passing a law for the collection of duties. That law, which passed seven weeks before the amendments were adopted for state consideration, contained a clause on search and seizure. It allowed collectors and naval officers to enter and search any ships suspected of having uncustomed goods and to seize such goods. That is, Congress authorized general searches for the search and seizure of ships—warrantless, general searches. By contrast, if an officer suspected the concealment of uncustomed goods in a building on land, he must apply for a specific warrant before a magistrate and under oath state the cause of his suspicion, and he "shall . . . be entitled to a warrant to enter such house, store, or any place (in the day time only)" and to conduct the search for and seizure of uncustomed goods.[76] Thus the statute enacted before the framing of the Fourth Amendment required magistrates to issue the warrant on the basis of the officer's suspicion, not on the magistrate's independent judgment of the question of whether probable cause existed.

Allowing the officer who executed a warrant to determine its specificity put the fox in charge of the chicken coop. The magistrate in effect accepted the officer's sworn statement that he was

---

[75]Lee to Henry, Sept. 14, 1789, in William Wirt Henry, *Patrick Henry* (New York, 1891, 3 vols.), vol. 3, p. 399.

[76]Statutes at Large, 1st Cong., sess. I, chap. 5, sec. 24, July 31, 1789, An Act to Regulate the Collection of Duties, vol. I, p. 43.

acting in good faith. That is difficult to reconcile with the fact that the good-faith execution of a general warrant by a customs officer in the years before the Revolution did not, to American Whigs, validate the warrant or the seizures under it.

The adoption of the Fourth Amendment changed the situation drastically. In March 1791, before the amendment had been formally ratified but after approval by nine state legislatures, Congress enacted a tax on liquor, whether imported or distilled in the United States. The statute reflected the meaning of the Fourth Amendment. Unlike the collections act of 1789, the act of 1791 explicitly empowered magistrates to decide for themselves whether an officer had probable cause. Any judge with jurisdiction might issue a "special warrant" for the detection of fraudulently concealed spirits, but the warrant was lawful only "upon reasonable cause of suspicion, to be made out to the satisfaction of such judge or justice of the peace" and sworn under oath. That became the basis in federal law for the determination of probable cause.[77]

The amendment constituted a swift liberalization of the law of search and seizure. Its language was the broadest known at the time. It provided no remedy, however, for an illegal search or seizure, or for the introduction in evidence of illegally seized items. It contained principles that were as vague as they might be comprehensive; "probable" and "unreasonable," even if judicially determined, remained uncertain in meaning, and Congress made no provision for the liability, civil or criminal, of federal officers who violated the amendment. Moreover, no exclusionary rule existed. Consequently the right of privacy created by the amendment, while better secured by the fundamental law in comparison to previous practices and standards, depended then, as now, upon the interpretation of the "probable cause" that justified a specific warrant and, above all, on the reasonableness of searches and seizures.

[77]Statutes at Large, 1st Cong., sess. III, chap. 15, sec. 32, March 3, 1791, vol. I, p. 207.

Origins of the Fifth Amendment
and Its Critics

*O*rigins of the Fifth Amendment: The Right Against Self-Incrimination (Oxford University Press, 1968) won the Pulitzer Prize in history, making it an attractive target for critics.[1] I am pleased and honored that a generation after its publication the book is still read and provokes serious criticism. Five of the six contributors to a new book on the Fifth Amendment make my *Origins* the target of their essays—R.H. Helmholz, Charles M. Gray, John H. Langbein, Eben Moglen, and Henry E. Smith.[2] All but Smith had earlier published articles devoted to criticizing my *Origins of the Fifth Amendment*, as had M. R. T. MacNair, who is not included in the new book. Helmholz writes that this book is intended to "supply a better understanding of the history of the subject" than is provided by my book, which he mischaracterizes as overlooking the legal context of evidence and as concentrating "too exclusively" on show trials.[3]

---

[1]My productivity and reputation have enlarged the target. In Harold M. Hyman and William M. Wiecek, *Equal Justice Under Law: Constitutional Development, 1835–1875*, p. 536 (New York, 1982), appears the following passage: "Constitutional history is one of the classical fields of American historical scholarship. . . . This tradition produced giants whose work has never been entirely superseded. It includes John W. Burgess, Edward S. Corwin, Howard J. Graham, Homer C. Hocket, Leonard Levy, Andrew C. McLaughlin, Alpheus T. Mason, Allan Nevins, Herman Pritchett, James G. Randall, James Schouler, Carl B. Swisher, James N. Thorpe, William W. Willoughby, and Benjamin F. Wright." Among these I am the sole survivor.

[2]R. H. Helmholz, ed., *The Privilege Against Self-Incrimination: Its Origins and Development* (Chicago, 1997). Hereafter cited as *The Privilege*.

[3]Ibid., pp. 6–7.

The first one to make my book the subject of an entire essay was Charles Gray of the University of Chicago's history department in 1982.[4] His 1997 essay adds nothing significant to his previous criticism. Gray misunderstands the right against self-incrimination because he thinks of it as a person's privilege "not to be asked to incriminate himself."[5] It is, rather, a right to refuse answer, not a right to be immune from questioning or exposure to incrimination.

To appreciate Gray's 1982 essay on "Prohibitions and the Privilege," some background on the writ of prohibition is appropriate. It was devised in the twelfth century to enable the king's courts to enforce their claims against rival courts, whether feudal or ecclesiastical. The writ enjoined the hearing and decision of a suit by a court of rival jurisdiction in a matter supposedly within the cognizance of the king or the common law. Henry III's writs of prohibition against Bishop Grosseteste of Lincoln in 1246 and 1252 commanded that laymen should not be examined under oath in ecclesiastical courts except in matrimonial and testamentary cases.[6]

But the *inquisitio*, a canon law procedure introduced in 1215, required that suspects swear an oath to answer truthfully any interrogatories that might be asked. That oath was called the oath *ex officio* since the judge who exacted it served *ex officio* as accuser, prosecutor, judge, and jury. Because confession was central to the entire inquisitional process, the oath was in-

---

[4]Charles Gray, "Prohibitions and the Privilege Against Self-Incrimination," in Delloyd J. Guth and John W. McKenna, eds., *Tudor Rule and Revolution: Essays for G. R. Elton* (Cambridge, England, 1982), pp. 345–367. Parenthetically I must observe that although the legal profession customarily refers to the right against compulsory self-incrimination as a "privilege," I call it a "right" because it is one. Privileges are concessions granted by government to its subjects and may be revoked. The right originated in England where it was a common-law privilege, but in the United States the Fifth Amendment made it a constitutional right, clothing it with the same status as other rights, such as freedom of religion, that we would never denigrate by describing them as mere privileges.

[5]Charles Gray, "Self-Incrimination in Interjurisdictional Law," in Helmholz, ed., *The Privilege*, p. 63.

[6]Henry III's writs are in 4 Matthew Paris, *Chronica Majora*, ed. H. R. Luard (London, 1876), pp. 579–580; *Close Rolls of the Reign of Henry III, 1247–51*, ed. E. G. Atkinson (London, 1922), pp. 221–222, 554; and *Close Rolls of the Reign of Henry III, 1252–53*, ed. A. E. Stamp (London, 1927), pp. 224–225.

dispensable in securing a conviction; it was virtually a self-incriminatory oath, especially in cases involving religious belief. No man had to reveal an unknown crime, but if strongly suspected he was obliged to answer truthfully under the oath.[7] The Court of High Commission, England's supreme ecclesiastical court, always proceeded *ex officio* so that it might exact the oath *ex officio*, as a High Commissioner stated in 1593, "to the intent, he [the defendant] may not be privileged to say, that he is not bounde to answere."[8] Suspects often relied on a canon law maxim, *Nemo tenetur seipsum accusare* (nobody has to accuse himself), but it never vested a right against self-incrimination.[9] The maxim notwithstanding, one who was reasonably suspected had to answer pertinent questions however incriminating, though he or she was under no obligation to disclose an unknown crime.

In 1568, for the first time, a common-law court, the Court of Common Pleas, speaking unanimously through Chief Justice James Dyer, endorsed the *nemo tenetur* maxim.[10] In the 1580 Star Chamber case of Sir Thomas Tresham, Lord Chief Justice Christopher Wray of the King's Bench asserted "that no man by lawe ought to sweare to accuse hymselfe when he might loose lyfe or lymme. . . ."[11] These early cases show the amenability of the secular courts to the principle that no person had an obliga-

---

[7]Aemilius Friedberg, ed., *Corpus Juris Canonici*, 1881, book V, title I, de accusat., ch. 24, pp. 745–747; Henry Charles Lea, *A History of the Inquisition of the Middle Ages* (New York, 1907), pp. 408–415.

[8]Richard Cosin, *An Apologie for Sundrie Proceedings Ecclesiasticall* (London, 1593, 2nd ed.), Short Title Catalogue #5821, Reel 210, Part II, pp. 49–51.

[9]For the Latin maxim, John Strype, *Life and Acts of John Whitgift* (Oxford, 1822), vol. 3, pp. 234–235: "Licet nemo tenetur seipsum prodere; tamen proditus per famam, teneture seipsum ostedere, utrum possit suam innocentiam ostendere, et seipsum purgare." Literally translated, it is: No one is bound to produce against himself, but when exposed by common report he is bound to show whether he can show his innocence and is permitted to purge himself.

[10]Case of Thomas Leigh, 2 Brownlow & Goldesborough 271–272; 12 Coke's Rep. 26, 27; 3 Bulstrode 48, 50.

[11]Tresham's case, "Narrative of Proceedings in the Star-chamber against lord Vauyx, sir Thomas Tresham, sir William Catesby, and others, for a contempt in refusing to swear that they had not harboured Campion the Jesuit," in 30 *Archaeologia: or, Miscellaneous Tracts Relating to Antiquity* 80, 102–103 (London, 1844).

tion to reveal a crime. The common-law courts, especially in the time of Sir Edward Coke, issued many prohibitions against the Court of High Commission, on the ground that it exceeded its jurisdiction by using the incriminatory oath *ex officio* against laymen in cases not matrimonial or testamentary.[12]

Gray's 1982 essay narrates some of the history of the right against self-incrimination without challenging my work and without indicating that he offers nothing on self-incrimination not in my book. He asserts that much in his essay depends on his "extensive, unpublished study of Prohibitions in Tudor-Stuart England and is too multifarious to document briefly."[13] But a good deal of Gray's discussion on the writs of prohibition and the cases in which they were issued has nothing whatever to do with the right against self-incrimination. The thesis of the essay is that although my book is "useful for the larger political and intellectual history of the privilege against self-incrimination," it "clearly misreads the aspect discussed in this essay"—prohibitions. According to Gray, from a technical standpoint the common-law courts relied on jurisdictional grounds to issue writs of prohibition that curbed ecclesiastical courts from exacting incriminating information; that is, without holding that no person may be forced involuntarily to incriminate himself, the common-law courts merely ruled that the ecclesiastical courts lacked authority to adjudicate. "The [High] Commission," Gray tersely says, "was prohibitable, or an imprisonment could be adjudged unlawful, simply because it had exceeded its jurisdiction."[14] A footnote at that point in his essay acknowledges that I recognize that writs of prohibition against the High Commission "were more often than not based on grounds other than objection to incriminating examination."

With respect to a collection of seventeen manuscript prohibi-

[12] Roland G. Usher, *The Reconstruction of the English Church* (1909), pp. 206–207; Usher, *The Rise and Fall of the High Commission* (1913), pp. 181–182; British Library, London, Stowe MSS 424, fols. 158a–163b.

[13] Gray, "Prohibitions," p. 345 n.1.

[14] Ibid, p. 354.

tion cases decided by Chief Justice Edward Coke and his Court of Common Pleas between 1609 and 1611,[15] Gray adds that I "associate" some of the cases "too clearly" with objections against incriminating examinations. He correctly observes that none of these seventeen cases was grounded on the right, but he misleads when declaring that his analysis of these seventeen cases shows "that they are worthless" as to the right's history.[16] He later adds that all references to the right in these cases meant "practically nothing."[17] I believe that Coke's references to the right, even if only in *obiter dicta*, were significant because he and his court so obviously endorsed it. In addition to my not distinguishing between the worthy and the worthless, I am also accused by Gray of confusing lawyers' arguments with court decisions, for, he continues, although counsel may have complained about incriminating procedures, the cases don't prove that the court "attended to that aspect of the complaint when the cases were more easily disposable," that is, on purely jurisdictional grounds.[18] In view of this criticism, I shall focus here on court decisions rather than arguments of counsel.

I concede that I associate Coke with objections to incriminating examinations. The reason is that he issued writs of prohibition against the High Commission explicitly based on objections to the incriminatory oath *ex officio*. Among the 1609–1611 manuscript cases involving the oath *ex officio* was that of Rochester and Mascall, who had been convicted by the High Commission for notorious adultery. Coke stated "*nemo tenetur* in *Causis criminalibus prodere seipsum.*" In the case of Giles and Symonds, who were also convicted for adultery, Coke declared that the defendants, being free subjects, were entitled to enjoy "the freedom of all Laws and privileges of the Kingdom, and that they are not bound to answer articles touching these premises on their oathes." In the Pierces' case, Coke said that "all cannons

[15]Stowe MSS 424, fol. 158a–164b.
[16]Gray, "Prohibitions," p. 355 n.13, and Gray, "Self-Incrimination," p. 92.
[17]Gray, "Self-Incrimination," p. 93.
[18] Ibid.

and constitutions, &c. made to compell any person (questioned in a court Ecclesiasticall) to take his oath against his will, except in causes *Testimentariis* or *Matrimonialibus*, are void." On another occasion the Commission convicted Edward and Anne Jenner for having disturbed church services, defended Brownist separatists, published schismatical books, and called the minister's wife "a priests whore." Yet Coke said, in Latin, "no free man should be compelled to answer for his secret thought and opinions."[19]

Coke's statement in the Jenners' case was preceded by the advisory opinion that he and Sir John Popham of the Kings Bench had given to the Privy Council in 1607 and by Coke's opinion in the case of Thomas Edwards in 1609. Coke and Popham, in response to the question whether an ecclesiastical judge might examine a person on the oath *ex officio*, declared that if the individual had not received a copy of the charges against him in advance of the questions, "he need not answer"; moreover, no layman could be examined except in matrimonial and testamentary cases, because "they may easily be inveigled and entrapped, and principally in heresy and errors of faith."[20]

Gray makes no issue over the Coke-Popham opinion, which shows Coke's opposition to the oath, but Gray wrongly dismisses Edwards's case as merely an application by Coke of the "secret thoughts" limit "on a minor point." Edwards's case appears in Coke's *Reports*, where it could be read by all who objected to compulsory self-incrimination. Charged with having libeled a bishop, Edwards refused the oath *ex officio* when required to swear to the meaning of certain remarks about the bishop and his wife. On granting the application for a prohibition, Coke found that the cause belonged to temporal jurisdiction and that "the Ecclesiastical Judge cannot examine any man upon his oath,

---

[19]Case of Rochester and Mascall (1609), in ibid., Stowe MSS 424, fol. 160b; see also "The L. Cook's Argument touching Rochester's Case," Cotton MSS, Cleo. F. II, fols. 467–478. Case of Giles and Symonds (1611), Stowe MSS 424, fols. 158a–159b; Case of Richard, David, and Joan Pierce (1611), in ibid., fols. 158b–159a; and Case of Edward and Anne Jenner (1611), in ibid., fols. 159b–160a.

[20]Of "Oaths before an Ecclesiastical Judge Ex Officio," 12 Coke's Rep. 26 (1607), 77 Eng. Rep. 1308.

upon the intention and thought of his heart, for *cogitationis poenam nemo emeret* [no man may be punished for his thought]. And in cases where a man is to be examined upon his oath, he ought to be [examined] upon acts and words, and not of the intention or thought of his heart; and if any man should be examined upon any point of religion, he is not bound to answer the same; for in time of danger, *quis modo tutus erit* [how will he be safe] if everyone should be examined of his thought . . . for it has been said in the proverb, thought is free."[21] And in a case of 1611, Coke declared that the High Commission should not "examine any man upon his oath, to betray himself, and to incur any penalty pecuniary or corporal."[22] These cases illustrate Coke's deep concern for substantive matters, not just Gray's purely jurisdictional ones.

James I was resentful of Coke's challenges to his prerogative powers. Coke had said, for example, that "the king hath no prerogative but that which the law of the land allows."[23] So in 1611 the king acted to bolster the High Commission. He issued new royal letters patent authorizing the Commission to use the oath *ex officio*. He also empowered the Commission to fine and imprison defendants whom it convicted as well as anyone who refused the oath and anyone who having taken it failed to answer "fully and directly."[24] Yet Coke's prohibitions continued. He issued two of the most extreme prohibitions in 1611 after the new letters patent had gone into effect.[25]

A substantial part of Gray's essay has nothing to do with prohibitions or with jurisdictions, just as much of his section on prohibitions has nothing to do with self-incrimination. For example, he amply covers the Coke-Popham advisory opinion of 1607, and the 1611 habeas corpus case of Ladd and Mansell, and the 1616

[21]13 Coke's Rep. 9, at 10 (1609), 77 Eng. Rep. 1421, 1422.
[22]*Huntly v. Cage*, 2 Brownlow & Goldsborough 14–16 (1611), Eng. Rep. 787–788.
[23]Quoted in Usher, *Rise and Fall of High Commission*, p. 210.
[24]Sect. 11, Letters patent 1611, reprinted in G. W. Prothero, ed., *Selected Statutes and Other Constitutional Documents Illustrative of the Reign of Elizabeth and James* (Oxford, 1894), p. 429.
[25]Pierces' case, Nov. 21, 1611, and Jenners' case, Nov. 28, 1611, both cited in note 19 above.

habeas corpus case of Burrowes *et al.*, none of which concerned prohibitions. Gray has no quarrel with my treatment of Ladd and Mansell, and I have none with his. But he alleges that the Burrowes case "has virtually the opposite significance from that which has been attributed to it [by me], for it has been acclaimed as Coke's finest hour in broad opposition to self-incrimination. In fact, it shows Coke and his brethren leaning over backwards to avoid being harder on the High Commission than they could help."[26]

Gray misrepresents me. I said nothing of the kind nor anything remotely about Coke's finest hour. I called the case "the most important" of Coke's career on the oath *ex officio*, because he deliberately set out to make it the leading case on the subject, and he described it as a case "of very great consequence." Relying on the *nemo tenetur* maxim, he elaborately condemned as illegal the oath *ex officio* because it forced self-incrimination. He gave three reasons for sustaining the writ of habeas corpus and releasing the eight Puritan prisoners: the Commission had required the oath; it failed to give the prisoners a copy of the charges; the Magna Carta protected the liberty of the subject. I add, however, that Coke "inexplicably balked at issuing the writ after having given all the reasons why he should." He released the prisoners on bail and advised them to submit to the High Commission and conform. When the prisoners again applied to Coke for discharge on habeas corpus at the court's next session, he observed that although the Commission could not imprison them for refusing the oath, it could imprison them for obstinate heresy and schism, whereupon the court remanded the prisoners to the Commission.[27] Treating the case that way does not depict Coke's "finest hour"; Gray, on the other hand, regards Coke's record in the case as "statesmanly."[28] He adds that Burrowes was definitely not a triumphant moment for the privilege against self-

[26]Gray, "Prohibitions," p. 365.
[27]Levy, *Origins of the Fifth Amendment* pp. 254– 257.
[28]Gray, "Prohibitions," p. 366.

incrimination. Contrary to his insinuation, I never indicated that it was.

Gray concludes that Magna Carta "made as little impression on the courts as it deserved to."[29] The sarcasm is unwarranted and the statement is wrong. In the Stowe manuscripts describing seventeen prohibition cases between 1609 and 1611, Coke quoted chapter 39 of Magna Carta in every one; the clerk rendered the Latin in progressively shorter phrasing from case to case until he ended with *"nullus liber homo* etc."[30] And Coke connected Magna Carta to the illegality of the incriminatory oath.

Gray ends by declaring that the common-law courts "never said that the jurisdictions using civil-canon procedure could not expose individuals to self-incrimination."[31] Of course they could, but phrasing the point that way misleads, because even if a well-established right against self-incrimination existed, the courts could still ask questions, the answers to which might expose one to self-incrimination. The right does not ensure against incriminatory questions. Nevertheless, in view of the fact that exaction of the oath *ex officio* exposed individuals to self-incrimination, the common-law courts did in fact uphold a right against self-incrimination by declaring, frequently, that the oath was illegal when employed against laymen in cases not testamentary or matrimonial.

We have only Gray's *ipse dixit* that the prohibitions he says were decided on jurisdictional grounds were in fact so decided. Gray, whose essay lacks focus, does not analyze a single prohibition case. Despite his title, much of his essay is not about prohibitions. The Ladd and Mansell case and the Burrowes case, for example, deal with the writ of habeas corpus. Gray is discursive and can be irrelevant. But my critics admire and exaggerate his

[29]Ibid., p. 367.
[30]Stowe MSS 424, fols. 158a–164b. Ch. 39 says, *"Nullus liber homo capiatur vel imprisonetur, aut disseisiastur, aut utlagetur, aut exuletur, aut aliquo modo destruatur super eum ibimus, nec super eum mittemus, nisi per legale judicium parium suorum vel per legem terrae, nec."* William Sharp McKechnie, *Magna Carta* (Glasgow, 1914), p. 375.
[31]Gray, "Prohibitions," p. 367.

work. One, M. R. T. MacNair, a lecturer in law at the University of Leeds, alleged that Gray undermined my presentation "by identifying the prohibition cases of the reign of James I as cases of jurisdiction."[32] But not even Gray alleged that prohibitions never related to self-incrimination or that they were decided on jurisdictional grounds exclusively. Indeed, he said, "In several cases, ecclesiastical courts were prohibited from interrogation when the effects would be to force someone to supply sworn confessional evidence that could be used against him in a secular prosecution for the same offense."[33] MacNair's facts are wrong.

John H. Langbein, another of my critics, says that Gray corrects me by showing that when the common-law courts issued writs of prohibition, those courts did not reflect "any consistent notion of a privilege against self-incrimination." I never said the common-law courts were consistent. Langbein also approvingly quotes Gray as showing that at "the level of technical law . . . a general privilege cannot be asserted."[34] Langbein, nor Gray, nor anyone else quotes me to the contrary. They leave the impression that they had scored a point when in fact they had not joined the issue.

In 1900 Richard H. Helmholz, a medievalist and canon-law specialist at the University of Chicago Law School, published a sustained attack on my book in a law review article that focused on the role of Europe's *ius commune*, the continental blend of canon and Roman law ordinarily referred to as the civil law system.[35] The theme of his article is that the canon law protected the "privilege" against self-incrimination. That is a preposterous theme, because in its canon-law form the privilege merely protected a person against revealing an unknown crime but otherwise obligated him to respond to incriminating questions. When

[32]M. R. T. MacNair, "Early Development of the Privilege against Self-Incrimination," 10 *Oxford Journal of Legal Studies*, p. 68.

[33]Gray, "Prohibitions," pp. 352–353.

[34]John H. Langbein, "Historical Origins of the Privilege Against Self-Incrimination at Common Law," 92 *Michigan Law Review*, pp. 1047, 1073 n.121.

[35]R. H. Helmholz, "Origins of the Privilege Against Self-Incrimination: The Role of the European *Ius Commune*," 65 *New York University Law Review*, p. 962.

exposed by public rumor or common report, the individual must answer. In 1593 Dr. Richard Cosin, a member of the High Commission and an expert on the civil and canon law, said that one must confess if suspected by common report.[36] The canon law's inquisitorial system of criminal justice, which operated in cases of offenses against religion, privileged only secret or unknown crimes. The English common law's accusatorial system of criminal justice was, by contrast, hospitable to a far broader privilege.

Helmholz claims that I depict the rack and the auto-da-fé as the "goal and glory of civil procedure." That is false. I spoke of the rack and auto-da-fé only in connection with the Inquisition in heresy cases, and in that regard my characterization is accurate.[37] The most astonishing aspect of Helmholz's 1990 article is that he never refers to the Inquisition or to heresy cases—enormous omissions of considerable significance to anyone seeking to understand the origins of the right at issue. If speech and belief had been free, rather than subject to the laws of heresy and seditious libel, the right against self-incrimination might never have developed. In his 1997 essay Helmholz emphasizes that people suspected of heresy were obliged to answer, but he claims that few Englishmen were accused of heresy in the ecclesiastical courts. Their Puritan victims would not likely have agreed.[38]

Helmholz insists, nevertheless, that the right originated in ecclesiastical courts and that they respected it. The crux of his entire argument focuses on the old maxim, *nemo tenetur prodere seipsum*, no person is obliged to betray or produce against himself, which Helmholz, a bit loosely, translates as no one is compelled "to give evidence against himself."[39] He finds the maxim in medieval guides to the canon law and accurately observes that I cast doubt on the maxim's origins, regard them as mysterious, and say

[36]Cosin, *An Apologie*, Part III, pp. 81–82. Archbishop John Whitgift asserted, in 1584, writing in Latin, that "whoever is accused by the denunciation of others or by common report is obliged to reveal himself, to avoid scandal, and to clear himself." 1 Strype, *Whitgift*, p. 318.
[37]Helmholz, "Origins of the Privilege," at p. 963.
[38]Helmholz, "The Privilege and the *Ius Commune*," p. 40.
[39]Helmholz, "Origins of the Privilege," p. 962.

that the maxim never existed in any canon-law text. The origins of the maxim are indeed mysterious, though I trace it back to antiquity, which no one else had done. I cannot imagine, however, what possessed me to say that the maxim never existed in canon-law texts. That was incorrect, as my statement contradicts my own evidence, because after I traced the maxim to Saints Chrysostom and Augustine, I showed that it was present in Aquinas's *Summa* and Gratian's *Decretals*; moreover, in a note I observed that Durantis, Gandinus, and Panormitanus mentioned the maxim and its qualification that obligated a need to reply if publicly suspected.[40]

My guess is that I erred on the question whether canon-law texts recognized the maxim because I was so impressed by the fact that by the mid-thirteenth century the need of the Church to protect itself from heresy dissolved any protection afforded by the maxim. That is the reason why Helmholz's neglect of the Inquisition and of heresy invalidated his thesis in his original article. In matters of heresy, the law denied all safeguards. In 1593 Cosin, the High Commissioner, observed that if a case involved treason against the monarch, a person should be tortured, and Cosin added, "But if this be lawful for treason against man, much more then, for that which is heresie indeede; being no lesse than treason against the devine majestie of God himselfe, who is King of kings, and Lord of lords."[41] Aquinas, who had advocated death for heretics, required truthful answers to incriminating questions about religious belief.[42] Beginning with Innocent III's introduction of the inquisitio as a criminal procedure of the canon law in 1215, the maxim lost any validity it had as a means of ensuring a right of silence, if probable grounds existed for the *inquisitio*. In canon law, *fama*, or common report, established probable grounds. The inquisitor himself was the sole judge of the existence of *fama*; his suspicions, however based or baseless, justified

---

[40]Levy, *Origins of the Fifth*, pp. 21, 446 n.27.
[41]Cosin, *Apologie*, vol. 3, pp. 213–214.
[42]Thomas Aquinas *Summa Theologica* vol. 10, pp. 255–258 (Quest. LXIX, 1st and 2nd Articles).

putting a suspect to the inquisition. He administered the oath *ex officio* and sought a confession of guilt. Helmholz's 1997 essay is distinguished by the fact that he emphasizes the conditions necessary to establish *fama* and the exceptions to the need for showing it. He generalizes that the right against self-incrimination was driven "by the rule of the European *ius commune*" rather than the English common law.

Helmholz alleges that I am "consistent only in treating any canonical precedent against the legality of the *ex officio* oath as of negligible importance in the privilege's development."[43] Since the precedent to which he refers is the *nemo tenetur* maxim, his statement is astonishingly misrepresentative. I refer to the maxim on my first page and with considerable frequency throughout the book. I close chapter 1 by noting that the history of the right against self-incrimination is enmeshed in the contests for supremacy between the accusatory and inquisitorial systems of criminal procedure, and between the common law and its rivals, canon and civil law. "The origins of the concept that 'no man is bound to accuse himself' (*nemo tenetur seipsum prodere*) can be seen only with a view of this breadth."[44] I track the acceptance of the maxim by common-law judges, beginning with Chief Justice Dyer in Leigh's case of 1568; I trace its appearance in manuals for justices of the peace and other law books, beginning with Anthony Fitzherbert's in 1583 and William Lambard's in 1588 to Geoffrey Gilbert's *Law of Evidence* in 1756 and Blackstone's *Commentaries* in 1776. I stress both the Catholic and the Puritan reliance on the maxim, its use by Chief Justice Coke, and its association with Magna Carta by advocates of the maxim.[45] In my last chapter on the establishment of the right in England, I observe that the *nemo tenetur* maxim had come a long way from its mysterious origins. In the final chapter of my book I say, "By

---

[43]Helmholz, "Origins," p. 967 n.25.

[44]Levy, *Origins of the Fifth* p. 42.

[45]Ibid., pp. 373–374. My ch. 3 is on Catholic reliance on the maxim, and the next several chapters deal with the Puritans and their lawyers' arguments relying on Magna Carta. See also notes 61–63 below.

1776 the principle of the *nemo tenetur* maxim was simply taken for granted and so deeply accepted that its constitutional expression had the mechanical quality of a ritualistic gesture in favor of a self-evident truth needing no explanation."[46] Again and again throughout the book I return to the maxim. I add emphatically that I consistently regard it as extremely important in the development of the right and give it substantial coverage.

The maxim undoubtedly protected against an obligation to disclose an unknown transgression. Requiring answers to incriminating questions, Helmholz says, "evidently ran counter to this principle."[47] Maybe it did, but the High Commission ignored that principle consistently. Helmholz knows this because he later observes that the rule against forced self-incrimination "was held not to apply where there was public knowledge that a crime had been committed, where the public had an interest in punishing the crime, and where there were legitimate indicia that the defendant being questioned had committed it." Under such circumstances, he acknowledges, "defendants had no right to refuse to plead or [to refuse] to answer specific questions about their crimes."[48] The "privilege did not then have an absolute character," he adds. That is a peculiar way to make the point that the privilege had an extraordinarily limited character: it was inapplicable when the Commission, which was the sole judge whether it could administer the oath, asked incriminating questions to which it demanded truthful responses. Failure to take the oath meant conviction *pro confesso*.[49]

Helmholz wrongly declares that "Levy's *Origins* wholly ignores evidence that actual arguments about the oath [*ex officio*] were being made at the time by ecclesiastical lawyers."[50] In fact I have an entire chapter on arguments about the oath by Archbishop John Whitgift and his Court of High Commission, in the

[46]Levy, *Origins of the Fifth*, p. 430.
[47]Helmholz, "Origins," pp. 981–982.
[48]Ibid., p. 983.
[49]Cosin, *Apologie*, vol. 3, pp. 43, 116.
[50]Helmholz, "Origins," p. 968.

course of which I present the views of Richard Cosin, a member of the Commission who was the foremost civil and canon lawyer of the time. I devote eight pages just to Cosin and to his book, *An Apologie for Sundrie Proceedings Ecclesiasticall* (London, 1593, 2nd ed.). I also give the arguments in Burrowe's case of Sir Henry Martin, another ecclesiastical lawyer who was the King's Advocate for the Commission.[51]

Without doubt Helmholz demonstrates the existence of the *nemo tenetur* maxim in canon and civil law—the *ius commune*—and he shows that those who relied on the maxim claimed that the Commission violated its own procedures in requiring the oath. I never thought otherwise. We differ, however, in salient respects. One is my emphasis on the legitimacy of requiring the oath and truthful responses to interrogatories if *fama* or reasonable suspicion existed as a preliminary condition. That is, the maxim had no effectiveness or applicability if the ecclesiastical court administering both the oath and the incriminating interrogatories alleged that it had reasonable suspicion. Common report or reasonable suspicion (*fama*) justified the inquisitorial procedure. The court itself, as observed earlier, possessed utter discretion to determine whether such suspicion existed.

Helmholz is not ignorant of this last fact. In 1990 he simply buried it or relegated it to a position of unimportance as an afterthought. Having stressed that the *nemo tenetur* doctrine was the canon-law basis for objections to the oath procedure and was the foremost basis of such objections, Helmholz several pages later found an exception to the "established rule" that the privilege existed in the civil and canon law. He did not reveal the exception until several more pages; then we finally learn that an ecclesiastical judge could "interrogate on his own authority when public fame circulated that a specific person had committed an offense," and a note adds the translation of a line from a canon-law treatise saying, "If the offense is notorious or famous he must

---

[51]Levy, *Origins of the Fifth*, pp. 109–135; on Cosin, see ibid., pp. 126, 129–133, 159–161, 255, 258.

respond."[52] In 1997 Helmholz's emphasis on *fama* as providing an obligation to reply accorded with my presentation for the most part, but he is inconsistent because he claims, "That there was a privilege against self-incrimination in the *ius commune*, there can be no doubt."[53] Oddly, Helmholz compares the right to "something like probable cause in our legal system, permitting a magistrate to carry out an essentially neutral role in criminal proceedings."[54]

And, although in 1997 Helmholz discourses at length on public fame, he reaches conclusions in which he rides off in all directions at once. The right against self-incrimination, he repeatedly says, existed in the *ius commune*, though he fails again and again to recall that public fame obligated a reply to incriminating interrogatories.[55] On the other hand, he acknowledges that the right against self-incrimination in the *ius commune* was "a limited right" and "it is even questionable whether one could actually speak of the privilege in the *ius commune* as an operative rule of law. . . ." There were "too many exceptions to the rule. . . ."[56] Nevertheless his thesis is that the right against self-incrimination was "driven" not by the common law but "rather by the rules of the European *ius commune*. . . ." If so, why was the right against self-incrimination alien to the law of continental nations? Helmholz cannot mean that the right derived from Spain, France, and Germany.

Among the various exceptions to the rule, one, in my opinion, derived from the role of the inquisitor who was hardly a neutral judge; he sat as accuser, prosecutor, judge, and jury, and his ob-

---

[52]Helmholz, "Origins," pp. 969, 972.

[53]Helmholz, "The Privilege and the *Ius Commune*: The Middle Ages to the Seventeenth Century," in Helmholz, ed., *The Privilege*, p. 9. See also, ibid., p. 23, where he repeats that because of the *nemo tenetur* maxim, "Long before any appearance of a privilege against self-incrimination in the common law, therefore, its underlying principle was found and discussed within the copious traditions of the European *ius commune*." Once again he neglected to observe that *fama* effaced the maxim.

[54]Helmholz, "The Privilege and the *Ius Commune*," pp. 9, 31, and "Origins," p. 977.

[55]E.g., Helmholz, "The Privilege and the *Ius Commune*," pp. 35, 48, 53, 61. See also ibid., pp. 27, 30–32, 295 n.66.

[56]Helmholz, "The Privilege and the *Ius Commune*," pp. 61, 62.

jective was to secure a confession of guilt. Moreover, Helmholz does not report that the inquisitor determined for himself whether public fame existed. From the time of the Fourth Lateran Council in 1215, no forum for the establishment of *fama* existed if the judge decided to proceed *ex officio mero*, that is, of his own accord or at his discretion. Helmholz claims that public fame had to meet strict requirements under the *ius commune*, but he adds, later, that opponents of the High Commission argued that "in practice, the High Commission judges and those in all English ecclesiastical courts were at fault for presuming the existence of the *fama publica*, routinely denying defendants' requests for an inquest into the issue."[57] Helmholz adds that the Commission's defenders had "continental authority" on their side. He fails to observe that in heresy cases the existence of public fame did not need to be proved by the testimony of trustworthy persons. The High Commission simply assumed that it existed. That's how the High Commission operated for decades.[58]

Helmholz insists that objection to the oath rested on "the letter of the Roman canon law" and that it did not rest "on the basis of supposed rights of conscience or as derived from Magna Carta or as a common law invention, as Levy's account suggests."[59] Helmholz's dismissal of conscience as a source of the right robs him of any understanding. Conscience was the most common basis of the claims that no person should be compelled to accuse himself in a case dealing with religion. Having ignored the Inquisition and the problem of heresy, Helmholz has blinded himself to claims based on conscience. He ought to scan the pages of John Foxe's *Book of Martyrs* (1563), which was the most influential and popular book in the English language, excepting the Bible. Foxe gave instance after instance of a right against involuntary self-incrimination having been claimed by victims of religious persecution, who, like Ralph Allerton in 1557, declared,

---

[57]Helmholz, "Origins," p. 978.
[58]Usher, *Rise and Fall of the High Commission*, remains the leading account.
[59]Helmholz, "Origins," p. 969.

"my conscience doth constrain me to accuse myself before you."[60]

It is nonsense to believe as Helmholz does that the right against self-incrimination derived from the canon law, which embodied inquisitional procedures whose objective was to coerce confessions; coercion even by torture was justified on the continent, where Helmholz's *ius commune* prevailed. The canon law did not recognize a right against self-incrimination beyond the maxim whose protection was extinguished by *fama*. If Helmholz's arguments were valid, continental nations would have developed a right against compulsory self-incrimination.

Because the canon law was against them, suspects had to be creative and invented the claim that conscience and Magna Carta authorized a right against self-incrimination. My book is thick with opponents and victims of ecclesiastical courts relying on conscience. As for Magna Carta, Robert Beale, clerk of the Privy Council and an aggressive champion of Puritan victims of the High Commission, was the first, in 1589, to conscript Magna Carta into service against the oath *ex officio* and all inquisitorial proceedings by the High Commission. He invented a significant fiction, which in time reached the stature of an article of constitutional faith, that Magna Carta outlawed forcing a person to be a witness against himself.[61] James Morice, another Puritan lawyer, published a book in 1598 in which he argued at length that the *nemo tenetur* maxim derived from Magna Carta.[62] A third Puritan lawyer, Nicholas Fuller, who had served in the Commons with Beale and Morice, elaborately advocated the same thesis.[63]

Helmholz restates his thesis about the canon law and the *ius commune* in different terms. "Despite the existence of many ex-

[60]8 *The Acts and Monuments of John Foxe: A New and Complete Edition*, ed. Stephen R. Cattley (London, 1837–1841), p. 368.

[61]Robert, Beale, "A Collection shewinge what jurisdiction the clergie hath . . . ," 1589–1590, Cotton MSS, Cleopatra F.I., fols. 1–49. See also 2 Strype, *Whitgift* 30.

[62]James, Morice, *A brief treatise of Oaths exacted by Ordinaries and Ecclesiasticall Judges* (London, 1598), pp. 8–18, 22, 26–32, 37, 47.

[63]*The Argument of Master Nicholas Fuller in the Case of Thomas Lad and Richard Maunsell, his clients* (1607), pp. 7–13, 28–29.

ceptions," he concludes, "the rule *nemo tenetur prodere seipsum* still applied in the absence of public notoriety indicating that an accused had committed a crime, and it still applied to prohibit judicial fishing expeditions to search out a defendant's private faults."[64] That may well have been true in cases of ordinary crime, but not in heresy cases, when merely to admit one's Protestant beliefs in Catholic Europe or deviance from the Church of England in Britain was sufficient to convict.

The fundamental errors throughout Helmholz's articles, until his 1997 essay, were his failures to acknowledge that the Inquisition changed the rules and that even in England the canon law, following the *inquisitio* in heresy cases, demanded self-incrimination. That a medievalist should ever have ignored the Inquisition is extraordinary. Moreover he did not merely relegate to the back pages the fact that the *nemo tenetur* maxim had no force if public fame existed. The thrust of his first article is that the canon law originated the maxim, as if public fame did not extinguish it. When Helmholz in a different article returns to his attack on me, he writes: "The principle that no one should be compelled to incriminate himself was found in the most basic guides to that law [*ius commune*], the *glossa ordinaria* to the Gregorian Decretals, and it was also stated prominently in many 16th and 17th century treatises on civilian procedure."[65] In the second article Helmholz does not even refer to the fact that the canon law allowed incriminatory questioning and demanded responses if public fame or common report existed, the maxim notwithstanding. When John H. Langbein commented on Helmholz's criticism of my book, Langbein did not refer to public fame either, though it subverted Helmholz's point. Langbein wrote:[66]

In a very important article, Richard Helmholz has recently shown how prominently the *nemo tenetur* maxim appeared in the

---

[64]Ibid., p. 984.
[65]R. H. Helmholz, "Continental Law and Common Law: Historical Strangers or Companions?" 1990 *Duke Law Journal* pp. 1207, 1218.
[66]Langbein, "Historical Origins," p. 1072.

Continental sources of the later Middle Ages and the renaissance. He has established that the *nemo tenetur* maxim influenced practice in the English ecclesiastic courts long before anybody in England started complaining about Star Chamber or the Court of High Commission. Helmholz's work ... delivers a devastating refutation of Leonard Levy's effort to portray the privilege against self-incrimination as an English invention intended to protect the indigenous adversarial criminal procedure against incursions of European inquisitorial procedure.

Perhaps Langbein believes that the *nemo tenetur* maxim triumphed effectively in the High Commission even when it discerned the existence of public fame. If so, he is wrong in that regard as well as in his belief that Helmholz's criticism of my book has validity.

M. R. T. MacNair, another of my critics, understands that an accused person if reasonably suspected could be required to swear answers to incriminating interrogatories. He knows that the *nemo tenetur* maxim had no effectiveness once the need to combat heresy induced canon-law authorities to find a way around the maxim, and he realizes that what once had been an extraordinary process of interrogating the accused became the normal practice in the *ius commune*. But MacNair and I disagree on several other significant matters.

He argues that the right first emerged on behalf of witnesses and in civil cases involving allegations of crime before the criminal defendant won a right to refuse answering incriminating questions. Like Helmholz, MacNair also believes that the right came into English law from the canon law and the continental civil law. Furthermore he asserts that "it is only in the very late seventeenth or early eighteenth centuries that there are signs in the cases of the idea of a general right to silence in a face of charges of crime, distinctive to the common law."[67] In fact the "signs" go back to Leigh's case of 1568 in which the opinion of

[67]MacNair, "Early Development." p. 67.

Chief Justice James Dyer for his Court of Common Pleas has been quoted above.[68]

The reason that MacNair dates the emergence of the right so late is that he entirely misconceives it. He rejects my dating the establishment of the right in the Restoration, because, he claims, "judges continued to put incriminating questions to the accused in ordinary criminal trials until considerably later."[69] Indeed they did, but the right against self-incrimination is not a right that bars incriminatory interrogation; it is, rather, a right to remain silent in the face of such interrogation. On the basis of MacNair's faulty logic one could argue that the right did not exist until after the decision of *Miranda v. Arizona* in 1966, in which the Supreme Court held that the inherently compulsive character of in-custody interrogation had to be offset by procedural safeguards to insure obedience to the right to silence.[70] MacNair reasons that since the *nemo tenetur* maxim derived from the canon law, then equity law, which shared a similar background, could be expected to respect the rule. He produces several cases in which Chancery applied a version of the *nemo tenetur* maxim. He also finds that the rule that one need not respond to charges carrying a criminal liability, "in its application to witnesses is stated in Cosin and was affirmed, as far as the church courts went, by Whitgift in 1603."[71] MacNair cites me as his authority; for Whitgift I rely on a Hampton Court Conference reported in *State Trials*.[72] But its date is 1604, not 1603, and Whitgift referred not to witnesses but to the party: ". . . if the Article touch the party for life, liberty, or scandal, he may refuse to answer."[73] Mac-Nair accurately says that Cosin declared that the maxim applied to a witness, but he neglects to say that Cosin also applied it to

---

[68]Case of Thomas Leigh, 2 Brownlow & Goldesborough 271–272; 12 Coke's Rep. 26, 27; 3 Bulstrode 48, 50.

[69]MacNair, "Early Development," p. 69.

[70]384 U.S. 436 (1966).

[71]MacNair, "Early Development," p. 78.

[72]"Proceedings in a Conference at Hampton Court," 2 *State Trials* 86.

[73]Levy, *Origins of the Fifth*, p. 212.

a defendant.[74] The Star Chamber, as MacNair affirms, also applied it to witnesses, but, again, he fails to say that the Star Chamber also applied it to parties. William Hudson, the Star Chamber lawyer whose book MacNair cites, said that a defendant might, with the advice of counsel, demur to questions for many reasons, among them "that the matter in charge tendeth to accuse the defendant of some crime which may be capital; in which case *nemo tenetur prodere seipsum....*" And Hudson added, "neither must it question the party to accuse him of crime."[75]

"At common law," MacNair writes, "there is a dictum of Hyde CJ in Fitzpatricks' Trial (1631) in the *State Trials* which suggests that the principle was already recognized then."[76] That is true, but oversimplifies. After my discussion of Fitzpatrick's case, I add:[77]

> Even in such a case, however, the right against self-incrimination existed in a common law court only in the sense that the defendant could not be required to answer involuntarily; nevertheless, his silence customarily spoke against him. It invited adverse comment from the prosecution and perhaps even from the trial judge, prejudicing the jury's deliberations.... [I]f the defendant, whose testimony was the focal point of the trial, did not satisfactorily contest the prosecution's case, if, that is, he remained silent, resting on a claim that the law did not oblige him to accuse himself, he could rely on a verdict of guilty.

As for MacNair's point that the case of 1631 suggests that the principle was already recognized, the response must be that the principle went back more than sixty years to Leigh's case in

---

[74]Cosin, *Apologie*, Part III, pp. 113–114.

[75]William Hudson, *A Treatise of the Court of Star Chamber* (ante 1621), in 2 Francis Hargrave, ed., *Collectanea Juridica*, pp. 64, 164, 169, 208–209.

[76]MacNair, "Early Development," p. 78.

[77]Levy, *Origins of the Fifth*, pp. 264–265.

1568. MacNair's statement that witnesses before the Star Chamber were not compelled to incriminate themselves neglects to notice that the Star Chamber recognized the right as early as 1580 in the case of Thomas Tresham.[78]

"The privilege and the *nemo tenetur* maxim are clearly applied to a witness," MacNair adds, "in KB [Kings Bench] in Anon (1647), before Lilburne's trial for treason in 1649, which both Wigmore and Levy take to be the starting point of the privilege at common law. . . ."[79] That is also mistaken. I never said that Lilburne's trial of 1649 marked a "starting point" because, as noted, I relied on Leigh's case of 1568 as the starting point. As for Lilburne's case, I said that after 1649, the right was "established," meaning that in subsequent cases the common-law courts acknowledged it without dispute.[80]

Despite MacNair's finding that the common law by 1631 recognized the principle that no one should be forced to incriminate himself, he contends that the right did "not become established after the trial of John Lilburne in 1649. The basic reason is the continuation of the practice of interrogating the accused (not on oath) in felony trials on indictment up to the mid-eighteenth century."[81] As noted above, MacNair does not understand that the right protects a person from the need to reply truthfully to incriminating questions but does not bar the questions. I find difficulty in reconciling his views that the right was clearly applied to a witness in 1647 but was not established until the practice of interrogating the accused at his trial ceased.

MacNair dates the establishment of the right in "the period after the Revolution of 1688." Although he notices that I relied on earlier cases respecting the right—Lilburne's in 1649, Scroop's in 1660, and Penn and Mead's in 1670—he asserts, without any evidence to back up his point, that "these were all very

[78]Ibid., p. 105; see note 11 above for citation to Tresham's case.
[79]MacNair, "Early Development," pp. 78–79.
[80]Levy, *Origins of the Fifth*, p. 313.
[81]MacNair, "Early Development," p. 79.

unusual cases, in which the judges may have been exceptionally concerned to show how fair they were."[82] Adrian Scroop was a Puritan regicide who was tried for treason. Chief Justice Kelyng asked whether Scroop confessed to having sat on a tribunal on the day it handed down its sentence against Charles I, but Kelyng added: "You are not bound to answer me, but if you will not, we must prove it."[83] In *Origins of the Fifth*, I pointed out that this was the first time a trial judge voluntarily apprised the defendant of his right to remain silent.[84] In that sense alone, the case was unusual. William Penn and William Mead, of course, were Quaker leaders who refused to swear allegiance to Charles II.[85] They were aggressive about refusing to incriminate themselves, and the judge in their case defensively insisted that he was not trying to incriminate them. He was not bending over backward to be fair.[86]

The fact is that during the Restoration, the right was routinely acknowledged by judges, even by those with reputations for severity and even in sensational trials. In 1679, at the treason trial of Father Thomas White, head of the Jesuits, the notorious Titus Oates wanted to ask a defense witness whether he was a priest, and Lord Chief Justice Scroggs, whose misbehavior on the bench during these trials was compared by Sir James Fitzjames Stephen "unfavourably even with the brutality of Jeffries [a high court justice infamous for his cruelty]," interposed to protect the witness: "That would be a hard question to put to him to make him accuse himself. It would bring him a danger of treason."[87]

MacNair, having dismissed Lilburne's, Scroop's, and Penn and Mead's cases as unusual, ignored other cases that I discussed because, he alleged, they "are not at common law." But they were. Reading's case of 1679 was a common-law case[88] as was

[82]Ibid., p. 82.
[83]Trial of Adrian Scroop, 5 *State Trials* 1034, 1039 (1660).
[84]Levy, *Origins of the Fifth*, p. 314.
[85]Trial of William Penn and William Mead, 6 *State Trials* 951 (1670).
[86]Ibid., pp. 957–958, 960. See my discussion in *Origins of the Fifth*, pp. 314–315.
[87]The Trial of Thomas White, 7 *State Trials* 311, p. 361.
[88]The Trial of Nathanael Reading, 7 *State Trials* 259, pp. 296–297 (1679).

Langhorn's of the same year.[89] Moreover, Judge George Jeffries respected the right in Thomas Roswell's trial in 1684 and in Titus Oates's trial in 1685, also common-law cases.[90] Indeed, the common-law courts developed so indulgent an attitude toward the right against self-incrimination that they sometimes prevented incriminatory questions from being asked, as in the example of Thomas White's case given above, and they extended the right to prevent not only self-incrimination but self-disgrace. They also applied the right in civil cases with respect to questions that could be used against a person in a criminal proceeding, and even with respect to questions that might expose one to the forfeiture of property by way of a penalty. A ruling of 1704 foreshadowed the development of a new doctrine that the right, which originated to protect against the compulsion of oral testimony, applied also to papers and documents that might incriminate.[91] In sum, MacNair's work is unreliable, his criticisms invalid.

John H. Langbein, another critic, is driven by the fixed idea that if a person can be questioned, no right against self-incrimination can exist.[92] Langbein, like Gray and MacNair, simply fails to understand that the right had to be claimed by the defendant. Historically it was a fighting right: unless invoked it offered no protection. It vested an option to refuse answer but did not ban interrogation nor taint a voluntary confession as improper evidence. Incriminating statements made by a suspect at his preliminary examination or even at arraignment could always be used with devastating effect at his trial. That a person might

[89]Trial of Richard Langhorn, 7 *State Trials* 418, p. 435 (1679).

[90]Trial of Thomas Roswell, 10 *State Trials* 147, p. 169 (1684), and Trial of Titus Oates, 10 *State Trials* 1079, 1099–1100 (1685).

[91]On disgrace, see Trial of Peter Cook 13 *State Trials* 311, pp. 334–335 (1696), and for earlier precedents Levy, *Origins of The Fifth*, pp. 196, 198, 317; for the citation of dozens of civil cases, and for extension of the right to personal papers, see Levy, *Origins of the Fifth*, pp. 491–492, n.30.

[92]Langbein, "Historical Origins," p. 1047, and John H. Langbein, "The Privilege and Common Law Procedure," ch. 4 in Helmholz, ed., *The Privilege*, pp. 112, 312 n.3. Langbein's 1997 essay is substantially the same as his earlier one, even as to phraseology.

unwittingly incriminate himself when questioned in no way impaired his legal right to refuse to answer.

According to Langbein, the right cannot be said to exist until such time as defense counsel made it possible for the defendant not to speak at all. The right, he believes, could not function unless the defendant had counsel.[93] That is the sole string in his bow. He dates the "true origins" of the right "at the end of the eighteenth century."[94] That overlooks too much evidence. Langbein leapfrogs evidence rather than confront and evaluate it. Dating the origins of the right as late as he does ignores Leigh's case as well as later ones such as Lilburne's, Scroop's, and Penn's cases, and others such as the witness Mr. Holder, in 1649. Moreover Lord Chief Baron Geoffrey Gilbert, in his *Law of Evidence*, written before 1726 (though not published until thirty years later), stated that confessions "must be voluntary and without Compulsion; for our Law in this differs from the Civil Law, that it will not force any Man to accuse himself; and in this we do certainly follow the Law of Nature, which commands every Man to endeavour his own Preservation. . . ."[95] Obviously Gilbert was stating a familiar and long-established right. In 1730 Sollom Emlyn, introducing his edition of the collected state trials, boasted that Englishmen enjoyed "the benefit of that just and reasonable Maxim, *Nemo tenetur accusare seipsum*."[96] So too Benjamin Franklin, writing in 1735, declared, "It was contrary to the common Right of Mankind no Man being obliged to furnish Matter of Accusation against himself."[97] Emlyn, Gilbert, and Franklin all made their points in a manner indicating that the right was an old one.

Langbein's thesis is that the right "was the work of defense

[93]Langbein, "The Privilege and Common Law Criminal Procedure," in Helmholz, ed., *The Privilege*, p. 110.

[94]Langbein, "Historical Origins," p. 1047.

[95]Geoffrey Gilbert, *The Law of Evidence by a Late Learned Judge* (London, 1756), pp. 139–140.

[96]*State Trials*, p. xxv.

[97]Benjamin Franklin, "Some Observations on the Proceedings against the Rev. Mr. Hemphill," in Leonard W. Labaree et al., eds., *Papers of Benjamin Franklin* (New Haven, Conn., 1959), vol. 2, p. 37; see also pp. 44, 45, 47, 49.

counsel" who entered the ordinary criminal trial in the 1730s.[98] I do not disagree about the importance of counsel, but they did not originate the right; its early advocates, such as Lilburne and Penn, had no counsel. Counsel solidified the right rather than created it. Langbein ignores the credit that I attribute to counsel. He has a habit of saying something as if no one had ever said it before. Many of his points merely rephrase passages in my book. Yet he writes about justices of the peace as if no one else knew about them.[99] He writes about the importance of counsel as if I had not declared that "the right to counsel was easily the most valuable to the accused's armory of defense" and that the right against self-incrimination was "associated with the right to counsel and to have witnesses on behalf of the defendant, so that his lips could be sealed against the government's questions or accusations."[100]

I also argued that by the mid-eighteenth century a practice had developed of permitting counsel to do everything for the defendant accused of felony except address the jury for him. By then both judicial and statutory alterations in procedure made it possible for a defendant to present his defense through witnesses and by counsel. As a result, though the defendant always retained the right to address the court unsworn at the close of his trials, and to range freely over matters of his choice, he was no longer obliged to speak out personally in order to get his story before the jury, to rebut incriminating evidence, or to answer accusations by the prosecution.

Pressing, urging, and bullying the defendant began to die out, and after Lord Holt died in 1710, the prosecution began making its case without interrogating him at all at his trial.[101] The security of the state after the revolution of 1689 was the most important force working for greater fairness in criminal trials. The incidence of treason trials dropped precipitously, and political tri-

---

[98]Langbein, "Historical Origins," p. 1047.
[99]Langbein, "Historical Origins," pp. 1059–1061, and Levy, *Origins of the Fifth*, pp. 35, 325, 492–494.
[100]Levy, *Origins of the Fifth*, p. 322.
[101]Ibid., p. 323.

als of any sort also became far fewer. John Pollock, the historian of the Popish Plot, describing the late Restoration period, ably summarized the matter:[102]

> The inquisitorial nature of the old trial was gradually disappearing. [T]he prisoner was no longer systematically questioned in court. When he was questioned, it was now, as if he were innocent, in his favour. His examination was no longer what it had been in the days of Elizabeth and James I, the very essence of the trial. Questions were still put to him, but now they were directed by judges and not by the prosecution. The prisoner moreover could, if he wished, refuse to answer questions put to him.

Langbein argues that the right could not emerge as long as defendants had to conduct their own defense. In fact, however, the right emerged because defendants without counsel asserted that they had no obligation to accuse themselves. Langbein flirts with deception to make his point, saying, for example, that the pretrial system of the later seventeenth century, when I claim that the right "prevailed supreme" during a criminal trial, was "antithetical to any such privilege."[103] That gives the impression that I don't know the nature of the pretrial system. In later pages, however, Langbein quotes me as saying that in the pretrial stages of a case, "inquisitorial tactics were routine" and, "For all practical purposes, the right against self-incrimination scarcely existed in the pretrial stages of a criminal proceeding."[104]

Then Langbein says that I have made an important "admission," as if I have been compelled to concede a point that I deplore. I did not admit anything; I merely described a fact. "Levy requires us to believe," Langbein adds, "that the seventeenth-century common law courts and their supporting political authorities created a self-evidently schizophrenic crimi-

---

[102]John Pollock, *The Popish Plot: A Study in the History of the Reign of Charles II* (Cambridge, England, 1944), pp. 294–295.

[103]Langbein, "Historical Origins," p. 1059, and Langbein, "The Privilege," in Helmholz, ed., *The Privilege*, pp. 122, 123.

[104]Levy, *Origins of the Fifth*, p. 325.

nal procedure—that they enshrined a privilege against self-incrimination at trials while busily gutting it in the pretrial."[105] My response is that in the very late eighteenth century, when defense counsel, according to Langbein, had made the right possible at last, it was still being gutted by justices of the peace in the pretrial stages of a criminal case. Indeed, a suspect lacked the right to be warned that he need not answer, because the authorities were under no legal obligation to apprise him of his right. That reform did not come in England until Sir John Jervis's Act in 1848, and in the United States more than a century later the matter was still a subject of acute constitutional controversy.

Langbein rightly says that before defense counsels were able to manage a prisoner's defense, the system "pressured the criminal defendant to speak."[106] He finds that invocations of the right were "isolated" during a trial, when the defendant spoke constantly, supposedly in disregard of the right.[107] The fact that they spoke does not mean that defendants were forced to confess their guilt at their trials. They spoke to deny the charges against them and to repudiate the prosecution's evidence. They invoked the right only when necessary to respond to a question, the answer to which might incriminate. Langbein does not show otherwise. He does not seem to know the difference between a defense that rebuts the prosecution and an answer relying on the right.

Like Helmholz and MacNair, whose work he praises, Langbein find that the *ius commune*, thanks to its canon-law antecedents, was familiar with the *nemo tenetur* maxim. Langbein decidedly gives the impression that I would be surprised to learn that, because I portray the right as an English invention. Indeed it was. It was not a canon-law invention because the canon law merely protected the revelation of an unsuspected crime but required a suspected person to incriminate himself. Langbein

---

[105]Langbein, "Historical Origins," p. 1062, and Langbein, "The Privilege," in Helmholz, ed., *The Privilege*, p. 124.
[106]Ibid., p. 1069.
[107]Ibid., p. 1071.

never refers to public fame or ill repute, the existence of which the ecclesiastical court determined for itself, and having done so compelled replies to incriminating interrogatories; ill repute or reasonable suspicion extinguished a right to rely on the *nemo tenetur* maxim. Langbein also writes about the oath *ex officio* without citing my work, though I have a forty-page chapter on the oath and refer to it elsewhere frequently.

"It seems odd to assert, as Levy does," says Langbein, "that the privilege 'prevailed supreme' at trial when the pretrial procedure was so resolutely organized as to render any such trial privilege ineffectual."[108] Given the significant differences between the pretrial and trial stages, I don't know why Langbein sees oddity. I think it much odder that after defense counsel, according to Langbein, had established the right, the pretrial examination of a suspect remained as inquisitorial as it had been before counsel was common at trials, and it continued that way until the mid-nineteenth century. I think it odd too that Langbein should believe that the right against self-incrimination "originated" within the European tradition, as a subprinciple of inquisitorial procedure," centuries before the adversary system of criminal procedure finally produced the right in England in the late eighteenth century.[109] It is odder still that Langbein favorably quotes Gray's remark that the common-law courts never said that the civil/canon-law courts "could not expose individuals to self-incrimination."[110] They could and did expose people to self-incrimination, notwithstanding the supposed shield of the *nemo tenetur* maxim. If Gray is the right on this point, as I believe he is, Helmholz, MacNair, and Langbein cannot be right in their belief that the canon law protected against self-incrimination.

Langbein can't distinguish between a defendant's answering a question by denying the charges and a defendant's refusal to answer on grounds of self-incrimination. He says that defendants

[108]Ibid., p. 1061.
[109]Ibid., p. 1072.
[110]Ibid., p. 1073 n.121.

claimed the right "in isolated remarks, while utterly disregarding any supposed privilege against self-incrimination."[111] Supposed? Is he implying that the "privilege" was just a fiction? The point misleads, for the defendant spoke to answer charges, invoking his right only when an answer might incriminate him.

Langbein says that Lilburne "responded at his trial to prosecution evidence and questioning as did other defendants of the age. . . . This behavior is quite difficult to reconcile with Levy's claim that Lilburne was insisting on a privilege against self-incrimination."[112] Lilburne demanded many rights—among them a copy of the indictment, representation by counsel, and compulsory production of witnesses in his behalf—and invoked a right to silence only when necessary to support his refusal to respond to any questions "concerning" himself.[113] Langbein actually declares that Lilburne "was an insignificant figure in the development of the privilege" and that his reputation "derived mainly from his spirited defense to treason charges" in 1649.[114] In fact Lilburne, who was the leader of the Leveller faction and the most popular man in England, was the first to claim the right against self-incrimination before a legislative investigating committee; he defended the right in widely read pamphlets; he incorporated it within constitutional documents which he advocated; and he justified the right at some length, relying, however factually wrong, on Magna Carta and the Petition of Right.[115] Leveller documents, one after the other with monotonous regularity, demanded the right. It appeared most importantly in a clause drafted by Lilburne in the magnificent 1648 "Second Agreement of People" and again in 1649 in the democratic "Third Agreement of the People." Lilburne's example of relying on the right to refuse to testify against himself inspired

[111]Ibid., p. 1081.
[112]Ibid., p. 1077 n.131.
[113]Levy, *Origins of the Fifth*, pp. 288–290, 296, 298, 299, 304, 307.
[114]Langbein, "Historical Origins," p. 1076 n.131, and Langbein, "The Privilege," in Helmholz, ed., *The Privilege*, pp. 138, 357.
[115]Levy, *Origins of the Fifth*, pp. 288–291.

many others to do likewise. One person colorfully refused "to cut our owne throats with our tongues."[116] Lilburne's advocacy of the right and his exceptional prominence made him its foremost champion, especially because it was he who first won judicial respect for it.

Langbein asserts that judges who "supposedly" vindicated the right in the notorious Popish Plot trials were the Stuart bullies, Scroggs and Jeffries. He finds it "difficult to imagine" that such judges should have recognized the right, and he criticizes me for being "untroubled" in "celebrating the spectacle of the late-Stuart judiciary serving as the engine that crafted the privilege." He says I "exult" in showing how scrupulously the courts adhered to the right against self-incrimination.[117] Langbein's emotional reaction to Scroggs and Jeffries seems to have impoverished his imagination, but no imagination is necessary in the face of facts. The two notorious judges did in fact respect the right, and I give chapter and verse as proof, none of which Langbein challenges. I am untroubled by their having respected the right but not exultant, because I have no personal stake in the outcome. I did, however, say of the two that they "made their names synonymous for judicial tyranny."[118] I also said that as a result of the Popish Plot trials, fourteen innocent men were executed for treason, but I must add there that an hysterical government prosecuted them and hysterical juries convicted them, not the presiding judges. Indeed, in my book and above in this article I quote John Pollock, the master historian of the Popish Plot, on the fairness of the trials. Scroggs did protect a defense witness in the case of Father Thomas White, and Jeffries, as I showed, displayed "tenderness toward the witness's right not to be questioned against himself."[119]

Langbein sarcastically says that I depict the right "as such an

[116]Ibid., p. 297.
[117]Ibid., p. 318, and Langbein, "Historical Origins," p. 1082, and Langbein, "The Privilege," in Helmholz, ed., *The Privilege*, p. 125.
[118]Levy, *Origins of the Fifth*, p. 316.
[119]Ibid., p. 319.

historical inevitability that the only puzzle is to wonder why it took the dummies so long to see the light."[120] Nowhere in my book do I use such a tone or such language. In what appears to me to be a non sequitur, Langbein immediately adds "as an example" of my belittling of others that I say I call the right a right because it is one. Saying so calls no one a dummy. I had no notion that describing a provision of the Bill of Rights as a right instead of a privilege was remarkable in any way. It was a privilege in England but not in the United States after ratification of the Fifth Amendment.

Eben Moglen of Columbia Law School has written an article against my book that I regard as error-prone and lacking in evidential support. Unlike other critics, Moglen emphasizes the American history of the right against self-incrimination during the colonial and early national periods. He purports to show that the criminal justice system showed less tenderness toward the defendant than I claimed it did, though I am not aware of making a claim about the system's tenderness. On the other hand, Moglen contradictorily says that in exalting the jury system "Americans discovered a tenderness concerning the process that extracted confessions."[121]

Moglen also asserts the mistaken notion that the first state constitutional provisions on self-incrimination were not acknowledgments of a long-accepted fundamental right but rather were "reflections of the contentious prerevolutionary constitutional debate, in which North American advocates made sweeping and often antiquarian legal claims protecting or expanding their power to resist Imperial control."[122] And in 1997, after noting American opposition to admiralty procedures, Moglen al-

---

[120]Langbein, "Historical Origins," p. 1080 and Langbein, "The Privilege," in Helmholz, ed., *The Privilege*, p. 142.

[121]Eben Moglen, "Taking the Fifth: Reconsidering the Origins of the Constitutional Privilege Against Self-Incrimination," 92 *Michigan Law Review*, p. 1112, and Eben Moglen, "The Privilege in British North America: The Colonial Period of the Fifth Amendment," in Helmholz, ed., *The Privilege*, p. 176. Moglen's second article substantially recapitulates the earlier one.

[122]Ibid., pp. 1086, 1087.

leged, "As the Admiralty grievance rose in intensity, after 1765, the idea of a fundamental law privilege against coercive testimonial pressure further embedded itself in the language of constitutional debate."[123] But during the course of the entire article he does not produce a single American complaint that Britain violated the right against self-incrimination, nor, as a matter of fact, does he produce a single example of any American argument against Britain having anything to do with the right against self-incrimination. He produces no such examples because none exists.[124] The constitutional debate between Britain and her American colonies dealt with other matters. Moglen ignores the 1768 cases of Henry Laurens and John Hancock, both of which I reported. He ignores too the 1770 instruction of Attorney General Andrew Allen to the collector of the port of Philadelphia: "I am very clear in the opinion that the Court of Admiralty cannot with propriety oblige any persons to answer interrogatories which may have a tendency to criminate themselves, or subject them to a penalty, it being contrary to any principle of Reason and the Laws of England."[125]

On the question whether the right was regarded as fundamental, I relied on the fact that the primary sources dealing with the framing of the first state constitutions reveal nothing about the right, which seven of the thirteen original states, plus Vermont, constitutionally protected. The fact that there was no discussion strikes me as revealing that none was needed because the right was accepted as a fundamental part of the common law. Attorney General Allen's 1770 statement affirms that, as does the

[123]Moglen, "The Privilege in British North America," in Helmholz, ed., *The Privilege*, p. 176.

[124]Moglen does give the humorous instance of a Boston pamphleteer imagining what might befall Samuel Adams if the customs commissioners sued him in an admiralty court, saying, "Once he was sworn, he should expect: 'Pray Sir, when did you kiss your maid Mary?—Where? and in what manner? ... Did you lay with her in the barn? Or in your own house?" in Moglen, "Taking the Fifth," p. 1116. This is hardly an example of exposure to criminal prosecution resulting from involuntary self-incrimination.

[125]Quoted in Oliver M. Dickerson, *The Navigation Acts and the American Revolution* (Philadelphia, 1951), p. 230, quoting the *Pennsylvania Journal*, Oct. 19, 1769.

testimony of Benjamin Franklin in 1735. In that year a special commission on inquiry of the Presbyterian synod of Philadelphia examined the unorthodox beliefs of Samuel Hemphill, a Presbyterian minister who had deistic ideas. The commission, censuring Hemphill's beliefs as "Unsound and Dangerous," suspended him from his ministry. Franklin, who liked Hemphill's sermons, wrote an indignant pamphlet, reporting that Hemphill had refused to submit his sermons to the commission because "It was contrary to the common Right of Mankind, no Man being obligated to furnish Matter of Accusation against himself." Franklin condemned the Presbyterian commission for aping "that hellish Tribunal the Inquisition" which extorted confessions.[126] I prefer Franklin's testimony to Moglen's on eighteenth-century beliefs on the question whether state constitutional provisions on self-incrimination acknowledged a fundamental right.

Moreover, in my book I produce considerable evidence that Moglen ignores to show that Franklin's view was a shared one. In Massachusetts, for example, in 1754, a liquor excise bill required consumers to report, on oath, to tax collectors on the amount spent by them for liquor; the bill was widely condemned as requiring self-incrimination, and the governor refused to sign it because it violated "natural Rights."[127] In the same year a witness before the Massachusetts House, Royal Tyler, parried all questions by invoking his right against self-incrimination: "and the only Answer he would make," the record states, "was *Nemo tenetur seipsum Accusare*; or, A right of Silence was the Privilege of every Englishman"—a magnificent free translation.[128]

Moglen seems also to be of the opinion that state adoption of

---

[126]Franklin, "Some Observations on the Proceedings against The Rev. Mr. Hemphill," in Labaree et al., *Papers of Benjamin Franklin*, vol. 2, p. 37; see also pp. 44, 45, 47, 49.

[127]*The Boston Post-Boy*, May 28, 1753. John Lovell, *Freedom, the First Blessings* (Boston, 1754), p. 1; Samuel Cooper, *The Crisis* (Boston, 1754), pp. 5–6; and, for the governor's remark, John F. Burns, *Controversies Between Royal Governors and Their Assemblies in the North American Colonies* (1923), pp. 132–133. See also Levy, *Origins of the Fifth*, pp. 385–386.

[128]*Journals of the House of Representatives of Massachusetts* (1754–1755) (Boston 1956), vol. 31, pp. 63–64.

the common law meant recognition of the "privilege."[129] I too have taken the position that in American thinking, "the common law was a repository of constitutional principles that secured individual rights against government intrusion," and that the right evolved in America as part of the reception of the common law's accusatorial system of criminal procedure.[130] But I recognize that in the four states that failed to protect the right constitutionally, adoption of the common law did not necessarily imply that protection of the right. Proof must be produced that the right was actually protected. Moglen does not do that; I do. He has nothing on the right in New York in the period before its first state constitution, which did not recognize the right.

New York substantially adopted the common law (excepting as to establishments of religion) yet also redundantly guaranteed trial by jury and the right to indictment, which were secured by the common law. I found the process of selecting rights for inclusion or exclusion in New York's constitution to be "baffling."[131] Contrary to Moglen, I did not describe as baffling the fact that although New York's constitution contained no provision on the right, the state recommended an amendment to the federal constitution protecting the right. Moglen is simply wrong as to what I described as baffling.[132] I found baffling the fact that New York, the locale of the Zenger case, did not constitutionally protect freedom of the press or, for that matter, the writ of habeas corpus, and New York failed also to protect against unreasonable search and seizure, ex post facto laws, and double jeopardy.

Despite the absence of a constitutional protection for the right in New York, that province did respect it. In 1702, for example, William Atwood, the provincial chief justice, and Samuel Shelton Broughton, the attorney general, acknowledged the right in connection with the treason trial of Bayard and Hutchins.[133] In

---

[129]Moglen, "Taking the Fifth," p. 1120.
[130]Levy, *Origins of the Fifth*, pp. 333, 338.
[131]Ibid., p. 411.
[132] Moglen, "The Privilege in British North America," in Helmholz, ed., *The Privilege*, p. 180.

1769, in the sensational McDougall case, the legislature offered to a witness immunity against prosecution so that his testimony could not be used against him criminally, while the subject of the investigation, Alexander McDougall, refused to answer on grounds of self-incrimination and double jeopardy.[134] These examples, two among several, invalidate the claim by Julius Goebel and T. Raymond Naughton, in their mammoth *Law Enforcement in Colonial New York: A Study in Criminal Procedure* (1664–1776): "We think that the existence before the Revolution of a privilege of defendants is an illusion. The fruit grown from the seed of the maxim *nemo tenetur prodere seipso* was an exotic of Westminister Hall, and of it neither the local justices in England nor in New York had eaten, or if they had, they took good care to keep their knowledge to themselves."[135] Goebel and Naughton added, again wrongly, "It is obviously idle to imagine that a 'principle' which even Baron Gilbert forbears to mention, should have been cosseted in our own courts."[136] Moglen endorses that conclusion, adding that the "flavor" of that exotic fruit was one with which "the provincial lawyers were unacquainted."[137]

But Gilbert did mention the principle, and New York lawyers, as well as those of other colonies, knew it. Gilbert's *Law of Evidence*, written before his death in 1726 but not published until 1756, was the first book on the subject of any analytic merit, as Goebel and Naughton say. Gilbert, whose words have been quoted above, stated that the law did not force any man to accuse himself—a principle of "the Law of Nature." His book was used

---

[133]Rex F. Bayard, 14 *State Trials* 471–506 (1702); Samuel Bayard to Adderly and Lodwick, Jan. 27 and 28, 1702, in B. O'Callaghan and B. Fernow, eds., *Documents Relative to the Colonial History of the State of New-York* (Albany, N.Y., 1853), vol. 4, pp. 945, 947; Sir Edward Northey to Board of Trade, Apr. 25, 1702, in ibid., p. 954; and 8 MS New York Council Minutes, New York State Library, Albany, N.Y., Jan. 21, 1702, 302–303. 13 "The Case of William Atwood, Esq." (1703), New-York Historical Society, *Collections*, 269.

[134]Alexander McDougall, "To the Freeholders," *New-York Gazette: or, the Weekly Post-Boy,* Dec. 24, 1770, ibid., Mar. 25, 1771. See Levy, *Origins of the Fifth,* pp. 399–401, on the McDougall case.

[135]Julius Goebel and T. Raymond Naughton, *Law Enforcement* (New York, 1944), p. 656.

[136]Ibid., pp. 656–657.

[137]Moglen, "Taking the Fifth," p. 1105, and "The Privilege in British North America," in Helmholz, ed., *The Privilege,* p. 164.

in New York even before it was published in England. On February 5, 1753, William Smith, Jr., one of the luminaries of the New York bar, received from John McEvers, a fellow attorney, a manuscript volume "supposed to be done by Baron Gilbert." Smith copied 173 pages of the manuscript, including the passage against self-accusing, and in the margin later wrote, "Now this book is printed under the title Law of Evidence in 8 vo. 1 June 1756." Smith, incidentally, not only knew of the right from many sources, in addition to Gilbert, but as an historian, councilor, and lawyer he respected the right.[138]

In 1963 I published an article in an historical journal proving that Goebel and Naughton were wrong.[139] and in my *Origins of the Fifth* I repeat some of the same material, developing the same thesis about Goebel's mistakes. As late as 1997 Moglen still does not refer to my article nor to the material from it in my book; he endorses Goebel as if I had not shown Goebel to be untrustworthy.[140] Consequently Moglen's work is also not trustworthy.

I singled out Gilbert's book here only because Moglen endorsed Goebel and Naughton who offered Gilbert's alleged silence on the right as proof that it was not even known in New York's English-minded courts. But almost any law book that touched criminal law might be used to prove that information about the right was available to the colonists, from the earliest discussion of the right in Edmond Wingate's *Maxims of Reason* (1658), copies of which were in the libraries of eminent New York lawyers, to Blackstone's *Commentaries*.[141] For example, in the most widely used English law dictionary, written by Giles

---

[138]William Smith, "A Treatise on Evidence," William Smith Papers, vol. 9, pp. 127–128, New York Public Library MSS.

[139]Leonard W. Levy and Lawrence H. Leder, "Exotic Fruit: The Right Against Self-Incrimination in Colonial New York," 20 *William and Mary Quarterly*, 3rd ser. (1963), pp. 3–22.

[140]Moglen, "The Privilege in British North America," in Helmholz, ed., *The Privilege*, p. 164.

[141]Edward Wingate, *Maxims of Reason: or the Reason of the Common Law of England* (London, 1658), sect. 125, pp. 486–487; Blackstone, *Commentaries on the Laws*, vol. 3, ch. 7, p. 101; ch. 23, p. 370; vol. 4, ch. 22, p. 296. Paul M. Hamlin, *Legal Education in Colonial New York* (New York, 1939), pp. 173, 179, 181, 187, 194.

Jacob, under "Evidence" appeared the proposition that "the witness shall not be asked any Question to accuse himself," and Jacob cited Coke's *Institutes*, Hobbes's *Leviathan*, and the *State Trials* as his authorities. In his *Every Man His Own Lawyer*, the seventh edition of which was published in New York in 1768, Jacob restated the proposition. It was in the most popular political tract on English rights. The right can also be found in Henry Care's *English Liberties* and in Lord Chancellor John Somers's *The Security of Englishmen's Lives*. The works of Care and Somers were reprinted in eighteenth-century America, each for a second time on the eve of the American Revolution.[142] Every popular manual for justices of the peace repeated the *nemo tenetur* maxim or gave the English equivalent, as did Hawkins's *Pleas of the Crown* and Nelson's *Law of Evidence*.[143]

Despite the titles of Moglen's articles, which lead the reader to believe that they are about the right against self-incrimination, much of his work, especially in the first article, has nothing to do with the right; it is, rather, about what Moglen calls the "trial rights cluster"—a batch of rights associated with trial by jury, above all representation by counsel.[144] Page after page of Moglen does not refer to or involve the right against self-incrimination. He covers justice-of-the-peace manuals in three pages only to show that "the prosecutorial system depended on the routine of

---

[142]Giles Jacob, *A New Law-Dictionary*, under "Evidence" (1732); Jacob, *Every Man His Own Lawyer* 93 (7th ed., New York, 1768, reprinted Philadelphia, 1769); Henry Care, *English liberties or the Free born Subject's Inheritance* (5th ed., Boston, 1721), pp. 198–199; a 6th ed. was published in Providence in 1774. John Somers, *The Security of Englishmen's Lives* (Boston, 1720, reprinted New York, 1773), and in an edition I used, the Appendix to [Anon.], *A Guide to the Knowledge of the Rights and Privileges of Englishmen* (London, 1757), p. 170.

[143]E.g., Michael Dalton, *The Countrey Justice* (1618) p. 264; (1619) p. 273; (1677) p. 411; (1742) p. 380; William Nelson, *The Office and Authority of the Justice of the Peace* (London, 1714, 4th ed.), p. 253; [James Parker?], *Conductor Generalis, or the Office, Duty and Authority of Justice of the Peace* (Philadelphia, 1722), p. 83, and in the 2nd ed. of 1749, Appendix, No. 5. William Hawkins, *A Treatise of the Pleas of the Crown* (London, 1716), vol. 2, ch. 46, sect. 20, p. 433; and William Nelson, *The Law of Evidence* (London, 1735), p. 51. See my *Origins of the Fifth*, pp. 505–506, for numerous other citations to law books containing the principle that no man need incriminate himself.

[144]Moglen, "The Privilege of British North America," in Helmholz, ed., *The Privilege*, p. 175.

self-incrimination in preliminary proceedings."[145] He ignores the pertinent fact that all the j.p. manuals observed that the suspect was entitled to remain silent in the face of a question the answer to which could incriminate him.

Moglen disregards historical accuracy and has a loose notion of what constitutes evidence. For example, he refers to a Virginia enactment of 1677 and Massachusetts data of 1641–1642, and he remarks that Pennsylvania did not conclude that conventional examination practices violated the privilege. On the basis of that slim evidence from three colonies, Moglen then draws conclusions about "criminal procedure in the American colonies."[146] He talks about what "the American records" disclose without citing any of them. He has a section in his law review article entitled "Constitutional Theory and the Privilege" that does not mention the privilege—except to crack wise about Sam Adams.[147] His section on "The Privilege and the State Constitutions" refers briefly and only to Virginia, Pennsylvania, Delaware, and Maryland, though seven states plus Vermont constitutionally protected the right.[148] His section entitled "After the Fifth—the Privilege in Practice" contains no material on the right against self-incrimination in practice but rather concludes with what purports to be "the common law position" by giving a long irrelevant quotation from a territorial judge on the subject of "Voluntary Confessions."[149] Elsewhere in the article Moglen's material is equally irrelevant when he speaks of forcing a witness to incriminate others. He persistently misrepresents me, even on trivial matters. For example, he notes that Maryland qualified its provision that no person should be compelled to give evidence against himself by fixing an exception "in such cases as have been usually prac-

---

[145]Ibid., and Moglen, "Taking the Fifth," p. 1098.

[146]Moglen, "Taking the Fifth," p. 1103, and "The Privilege in British North America," in Helmholz, ed., *The Privilege*, p. 162.

[147]Moglen, "Taking the Fifth," pp. 1115–1118; the reference to Adams is at p. 1116; see note 124 above.

[148]Moglen, "The Privilege in British North America," in Helmholz, ed., *The Privilege*, pp. 177–181.

[149]Moglen, "Taking the Fifth," p. 1121, citing Levy, *Origins of the Fifth*, p. 410.

ticed in this State, or may hereafter be directed by the Legislature."[150] Then he adds that my suggestion that this exception "concerned only cases of pardon or grant of immunity . . . is unsupported by any evidence." I never used "only" or any equivalent of it.[151]

Similarly, Moglen observes that a Rhode Island enactment of 1669 on the right to counsel limited that right "to plead any point of law," and then Moglen instructs readers to compare my treatment of the same enactment "where the restriction is ignored, supposedly showing the early establishment of the 'right to counsel.'"[152] But my language concerning the same enactment is that it provided that "it shall be the lawful privilege of any person that is indicted, to procure an attorney to plead any point of law that may make for the clearing of his innocencye."[153]

Moglen criticizes my treatment of Article 45 of the 1641 Massachusetts Body of Liberties because I say that it "provided in somewhat equivocal terms for the right against self-incrimination"—an "exaggeration" says Moglen. I explain that Liberty 45 abolished torture to force a confession of a person's guilt but permitted torture for the purpose of incriminating others only after the victim had been convicted in a case where it was obvious that he had confederates. Moglen acknowledges that Barbara Black, whom he regards as "authoritative," urged that the provision "should be read so as to deny any power to torture for self-incrimination," which is the position I advanced before she did.[154]

Moglen pronounces as "wrong" my view that the right to be free from self-incrimination continued to be observed more fully in Virginia than its stunted constitutional provision justified.[155] I can certainly make mistakes, but Moglen merely alleges that I

---

[150]Moglen, "Taking the Fifth," p. 1121 n.130.
[151]Levy, *Origins of the Fifth*, p. 410.
[152]Moglen, "Taking the Fifth," p. 1093.
[153]Levy, *Origins of the Fifth*, p. 356.
[154]Ibid., p. 345, and Moglen, "Taking the Fifth," p. 1101.
[155]Moglen, "Taking the Fifth," p. 1124.

am wrong in this instance without explaining why he thinks so and without evaluating or even noticing my evidence. His pronouncement that I am wrong is unsubstantiated. As for the problem of Virginia, its constitutional provision applied only to the accused in criminal prosecutions, yet in practice the right protected witnesses and applied to civil cases too, not just criminal ones. Moreover the right shielded the accused and witnesses against public obloquy. That is, even if their answers tended only to disgrace them but could not be used against them criminally, they could invoke the right.[156]

Moglen adds, mistakenly, that state constitutional protections of the right had "little or no" effect on practice in the new states, but he offers no evidence at all on the point and ignores my supporting evidence to the contrary.[157] He misleadingly credits me for the point that state practice changed "not at all" as a result of new state constitutional protections of the right. But he botches what I say. As a matter of fact, I point out that practice changed considerably, and some of the early state decisions in favor of the right went to the extreme.[158] Consider Pennsylvania's practice. The state constitution of 1790 narrowed the 1776 state constitution's protection by applying to "the accused" rather than to anyone. In an 1802 opinion, Chief Justice Edward Shippen spoke of the *nemo tenetur* maxim very broadly as if the 1776 constitution were still in effect:[159]

> It is founded on the best policy, and runs throughout the whole system of jurisprudence . . . it is considered cruel and unjust to propose questions which may tend to criminate the party. And so jealous have the legislatures of this commonwealth been of this mode of discovery of facts that they have refused assent to a bill brought in to compel persons to disclose on oath papers as well as facts relating to questions of mere property. And may we

[156]Richard Starke, *Office and Authority of a Justice of the Peace* (Williamsburg, Va., 1774), pp. 141, 145, 146.
[157]See Levy, *Origins of the Fifth*, pp. 515–517, where I review state cases.
[158]Ibid., p. 516.
[159]*Respublica v. Gibbs*, 3 Yeates (Pa.) 429, 437 (1802).

not justly suppose, that they would not be less jealous of securing our citizens against this mode of self-accusation? The words
'accusare' and 'prodere' are general terms, and their sense is not
confined to cases whether the answers to the questions proposed would induce to the punishment of the party. If they
would involve him in shame or reproach, he is under no obligation to answer them.

Other state courts which confronted the question decided similarly, and they also held that the right extended to a witness even
in civil suits where the questions asked might, if truthfully answered, supply a link in the chain, which would lead to a conviction for a crime.

Some of the early state decisions in favor of the right were far-
fetched, in effect taking literally the principle that a witness did
not have to answer questions "against himself," even if his answers did not incriminate him but might injure his civil interests.[160] An early federal case was similar.[161] In the first federal
case on the right, Justice James Iredell of the Supreme Court, on
circuit duty, ruled that a witness was not bound to answer a question that might tend to "implicate" or incriminate him.[162]

In one of the most famous cases in our constitutional history,
Marbury v. Madison, Attorney General Levi Lincoln balked at answering a question relating to his conduct of office as acting secretary of state when Jefferson first became president. Marbury's
commission as a justice of the peace for the District of Columbia
had been signed by the outgoing president and had been affixed
with the seal of the United States by the then–secretary of state,
John Marshall, who had had no time to deliver it. In *Marbury*,
Chief Justice Marshall asked Lincoln what he had done with that

---

[160]See, e.g., *Starr v. Tracy* 2 Root (Conn.) 528, at 529 (1797); *Connor v. Bradey*, An-
thon's Nisi Prius Rep. (N.Y.) 135, at 136 (1809); *Grannis v. Branden*, 5 Day (Conn.) 260, at
271–274 (1812); *Cook v. Corn*, 1 Overton (Tenn.) 340, at 341 (1808); *Bell's Case*, 1 Browne
(Pa.) 376 (1811).

[161]*Carne v. McLane*, Case No. 2,416, in 5 Fed. Cases (Circ. Ct., D.C.) 89 (1806).

[162]*U.S. v. Goosley*, Case No. 15,230 in 25 Fed. Cases (Circ. Ct., Va.) 1363 (undated but
before Iredell's death in 1799).

commission. Lincoln, who probably had burned it, replied that he did not think he was bound to disclose his official transactions while acting as secretary of state, nor should he "be compelled to answer any thing which might tend to criminate himself." Marbury's counsel, Charles Lee, who was himself a former attorney general of the United States, and Chief Justice Marshall agreed with Lincoln. Although Lincoln was in the peculiar position of being both a witness and counsel for the government in a civil suit, he was not obliged to disclose anything in either capacity.[163]

Henry Smith's contribution to Helmholz's *Privilege Against Self-Incrimination* is an essay on "The Modern Privilege: Its Nineteenth Century Origins."[164] In view of the fact that I conclude my book with the ratification of the Bill of Rights, Smith's subject does not bring him into collision with my work, but he does manage to criticize me for making a distinction between being "allowed" to testify and being "compelled" to. He thinks that a passage in my book dealing with the right of an individual not to be "compelled" to answer should be read as disqualifying him for interest. Perhaps, but Smith argues that the use of the word "compellable" "brings us no closer to the privilege." First, I never used the word "compellable." My word is "compelled." Second, compulsion brings us as close as possible to "the privilege," because the Fifth Amendment says, "no person shall be compelled in any criminal case to be a witness against himself." The alleged "confusion" is wholly on Smith's part, not mine.

On reflection, I must conclude that notwithstanding my critics, if I were rewriting the book I would make no significant changes.

---

[163]*Marbury v. Madison*, 1 Cranch (U.S.) 137, 144 (1803).
[164]Helmholz, ed., *The Privilege*, pp. 193–239.

America's Greatest Magistrate

*L*EMUEL SHAW served as chief justice of Massachusetts from 1830 to 1860, during an age which he said was remarkable for its "prodigious activity and energy in every department of life."[1] America was being transformed by the rise of railroads, steam power, the factory system, and the corporate form of business. A more complex society, urban and industrial, was superseding the older rural, agrarian one. Only a pace behind the astonishing rate of economic change came the democratization of politics and of society, while the federal system lumbered toward its greatest crisis. During this time Shaw delivered what is probably a record number of opinions for a single judge: more than 2,200, enough to fill about twenty volumes if separately collected.

At the time of his appointment to the bench, American law was still in its formative period. Whole areas of law were largely uncultivated, many unknown, and few if any settled. Although Shaw was not writing on a completely clean slate, the strategy of time and place surely presented an unrivaled opportunity for a judge of strength and vision to mold the law. His domain was the whole field of jurisprudence, excepting only admiralty. No other state judge through his opinions alone had so great an influence on the course of American law.

One of the major themes of his life work was the perpetua-

---

[1]Lemuel Shaw, "Profession of the Law in the United States" (extract from an address delivered before the Suffolk Bar, May 1827), *American Jurist*, VII (1832), 56–65.

tion of what Oscar and Mary Handlin have called "the commonwealth idea"[2]—essentially a quasi-mercantilist concept of the state within a democratic framework. In Europe, where the state was not responsible to the people and was the product of remote historical forces, mercantilism served the ruling classes who controlled the state. In America, men put the social contract theory into practice and actually made their government. The people were the state; the state was their "Common Wealth." They identified themselves with it and felt that they should share, as of right, in the advantages it could bring to them as a community. The state was their means of promoting the general interest.

The Commonwealth idea precluded the laissez-faire state whose function was simply to keep peace and order, and then, like a little child, not be heard. The people of Massachusetts expected their Commonwealth to participate actively in their economic affairs. Where risk capital feared to tread or needed franchises, powers of incorporation, or the boost of special powers such as eminent domain, the duty of the state was to subsidize, grant, and supervise the whole process in the interests of the general welfare. But regulation was not restricted to those special interests that had been promoted by government aid. Banks, insurance companies, liquor dealers, food vendors, and others were all subjected to varying degrees of control, although the public trough had not been open to them. The beneficent hand of the state reached out to touch every part of the economy.

The Commonwealth idea profoundly influenced the development of law in Massachusetts. It was largely responsible for the direction taken by law of eminent domain, for the development of the police power, and for the general precedence given by the courts to public rights over merely private ones. As employed by Shaw, the Commonwealth idea gave

[2]Oscar Handlin and Mary Handlin, *Commonwealth. A Study of the Role of Government in the American Economy: Massachusetts 1784–1861* (New York, 1947), p. 31.

rise to legal doctrines of the public interest by which the power of the state to govern the economy was judicially sustained.

The idea that "some privately owned corporations are more public in character than others," as Edwin Merrick Dodd noted, "had already begun to emerge in judicial decisions before 1830."[3] The grant of powers of eminent domain to early turnpike and canal companies had been upheld because these were public highways, although privately owned. The mill acts, which originated as a means of promoting water-powered gristmills, had also been sustained in early decisions on the ground that a public purpose was served. While the earlier judges regretted the extension of the old gristmill acts to new manufacturing corporations, Shaw, by contrast, warmly accepted these acts because he believed that industrialization would bring prosperity and progress to the Commonwealth. Accordingly he declared that "a great mill-power for manufacturing purposes" was, like a railroad, a species of public works in which the public had a great interest. He even placed "steam manufactories" in the same class as water-powered mills, as devoted to a public use, although steam-powered factories were never granted powers of eminent domain.[4]

The Commonwealth idea underlay those remarkably prophetic opinions of Shaw's that established the basis of the emerging law of public utilities. The old common law of common calling had considered only millers, carriers, and innkeepers as "public employments"; it "knew no such persons as the common road-maker or the common water-supplier."[5] The "common road-maker," that is, the turnpike, bridge, and canal companies, were added to the list of public employments or public works while Shaw was still at the bar. But it was Shaw who settled the

---

[3]Edwin M. Dodd, *American Business Corporations Until 1860* (Cambridge, Mass., 1954), p. 44.

[4]See *Hazen v. Essex Co.*, 66 Mass. (12 Cush.) 475 (1853); *Palmer Co. v. Ferrill*, 34 Mass. (17 Pick.) 58 (1835).

[5]Dodd, *American Business Corporations*, p. 161.

legal character of power companies,[6] turnpikes,[7] railroads,[8] and water suppliers[9] as public utilities, privately owned but subject to regulation for the public benefit. He would have included even manufacturers and banks. The Commonwealth idea left no doubt as to whether the state would master or be mastered by its creatures, the corporations, or whether the welfare of the economy was a matter of public or private concern.

The police power may be regarded as the legal expression of the Commonwealth idea, for it signifies the supremacy of public over private rights. To call the police power a Massachusetts doctrine would be an exaggeration, although not a great one. But it is certainly no coincidence that in Massachusetts, with its Commonwealth tradition, the police power was first defined and carried to great extremes from the standpoint of vested interests. Shaw's foremost contribution in the field of public law was to the development of the police-power concept.

The power of the legislature "to trench somewhat largely on the profitable use of individual property," for the sake of the common good, as Shaw expressed the police power in *Commonwealth v. Alger*,[10] was consistently confirmed over thirty years of his opinions. Three decades later, when judges were acting on the supposition that the Fourteenth Amendment incorporated Herbert Spencer's *Social Statics*, the ideas expressed in Shaw's opinions seemed the very epitome of revolutionary socialism. Shaw's name was revered, but the implications of his police-power opinions were politely evaded. In the period between

---

[6]See *Gould v. Boston Duck Co.*, 79 Mass. (13 Gray) 442 (1859); *Hazen v. Essex Co.*, 66 Mass. (12 Cush.) 475 (1853); *Murdock v. Stickney*, 62 Mass. (8 Cush.) 113 (1851); *Chase v. Sutton Mfg. Co.*, 58 Mass. (4 Cush.) 152 (1849); *Cary v. Daniels*, 49 Mass. (8 Met.) 466 (1844); *French v. Braintree Mfg. Co.*, 40 Mass. (23 Pick.) 216 (1839); *Williams v. Nelson*, 40 Mass. (23 Pick.) 141 (1839); *Palmer Co. v. Ferrill*, 34 Mass. (17 Pick.) 58 (1835); *Fiske v. Framingham Mfg. Co.*, 29 Mass. (12 Pick.) 68 (1831).

[7]*Commonwealth v. Wilkinson*, 33 Mass. (16 Pick.) 175 (1834).

[8]*City of Roxbury v. Boston & Providence R.R.*, 60 Mass. (6 Cush.) 424 (1850); *Newbury Tpk. Corp. v. Eastern R.R.*, 40 Mass. (23 Pick.) 326 (1839); *Boston Water Power Co. v. Boston & Worcester R.R.*, 33 Mass. (16 Pick.) 512 (1835); *Wellington, Petitioners*, 33 Mass. (16 Pick.) 87 (1834).

[9]*Lumbard v. Stearns*, 58 Mass. (4 Cush.) 60 (1849).

[10]61 Mass. (7 Cush.) 53 (1851).

Shaw and the school of Holmes and Brandeis, American law threatened to become the graveyard of general-welfare or public-interest doctrines, and doctrines of vested rights dominated. The trend toward legal Spencerianism was so pronounced by the end of the nineteenth century that legal historians concentrated on a search for the origins of doctrines of vested rights, almost as if contrary doctrines had never existed. When touching the pre–Civil War period, it is conventional to quote de Tocqueville on the conservatism of the American bench and bar, to present American law almost exclusively in terms of Marshall, Story, and Kent, and to emphasize that the rights of property claimed the very warmest affections of the American judiciary. If, however, the work of the state courts were better known, this view of our legal history might be altered. But Gibson and Ruffin and Blackford are little more than distinguished names, their work forgotten. Shaw's superb exposition of the police power is respectfully remembered, but it is usually treated as exceptional, or mistreated as an attempt to confine the police power to the common-law maxim of *sic utere tuo ut alienum non laedas*.[11]

Shaw taught that "all property . . . is derived directly or indirectly from the government, and held subject to those general regulations, which are necessary to the common good and general welfare."[12] Dean Pound, in discussing the "extreme individualist view" of the common law concerning the rights of riparian property owners, says the common law asked simply, "was the defendant acting on his own land and committing no nuisance?"[13] But Shaw believed that the common law of nuisances, which was founded on the *sic utere* maxim, inadequately protected the public, because it was restricted to the abatement of existing nuisances. He believed that the general welfare re-

<hr />

[11]Edward S. Corwin, *The Twilight of the Supreme Court* (New Haven, 1934), p. 68; Ernst Freund, *The Police Power* (Chicago, 1904), p. 425, §405. For an extended discussion of the police-power decisions by Shaw, see Leonard W. Levy, *The Law of the Commonwealth and Chief Justice Shaw* (Cambridge, Mass., 1957), chap. 13. (Trans.: so use your powers as not to injure others.)

[12]*Commonwealth v. Alger*, 61 Mass. (7 Cush.) 53, 83–84 (1851).

[13]Roscoe Pound, *The Spirit of the Common Law* (Boston, 1921), pp. 53–54.

quired the anticipation and prevention of prospective wrongs from the use of private property. Accordingly he held that the legislature might interfere with the use of property before its owner became amenable to the common law. So a man could not even remove stones from his own beach if prohibited by the legislature, nor erect a wharf on his property beyond boundary lines fixed by it. Even if his use of his property would be "harmless" or "indifferent," the necessity of restraints was to be judged "by those to whom all legislative power is intrusted by the sovereign authority." Similarly the "reasonableness" of such restraints was a matter of "expediency" to be determined by the legislature, not the court. The simple expedient of having a precise statutory rule for the obedience of all was sufficient reason for a finding of constitutionality.[14]

Thus Shaw, using the Commonwealth idea, established a broad base for the police power. He carried the law's conception of the public good and the power of government to protect it a long way from the straitjacketing ideas of Kent and Story. Their position may be summed up in Blackstone's language that "the public good is in nothing more essentially interested than the protection of every individual's private rights."[15]

A few other decisions of the Shaw court on the police power will illustrate that the chief justice's *Alger* opinion was more than rhetoric. The authority of the legislature to shape private banking practices in the public interest was unequivocally sustained in two sweeping opinions. In one, Shaw said that a statute intended to prevent banks from "becoming dangerous to the public" was attacked as unconstitutional on the authority of Marshall, Story, and Kent. The statute allegedly operated retroactively against the bank in question; constituted a legislative assumption of judicial power because it required the supreme judicial court to issue a preliminary injunction against banks on the findings of a government commission; and violated the federal

---

[14]Quotations are from Shaw's opinions in the *Alger* case and in *Commonwealth v. Tewksbury*, 52 Mass. (11 Met.) 55 (1846).

[15]Quoted by Pound, *The Spirit of the Common Law*, p. 53.

contract clause by providing for a perpetual injunction against the further doing of business, in effect a revocation of the charter. Rufus Choate probably never argued a stronger case. But Shaw sustained the statute and the injunction, peppering his opinion with references to the paramountcy of "the great interests of the community," the duty of the government to "provide security for its citizens," and the legitimacy of interferences with "the liberty of action, and even with the right of property, of such institutions."[16] In a second bank case of the same year, 1839, the court refused "to raise banks above the control of the legislature." The holding was that a charter could be dissolved at the authority of the legislature, under the reserved police power, without a judicial proceeding.[17]

It has been said that from the standpoint of the doctrine of vested rights, the most reprehensible legislation ever enacted was the prohibition on the sale of liquor. Such legislation wiped out the value of existing stocks and subjected violators to criminal sanctions, their property to public destruction. Similarly, buildings used for purposes of prostitution or gambling might, on the authority of the legislature, be torn down. The question presented by such statutes was whether the police power could justify uncompensated destruction of private property which had not been appropriated for a public use. The power of the Commonwealth over the health and morals of the public provided Shaw with the basis for sustaining legislation divesting vested rights.[18] On a half dozen occasions, the New York Wynehammer doctrine of substantive due process of law was repudiated in such cases.[19]

---

[16]*Commonwealth v. Farmers & Mechanics Bank*, 38 Mass. (21 Pick.) 542 (1839).

[17]*Crease v. Babcock*, 40 Mass. (23 Pick.) 334 (1839).

[18]*Commonwealth v. Howe*, 79 Mass. (13 Gray) 26 (1859); *Brown v. Perkins*, 70 Mass. (12 Gray) 89 (1858); *Fisher v. McGirr*, 67 Mass. (1 Gray) 1 (1854); *Commonwealth v. Blackington*, 41 Mass. (24 Pick.) 352 (1837). These are the leading cases among dozens.

[19]E.g., *Commonwealth v. Howe*, 79 Mass. (13 Gray) 26 (1859); *Commonwealth v. Logan*, 78 Mass. (12 Gray) 136 (1859); *Commonwealth v. Murphy*, 76 Mass. (10 Gray) 1 (1857); *Calder v. Kurby*, 71 Mass. (5 Gray) 597 (1856); *Commonwealth v. Hitchings*, 71 Mass. (5 Gray) 482 (1855); *Commonwealth v. Clap*, 71 Mass. (5 Gray) 97 (1855). For the Wynehammer doctrine, see *Wynehammer v. People*, 13 N.Y. 378 (1856); *People v. Toynbee*, 20 Barb. 168 (N.Y. 1855); *Wynehammer v. People*, 20 Barb. 567 (N.Y. 1855).

Regulation of railroad was another subject for the exercise of the police power, according to the Shaw court. The same principles that justified grants of eminent domain to railroads, or to canals, bridges, turnpikes, power companies, and water suppliers, also provided the basis for sustaining controls over their rates, profits, and services. Railroads, said Shaw, were a "public work, established by public authority, intended for the public use and benefit."[20] The power to charge rates was "in every respect a public grant, a franchise . . . subject to certain regulations, within the power of government, if it should become excessive."[21]

These dicta by Shaw became holdings at the first moment the railroads challenged the "reasonableness" of the rates and services fixed by government railroad commissions. "Reasonableness" was held to be a matter for determination by the legislature or the commission to which it delegated its powers. Those powers, in turn, were broadly construed. The court would not interfere with the regulatory process if the railroads had the benefit of notice, hearing, and other fair procedures.[22] Due process of law to the Shaw court meant according to legal forms, not according to legislation that the court approved or disapproved as a matter of policy.

The Shaw court's latitudinarian attitude toward the police power was influenced by the strong tradition of judicial self-restraint among Massachusetts judges, an outgrowth of the Commonwealth idea. Shaw carried on the tradition of the Massachusetts judiciary. During the thirty years that Shaw presided there were only ten cases, one unreported, in which the supreme judicial court voided legislative enactments.

Four of these cases in no way related to the police power. One involved a special legislative resolution confirming a private sale that had divested property rights of third persons without

---

[20]*Worcester v. Western R.R.*, 45 Mass. (4 Met.) 564, 566 (1842).
[21]*B.& L. R.R. v. S.& L. R.R.*, 68 Mass. (2 Gray) 1, 29 (1854).
[22]*B.& W. R.R. v. Western R.R.*, 80 Mass. (14 Gray) 253 (1859) and *L.& W. R.R. v. Fitchburg R.R.*, 80 Mass. (14 Gray) 266 (1859).

compensation.[23] The second concerned an act by which Charlestown was annexed to Boston without providing the citizens of Charlestown with representative districts and an opportunity to vote.[24] The third, an unreported case decided by Shaw sitting alone, involved the "personal liberty act," by which the state sought to evade Congress's Fugitive Slave Law.[25] Here Shaw felt bound by the national Constitution and by a decision of the Supreme Court of the United States. In the fourth case he invalidated a state act which dispensed with the ancient requirement of grand jury proceedings in cases of high crimes.[26] In each of these four, the decisions are above any but trifling criticism.

Of the six cases bearing on the police power, three involved legislation egregiously violating procedural guarantees that are part of our civil liberties.[27] The statutes in question had validly prohibited the sale of liquor. But they invalidly stripped accused persons of virtually every safeguard of criminal justice, from the right to be free from unreasonable searches and seizures to the rights that cluster around the concept of fair trial. Shaw's decisions against these statutes, like his decisions insuring the maintenance of grand jury proceedings and the right to vote, were manifestations of judicial review in its best sense. There were also dicta by Shaw on the point that the legislature cannot restrain the use of property by ex post facto laws, by bills of attainder, or by discriminatory classifications. Thus the limitations placed upon the police power by the Shaw court were indispensable to the protection of civil liberties.

The only exception to this generalization consists of the limitation derived from the contract clause of the United States Constitution. But there were only three cases during the long period of Shaw's chief justiceship in which this clause was the basis for the invalidation of statutes. In each of the three, the statutes

[23]*Sohier v. Mass. Gen. Hosp.*, 57 Mass. (3 Cush.) 483 (1849).
[24]*Warren v. Mayor and Aldermen of Charlestown*, 57 Mass. (3 Gray) 84 (1854).
[25]*Commonwealth v. Coolidge, Law Reporter*, 5 (Mass. 1843), 482.
[26]*Jones v. Robbins*, 74 Mass. (8 Gray) 329 (1857).
[27]*Robinson v. Richardson*, 79 Mass. (13 Gray) 454 (1859); *Sullivan v. Adams*, 69 Mass. (3 Gray) 476 (1855); *Fisher v. McGirr*, 67 Mass. (1 Gray) 1 (1854).

were of limited operation and the decisions made no sacrifice of the public interest. The legislature in one case attempted to regulate in the absence of a reserved power to alter or amend public contracts; the court left a way open for the legislature's purpose to be achieved under common law.[28] In the other two cases, regulatory powers had been reserved but were exercised in particularly faithless and arbitrary ways; in one case to increase substantially the obligations of a corporation for a second time, in effect doubling a liability which had been paid off; in the other case to repeal an explicit permission for a corporation to increase its capitalization in return for certain services rendered.[29] The legislature in all three cases had passed a high threshold of judicial tolerance for governmental interference with the sanctity of contracts. The decisions were hardly exceptional, considering the facts of the cases and their dates—they were decided between 1854 and 1860, after scores of similar decisions by Federalist, Whig, and Jacksonian jurists alike, in state and federal jurisdictions.

The striking fact is that there were so few such decisions by the Shaw court in thirty years. Handsome opportunities were provided again and again by litigants claiming impairment of their charters of incorporation by a meddlesome legislature. But the court's decisions were characterized by judicial self-restraint rather than an eagerness to erect a bulwark around chartered rights. The three cases in which statutes were voided for conflict with the contract clause were unusual for the Shaw court.

Generally the attitude of the court was typified by Shaw's remark that "immunities and privileges (vested by charter) do not exempt corporations from the operations of those made for the general regulation."[30] He habitually construed public grants in favor of the community and against private interests. When char-

---

[28]*Commonwealth v. New Bedford Bridge*, 68 Mass. (2 Gray) 339 (1854).

[29]*Central Bridge Corp. v. City of Lowell*, 81 Mass. (15 Gray) 106 (1860); *Commonwealth v. Essex Co.*, 79 Mass. (13 Gray) 239 (1859). For an extended discussion of judicial review and of constitutional limitations under Shaw, see Levy, *Law of the Commonwealth*, chap. 14.

[30]*Commonwealth v. Farmers & Mechanics Bank*, 38 Mass. (21 Pick.) 542 (1838).

tered powers were exercised in the public interest, he usually interpreted them broadly; but when they competed with the right of the community to protect itself or conserve its resources, he interpreted chartered powers narrowly. He did not permit the public control over matters of health, morals, or safety, nor the power of eminent domain; to be alienated by the contract clause.

In the face of such a record it is misleading to picture state courts assiduously searching for doctrines of vested rights to stymie the police power. Certainly no such doctrines appeared in the pre–Civil War decisions of the supreme judicial court of Massachusetts, except for the one doctrine derived by John Marshall from the contract clause and so sparingly used by Shaw. The sources from which vested-rights doctrines were derived by others—the higher law, natural rights, the social compact, and other sources of implied, inherent limitations on majoritarian assemblies—these were invoked by Shaw when he was checking impairments on personal liberties or traditional procedures of criminal justice.

If this picture does not fit the stereotype of conservative Whig jurists, the stereotype may need revision. On the great issue which has historically divided liberals from conservatives in politics—government controls over property and corporations—Shaw supported the government. Even when the Commonwealth idea was being eroded by those who welcomed the giveaway state but not the regulatory state, Shaw was still endorsing a concept of the police power that kept private interests under government surveillance and restraint. He would not permit the Commonwealth idea to become just a rationale for legislative subventions and grants of chartered powers, with business as the only beneficiary. To Shaw, government aid implied government control, because the aid to business was merely incidental to the promotion of the public welfare. No general regulatory statute was invalidated while he was chief justice. His conservatism tended to crop out in common-law cases where the public interest had not been defined or suggested by statute. In such cases the law was as putty in his hands, shaped to meet the press of business needs. Nothing illustrates this better than the personal injury cases and the variety of novel cases to which railroad corporations were parties. The roar of the first locomotive in Massachusetts signaled the advent of a capitalist revolution in the common law, in the sense that Shaw made railroads the beneficiaries of legal doctrine.[31] To be sure, he believed that he was genuinely serving the general interest on the calculation that what was good for business was good for the Commonwealth.

It was when he had a free hand, in the absence of government action, that the character of his conservatism displayed itself: he construed the law so that corporate industrial interests prevailed over lesser, private ones. An individual farmer, shipper, passenger, worker, or pedestrian, when pitted against a corporation which in Shaw's mind personified industrial expansion and public prosperity, risked a rough sort of justice, whether the issue involved tort or contract.[32] Shaw strictly insisted that individuals look to themselves, not to the law, for protection of life and limb, for his beloved common law was incorrigibly individualistic. The hero of the common law was the property-owning, liberty-loving, self-reliant reasonable man. He was also the hero of American society, celebrated by Jefferson as the freehold farmer, by Hamilton as the town merchant, by Jackson as the frontiersman. Between the American image of the common man

---

[31]See Levy, *Law of the Commonwealth*, chaps. 8–9, "The Formative Period of Railroad Law."

[32]*Denny v. New York Central R.R.*, 79 Mass. (13 Gray) 481 (1859); *Shaw v. Boston & Worcester R.R.*, 74 Mass. (8 Gray) 45 (1857); *Lucas v. New Bedford & Taunton R.R.*, 72 Mass. (6 Gray) 64 (1856); *Nutting v. Conn. River R.R.*, 67 Mass. (1 Gray) 502 (1854); *Norway Plains Co. v. Boston & Me. R.R.*, 67 Mass. (1 Gray) 263 (1854); *Brown v. Eastern R.R.*, 65 Mass. (11 Cush.) 97 (1853); *Lichtenheinz v. Boston & Providence R.R.*, 65 Mass. (11 Cush.) 70 (1853); *Props. of Locks and Canals v. Nashua & Lowell R.R.*, 64 Mass. (10 Cush.) 385 (1852); *Hollenbeck v. Berkshire R.R.*, 63 Mass. (9 Cush.) 478 (1852); *Kearney v. Boston & Worcester R.R.* 63 Mass. (9 Cush.) 108 (1851); *McElroy v. Nashua & Lowell R.R.* 58 Mass. (4 Cush.) 400 (1849); *Cary v. Berkshire R.R.*, 55 Mass. (1 Cush.) 175 (1848); *Snow v. Eastern R.R.*, 53 Mass. (12 Met.) 44 (1846); *Lewis v. Western R.R.* 52 Mass. (11 Met.) 509 (1846); *Draper v. Worcester & Norwich R.R.*, 52 Mass. (11 Met.) 505 (1846); *Worcester v. Western R.R.* 45 Mass. (4 Met.) 564 (1842); *Thompson v. Boston & Providence R.R., Daily Evening Transcript* (Boston), January 6, 1837; *Gerry v. Boston & Providence R.R.* ibid., December 29, 1836.

and the common law's ideal Everyman, there was a remarkable likeness. It harshly and uncompromisingly treated men as free-willed, self-reliant, risk-and-responsibility-taking individuals. Its spirit was Let every man beware and care for himself. That spirit, together with Shaw's belief that the rapid growth of manufacturing and transportation heralded the coming of the good society, tended to minimize the legal liabilities of business.

This was especially striking in cases of industrial accident and personal injury cases generally. For example, when an accident occurred despite all precautions, Shaw held railroads liable for damage to freight but not for injuries to passengers. They, he reasoned, took the risk of accidents that might occur regardless of due care. His opinions went a long way to accentuate the inhumanity of the common law in the area of torts, and simultaneously to spur capitalist enterprise. Here was the one great area of law in which he failed to protect the public interest. He might have done so without stymieing rapid industrialization, because the cost of accidents, if imposed on business, would have been ultimately shifted to the public by a rise in prices and rates.

The rigorous individualism of the common law was especially noticeable in the emergent doctrine of contributory negligence, of which Shaw was a leading exponent.[33] That doctrine required a degree of care and skill which no one but the mythical "prudent" or "reasonable man" of the common law could match. A misstep, however slight, from the ideal standard of conduct, placed upon the injured party the whole burden of his loss, even though the railroad was also at fault and perhaps more so. Comparative rather than contributory negligence would have been a fairer test, or perhaps some rule by which damages could be apportioned.

Probably the furthermost limit of the common law's individ-

---

[33]*Shaw v. B. & W. R.R.* 74 Mass. (8 Gray) 45 (1857); *Brown v. Kendell,* 60 Mass. (6 Cush.) 292 (1850).

ualism in accident cases was expressed in the rule that a right to action is personal and dies with the injured party. This contributed to the related rule that the wrongful death of a human being was no ground for an action of damages.[34] But for the intervention of the legislature, the common law would have left the relatives of victims of a fatal accident without a legal remedy to obtain compensation. Shaw would also have made it more profitable for a railroad to kill a man outright than to scratch him, for if he lived he could sue.[35]

The fellow-servant rule was the most far-reaching consequence of individualism in the law as Shaw expounded it.[36] The rule was that a worker who was injured, through no fault of his own, by the negligence of a fellow employee, could not maintain a claim of damages against his employer. Shaw formulated this rule at a strategic moment for employers, because as industrialization expanded at an incredible pace, factory and railroad accidents multiplied frighteningly. Since the fellow-servant rule threw the whole loss from accidents upon innocent workers, capitalism was relieved of an enormous sum that would otherwise have been due as damages. The encouragement of "infant industries" had no greater social cost.

The fellow-servant rule was unmistakably an expression of legal thinking predicated upon the conception that a free man is one who is free to work out his own destiny, to pursue the calling of his choice, and to care for himself. If he undertakes a dangerous occupation, he voluntarily assumes the risks to which he has exposed himself. He should know that the others with whom he will have to work may cause him harm by their negligence. He must bear his loss because his voluntary conduct has implied his consent to assume it and to relieve his employer of it. On the other hand, there can be no implication that the

---

[34]*Carey v. Berkshire R.R.* 55 Mass. (1 Cush.) 475 (1848).
[35]*Hollenbeck v. Berkshire R.R.*, 63 Mass. (9 Cush.) 478 (1852); *Kearney v. Boston & Worcester R.R.* 63 Mass. (9 Cush.) 108 (1851).
[36]*Farwell v. Boston & Worcester R.R.*, 45 Mass. (4 Met.) 49 (1842). See Levy, *Law of the Commonwealth*, chap. 10.

employer has contracted to indemnify the worker for the negligence of anyone but himself. The employer, like his employees, is responsible for his own conduct but cannot be liable without fault.

On such considerations Shaw exempted the employer from liability to his employees, although he was liable to the rest of the world for the injurious acts which they committed in the course of their employment. It is interesting to note that Shaw felt obliged to read the employee's assumption of risk into his contract of employment. This legal fiction also reflected the individualism of a time when it was felt that free men could not be bound except by a contract of their own making.

The public policy that Shaw confidently expounded in support of his reading of the law similarly expressed the independent man: safety would be promoted if each worker guarded himself against his own carelessness and just as prudently watched his neighbor; to remove this responsibility by setting up the liability of the employer would tend to create individual laxity rather than prudence. So Shaw reasoned. It seems not to have occurred to him that fear of being maimed prompted men to safety anyway, or that contributory negligence barred recovery of damages, or that freeing the employer from liability did not induce him to employ only the most careful persons and to utilize accident-saving devices. Nor, for all his reliance upon the voluntary choice of mature men, did it occur to Shaw that a worker undertook a dangerous occupation and "consented" to its risks because his poverty deprived him of real choice. For that matter, none of these considerations prompted the legislature to supersede the common law with employers' liability and workmen's compensation acts until many decades later. Shaw did no violence to the spirit of his age by the fellow-servant rule, or by the rules he applied in other personal injury cases, particularly those involving wrongful death. In all such cases his enlightened views, so evidenced in police-power cases, were absent, probably because government action was equally absent. On the other hand his exposition of the rule of implied malice in cases of homicide[37] and of the criminal responsibility of the insane[38] accorded with the growing humanitarianism of the day as well as with doctrines of individualism.

Shaw's conservatism tended to manifest itself in cases involving notable social issues of his time. For example, he handed down the leading opinion on the constitutionality of the Fugitive Slave Act of 1850;[39] he originated the "separate but equal" doctrine which became the legal linchpin of racial segregation in the public schools throughout the nation;[40] and in the celebrated Abner Kneeland case[41] he sustained a conviction for blasphemy that grossly abridged freedom of conscience and expression; still another opinion was a bulwark of the establishment of religion which was maintained in Massachusetts until 1833.[42]

But it would be misleading as well as minimally informing to conclude an analysis of Shaw's work by calling him a conservative, for the word reveals little about Shaw if it is also applied to Marshall, Kent, Story, Webster, and Choate.

When Story and Kent, steeped in the crusty lore of the *Year Books*, were wailing to each other that they were the last of an old race of judges and that Taney's *Charles River Bridge* decision[43] meant that the Constitution was gone,[44] Shaw was calmly noting

[37]*Commonwealth v. Hawkins*, 72 Mass. (6 Gray) 463 (1855); *Commonwealth v. Webster*, 59 Mass. (3 Cush.) 295 (1850); *Commonwealth v. York*, 50 Mass. (9 Met.) 93 (1845). See Levy, *Law of the Commonwealth*, pp. 218–228.

[38]*Commonwealth v. Rogers*, 48 Mass. (7 Met.) 500 (1844). See Leonard W. Levy, *Law of the Commonwealth*, pp. 207–218.

[39]Sims' Case, 61 Mass. (7 Cush.) 285 (1851). See Leonard W. Levy, "Sims' Case: The Fugitive Slave Law in Boston in 1851," *Journal of Negro History, XXXV* (1950), 39–74, and Levy, *Law of the Commonwealth*, chap. 6.

[40]*Roberts v. City of Boston*, 59 Mass. (5 Cush.) 198 (1849). See Leonard W. Levy and Harlan B. Phillips, "The Roberts Case: Source of the 'Separate but Equal' Doctrine," *American Historical Review, LVI* (1951), 510–518, and Levy, *Law of the Commonwealth*, chap. 7.

[41]*Commonwealth v. Kneeland*, 37 Mass. (20 Pick.) 206 (1838). See Leonard W. Levy, "Satan's Last Apostle in Massachusetts," *American Quarterly* 5 (1953), 16–30, and Levy, *Law of the Commonwealth*, chap. 5.

[42]*Stebbins v. Jennings*, 27 Mass. (10 Pick.) 172 (1830). See Levy, *Law of the Commonwealth*, chap. 3.

[43]*Charles River Bridge v. Warren Bridge*, 36 U.S. (11 Pet.) 420 (1837).

[44]John Theodore Horton, *James Kent* (New York and London, 1939), pp. 293–295; Carl B. Swisher, *Roger B. Taney* (New York, 1936), pp. 377–379.

that property was "fully subject to State regulation" in the interest of the "morals, health, internal commerce, and general prosperity of the community. . . ."[45] In 1860, at the age of eighty, in an opinion which is a little gem in the literature of the common law, he gave fresh evidence of his extraordinary talent for keeping hoary principles viable by adapting them—as he put it—"to new institutions and conditions of society, new modes of commerce, new usages and practices, as the society in the advancement of civilization may require."[46]

Shaw's mind was open to many of the liberal currents of his time. Witness his support from the bench of the free public education movement,[47] or his public-interest doctrines,[48] or his defense of trade union activities,[49] or his freeing of sojourner slaves. While Shaw was chief justice, all slaves whom fate brought to Massachusetts were guaranteed liberty, except for runaways. Whether they were brought by their masters who were temporarily visiting the Commonwealth or were just passing through, or whether they were cast up by the sea, they were set free by Shaw's definition of the law. Bound by neither precedent nor statute, he made that law. The principle of comity, he ruled, could not extend to human beings as property: because slavery was so odious and founded upon brute force, it could exist only when sanctioned by positive, local law. There being no such law in Massachusetts, Shaw freed even slave seamen in the service of the United States Navy if they reached a port within his jurisdiction.[50]

---

[45]*Commonwealth v. Kimball*, 41 Mass. (24 Pick.) 359, 363 (1837).
[46]*Commonwealth v. Temple*, 77 Mass. (14 Gray) 69, 74 (1859).
[47]Lemuel Shaw, "A Charge Delivered to the Grand Jury for the County of Essex, May Term 1832" (1832), pp. 15–16.
[48]See notes 6–9 above.
[49]*Commonwealth v. Hunt*, 45 Mass. (4 Met.) III (1842).
[50]The leading case is *Commonwealth v. Aves*, 35 Mass. (18 Pick.) 193 (1936). See also "Betty's Case," *Law Reporter*, XX (1857), 455; *Commonwealth v. Fitzgerald, Law Reporter*, VII (1844), 379; *Commonwealth v. Porterfield*, ibid., p. 256; *Commonwealth v. Ludlum, The Liberator* (Boston), August 31, 1841; *Anne v. Eames* (1836) in "Report of the Holden Slave Case," Holden Anti-Slavery Society pamphlet (1839); *Commonwealth v. Howard, American Jurist*, IX (1832), 490.

In the area of criminal law dealing with conspiracies, Shaw seems on first glance to have run counter to individualist doctrines. He held, in what is probably his best-known opinion,[51] that a combination of workers to establish and maintain a closed shop by the use of peaceable coercion was not an indictable conspiracy even if it tended to injure employers. Shaw also indicated that he saw nothing unlawful in a peaceable, concerted effort to raise wages.

But other judges had been persuaded by the ideology of individualism, or at least used its rhetoric, to find criminality in trade union activity and even in unions per se. Combination, labor's most effective means of economic improvement, was the very basis of the ancient doctrine of criminal conspiracy and the denial of individual effort. The closed shop was regarded as a hateful form of monopoly on the part of labor, organized action to raise wages as coercion, and both regarded as injurious to the workers themselves, as well as to the trade and the public at large. When so much store was placed on self-reliance, the only proper way in law and economics for employees to better themselves seemed to be by atomistic bargaining. Unions were thought to impede the natural operation of free competition by individuals on both sides of the labor market. Or so Shaw's contemporaries and earlier judges had believed.

Individualism, however, has many facets, and like maxims relating to liberty, the free market, or competition, can be conscripted into the service of more than one cause. If self-reliance was one attribute of individualism, the pursuit of self-interest was another. As de Tocqueville noted, where individualism and freedom prevail, men pursue their self-interest and express themselves by developing an astonishing proclivity for association. As soon as several Americans of like interest "have found one another out, they combine," observed de Tocqueville. Shaw

---

[51]*Commonwealth v. Hunt,* 45 Mass. (4 Met.) 111 (1842). See Levy, *Law of the Commonwealth,* chap. 11.

too noted the "general tendency of society in our times, to combine men into bodies and associations having some object of deep interest common to themselves."[52] He understood that freedom meant combination.

When the question arose whether it was criminal for a combination of employees to refuse to work for one who employed nonunion labor, Shaw replied in the disarming language of individualism that men who are not bound by contract are "free to work for whom they please, or not to work, if they so prefer. In this state of things, we cannot perceive, that it is criminal for men to agree together to exercise their acknowledged rights, in such a manner as best to sub-serve their own interests."[53]

He acknowledged that the pursuit of their own interests might result in injury to third parties, but that did not in his opinion make their combination criminal in the absence of fraud, violence, or other illegal behavior. To Shaw's mind the pursuit of self-interest was a hard, competitive game in which atomistic individuals stood less chance of getting hurt by joining forces. He seems also to have considered bargaining between capital and labor as a form of competition whose benefits to society, like those from competition of any kind, outweighed the costs. Finally, he was fair enough to believe that labor was entitled to combine if business could, and wary enough to understand that if the conspiracy doctrine were not modified, it might boomerang against combinations of businessmen who competed too energetically. Thus Shaw drew different conclusions from premises that he shared with others concerning individualism, freedom, and competition. The result of his interpretation of the criminal law of conspiracies was that the newly emerging trade union movement was left viable.

But the corporate movement was left viable too, a fact which helps reconcile the fellow-servant and trade union decisions. To

---

[52]Shaw, "Charge to the Grand Jury," pp. 7–8.
[53]*Commonwealth v. Hunt*, 45 Mass. (4 Met.) 111, 130 (1842).

regard one as "anti-labor" and the other as "pro-labor" adds nothing to an understanding of two cases governed by different legal considerations; on the one hand tort and contract, on the other criminal conspiracy. The fellow-servant case belongs to a line of harsh personal-injury decisions that were unrelated to labor as such. To be sure, labor was saddled with much of the cost of industrial accidents, but victims of other accidents hardly fared better. The fellow-servant decision also represented a departure of the maxim *respondeat superior* which might impose liability without fault; while the trade union decision, intended in part to draw the fangs of labor's support of the codification movement, represented a departure from Hawkins's conspiracy doctrine which might impose criminality on business as well as labor.

Despite the conflicting impact of the two decisions on labor's fortunes and the fact that they are not comparable from a legal standpoint, they harmonize as a part of Shaw's thought. He regarded the worker as a free agent competing with his employer as to the terms of employment, at liberty to refuse work if his demands were not met. As the best judge of his own welfare, he might assume risks, combine in a closed shop, or make other choices. For Shaw, workers possessed the same freedom of action enjoyed by employers against labor and against business rivals.

Compared to such Whig peers as Webster, Story, and Choate, Shaw was quite liberal in many respects. Indeed his judicial record is remarkably like the record one might expect from a jurist of the Jacksonian persuasion. Marcus Morton, during ten years of service as Shaw's associate, found it necessary to dissent only once, in *Kneeland's* case. No doubt the inherited legal tradition created an area of agreement among American jurists that was more influential in the decision-making process than party differences. Yet it is revealing that many of Shaw's opinions might conceivably have been written by a Gibson, but not by a Kent. It was not just the taught tradition of the common law that Shaw and Gibson shared; they shared also taught traditions of judicial self-restraint, the positive state, and the "Commonwealth idea," a term that is meaningful in Pennsylvania's history as well as in Massachusetts'.[54]

But personality makes a difference in law as in politics. It oversimplifies to say, as Pound has, that the "chiefest factor in determining the course which legal development will take with respect to any new situation or new problem is the analogy or analogies that chance to be at hand...."[55] There are usually conflicting and alternative analogies, rules, and precedents from among which judges may choose. The direction of choice is shaped by such personal factors as the judge's calculation of the community's needs, his theory of the function of government, his concept of the role of the court, inexpressible intuitions, unrecognized predilections, and perhaps doting biases. It is difficult to name a single major case decided by Shaw which might not have gone the other way had another been sitting in his place.

Shaw interpreted the received law as he understood it, and his understanding was colored by his own presuppositions, particularly in respect to those interests and values he thought the legal order should secure. Few other judges have been so earnestly and consciously concerned with the public policy implicit in the principle of a case.

Much of his greatness lay in this concern for principle and policy. "It is not enough," he observed, "to say, that the law is so established.... The rule may be a good rule.... But some better reason must be given for it than that, so it was enacted, or so it was decided."[56] He thought it necessary to search out the rule that governed a case, to ask "upon what principle is it founded?" and to deliver a disquisition on the subject, with copious illustrations for future guidance. From the bench he was one of the nation's foremost teachers of law.

[54]See generally Louis Hartz, *Economic Policy and Democratic Thought: Pennsylvania, 1776–1860* (Cambridge, Mass., 1948).

[55]Pound, *The Spirit of the Common Law*, p. 12.

[56]Shaw, "Profession of the Law in the United States" (extract from an address delivered before the Suffolk Bar, May 1827), *American Jurist*, VII (1832), 56–65.

His opinions did not overlook the question *"cui bono?"* which, he believed, "applies perhaps with still greater force to the laws, than to any other subject."[57] That is why he fixed "enlightened public policy" at the root of all legal principles, along with "reason" and "natural justice."[58] He understood that American law was a functioning instrument of a free society, embodying its ideals, serving its interests. It is not surprising, then, that he tended to minimize precedent and place his decisions on broad grounds of social advantage. Justice Holmes, attributing Shaw's greatness to his "accurate appreciation of the requirements of the community," thought that "few have lived who were his equals in their understanding of the grounds of public policy to which all laws must be ultimately referred. It was this which made him . . . the greatest magistrate which this century has produced."[59] To be sure, he made errors of judgment and policy. Yet the wonder is that his errors were so few, considering the record number of opinions he delivered, on so many novel questions, in so many fields of law.

Perhaps his chief contribution was his day-by-day domestication of the English common law. He made it plastic and practical, preserving its continuities with what was worthwhile in the past, yet accommodating it to the ideals and shifting imperatives of American life. The Massachusetts bar made a similar evaluation of his work when honoring the "old chief" upon his resignation. The bar, speaking through a distinguished committee, declared:

> It was the task of those who went before you, to show that the principles of the common and the commercial law were available to the wants of communities which were far more recent than the origin of those systems. It was for you to adapt those systems to still newer and greater exigencies; to extend them to the solution of questions, which it required a profound sagacity to foresee, and for which an intimate knowledge of the law often

[57]Ibid.
[58]*Norway Plains Co. v. Boston & Me. R.R.* 67 Mass. (1 Gray) 263, 267 (1854).
[59]Oliver Wendell Holmes, *The Common Law* (Boston, 1881), p. 106.

enabled you to provide, before they had even fully arisen for judgment. Thus it has been that in your hands the law has met the demands of a period of unexampled activity and enterprise; while over all its varied and conflicting interests you have held the strong, conservative sway of a judge, who moulds the rule for the present and the future out of the principles and precedents of the past. Thus too it has been, that every tribunal in the country has felt the weight of your judgments, and jurists at home and abroad look to you as one of the great expositors of the law.[60]

Time has not diminished the force of this observation. As Zechariah Chafee noted, "Probably no other state judge has so deeply influenced the development of commercial and constitutional law throughout the nation. Almost all the principles laid down by him have proved sound."[61]

He was sound in more than his principles. Like John Quincy Adams, his fellow Bay statesman whom he resembled in so many ways, he made his name a synonym for integrity, impartiality, and independence. Towering above class and party, doing everything for justice and nothing for fear or favor, he was a model for the American judicial character. And none but an Adams could compare with Shaw in his overpowering sense of public service and devotion to the good of the whole community. His achievement as a jurist is to be sought in his constructive influence upon the law of our country and in the fact so perfectly summed up in a tribute to him on his death: life, liberty, and property were safe in his hands.

---

[60]Address on Chief Justice Shaw's resignation, September 10, 1860, Supplement, 81 Mass. 599, 603 (1860).

[61]Zechariah Chafee, Jr., "Lemuel Shaw," *Dictionary of American Biography*.

A NOTE ON THE AUTHOR

Leonard W. Levy, whose *Origins of the Fifth Amendment* was awarded the Pulitzer Prize in history, is formerly Earl Warren Professor of Constitutional History at Brandeis University and Andrew W. Mellon All-Claremont Professor of Humanities and History at the Claremont Graduate School. His other writings, many of which have also won awards, include *Blasphemy*, *The Establishment Clause*, *Freedom of the Press from Zenger to Jefferson*, *Legacy of Suppression*, *Jefferson and Civil Liberties*, and *The Palladium of Justice*. Mr. Levy lives in Ashland, Oregon.